KB056396

Bada Humanities

This work was supported by the National Research Foundation of Korea Grant funded by the Korean Government (NRF-2018S1A6A3A01081098).

Bada Humanities

First Published on March 19th 2021 by Sunin Publishing

Authors | Jeong, Moon-Soo et al
Publisher | Youn Guan-Baek
Published by **SUNIN PUBLISHING**

Registration | 5-77(1998.11.4)
Address | 1st Floor Gotmaru B/D 4, Mapo-daero 4da-gil, Mapo-gu, Seoul, Korea
Tel | 02)718-6252 / 6257
Fax | 02)718-6253
E-mail | sunin72@chol.com
Homepage | www.suninbook.com

Price | 29,000 Won

ISBN | 979-11-6068-464-3 93300

The Series of Bada Humanities 005

Bada Humanities

Jeong, Moon-Soo et al.

S U N I N
PUBLISHING

Preface

The Institute of International Maritime Affairs (IMA) of Korea Maritime and Ocean University is carrying out the Humanities Korea Plus (HK⁺) Project from 2018 to 2025, supported by the Korea Research Foundation. The research agenda of the project is the "Bada Humanities." It is a successor to, and deepening of, the "Cultural Interaction Studies of Seaport Cities," which is a part of the Human Korea (HK) Project conducted by IMA over the past decade. The outline of "Bada Humanities" is as follows:

First of all, Bada Humanities study the relationship between the sea and humans. The 'sea' at this time is a physical ocean that has its own movements and principles that work regardless of human intentions. In this context, Bada Humanities pay attention to the relationship between Maritime/Marine Studies (海文, investigating aspects of sea's physical movement/principle) and Humanities (人文) that study facets of human society and culture. Humans are primarily land based mammals, so arguably, they have not been very interested in the effects of the sea on human life, for a long time. However, recent research on astronomy, cosmology, geology, oceanography, climatology and biology show that the sea's physical movements/principles and human social, economic and cultural activities have been influenced by each other.

Since time immemorial the physical movement of the sea has exerted great influence on the social economy and culture of mankind. On the other hand, it is only recently that mankind has begun to scientifically understand the physical movements and principles of the sea and has even influenced the sea's movements and environments. The relationship between the sea's physical movements and human activities has been dynamically developed through the times as follows: The ocean as the source of life, including human beings on Earth, the movement of the oceanic crust causing earth quakes and volcanic eruptions, the ocean's key role on the climate of earth by the Pacific and North Atlantic Oscillation, sea routes affording the exchange of people, goods, cultures, and species between continents, the creation of discourse and competition surrounding the sea space, intensification of globalization by containerization with global sourcing, and reversal of the sea-human relationship.

Against this backdrop of dynamic a sea-human relationships, first of all, the IMA is largely planning two categories of collective research topics: "The Encounter between the Sea and Humans in the Sea" during the first phase of the HK$^+$ Project (2018-2021) and "Studies on the Formation and Development of the Maritime Community," through solutions of impending issues in the relationship between the sea and humankind, during the second phase (2021-2025), will be produced as results of research.

Second, the academic methodology of Bada Humanities restores traditional academic research to overcome the discontinuation of modern projects that cut off interdisciplinary studies. In Bada Humanities, 'sea (bada)' is a modifier for 'accepting' (the Korean word 'bada' corresponds in English with 'sea,' and is accepting of all waters) research achievements related to other studies, especially maritime/marine studies, in addition to the meaning of 'sea' as a physical entity. The research methodology of Bada Humanities aims for interdisciplinary research. Our traditional methodology based on the principles of Heaven (天), Earth (地), and Human (人), placed the human principle in harmony with the other two principles. The emphasis on the interrelationship between the three principles valued the natural world and the human world, interdisciplinary research and consideration. However, regardless of being from the East or West, traditional academic methodologies have overlooked the relationship between the principles of the sea and humans. Bada Humanities suggests not only the principles of Heaven-Earth-Human, but also the principles of 'Sea' should be developed in relation to academic achievements. In this way, the methodology of studying the relationship between human beings and the sea could be applied. Bada Humanities is entirely novel, in that it combines sea-related academic achievements with humanities that have not been noted in traditional academic methodologies, beyond the restoration of academic research traditions.

Finally, 'Bada Humanities' responds more quickly to the needs of society. Humanities isolation from society, which has been pointed out as a relative weakness, would be overcome. Based on existing research achievements, Bada Humanities aims to be a "problem-solving humanities" that presents solutions to impending issues arising from sea-human relationships. IMA focuses on these issues that emerge in the relationship between sea and human beings, such as the history and prospect of maritime territorial conflicts, comparative studies on the re-development of old ports, China's One belt - One road, Korea's northward and new southward policies, drift and refugees, seamanship and ship officer's ethos, the vitalization of cultural heritages of seaport cities, and Anthropocene.

As was briefly introduced above, 'Bada Humanities: Problem Solving Humanities' seeks solutions to impending issues surrounding the relationship between the sea and human beings, aiming for interdisciplinary research of the physical movements of the sea and human studies. For this reason, the series of research will be published in two main types: One is the publication of the first and second phases of the HK$^+$ Project of collective research, and the other is the publication of research that deals with issues arising from sea-human relationships. Published primarily in Korean, it is our goal that the books be interrelated, and increase the integrity of the "Bada Humanities: Problem Solving Humanities" research. Therefore, I hope that these collective books will help the IMA to promote the academic and social spread of Bada Humanities and to establish itself as the cradle of production and communication of global discourse on the Bada Humanities.

In this context, the book titled Bada Humanities is published in English to share the achievements of the IMA's collective research with foreign scholars. In Chapter 1, What is Bada Humanities?, 'Studies on the Relationship between Maritime/Marine Studies and Humanities' describes the overall voyage course and coordinates of Bada Humanities. In Chapter 2, Open Sea, Closed Border, 'The Drift and Waters of Gyeongsang-Province and Ryukyu Drifters,' 'A Study on a British Sailing Ship Harbouring at Yongdanpo in 1797,' and 'The National and Transnational Characteristics of Korean Merchant officers - Focusing on the period of the shipping industry from 1960-1990' are included, and deal with various cultural interactions of people who enter closed boundaries through open waters. Chapter 3, The Projection of Nation State Sovereignty on the Oceanic Space includes 'A Study on Russia's Deer Island (絶影島) Leased Territory in the late 19th century,' 'A Sea Agreed upon as a 'Sea' : Territorial Dispute and Settlement of the Caspian Sea,' 'The Maritime Boundary Dispute between Slovenia and Croatia,' and 'A Study on Maritime Jurisdictions in the Constitutions of Asian Countries.' This section demonstrates how the projection of sovereignty over the oceanic space has evolved from the time of establishing modern nations up to now. Chapter 4, Discourse on Sea and Seaport Cities selected 'A Critical Review on the Japanese Waegu/Wako,' 'The Imperial Eyes towards Busan as Contact Zone,' and 'Life on the Sea: The Merchant Vessel as a Cultural Interaction Space.' The first article critically illustrates how the discourse on Japanese pirates, which claims to be a symbol for overcoming Eurocentrism and the Modern Project, has been gradually distorted in the Japanese academic community. The second paper analyzes how, as a contact zone, Busan was reflected in the eyes of imperialist intellectuals who visited during the Japanese colonial era. Lastly, the third article raises the issue of cultural interaction between crew members with diverse identities on shipboard and presents cultural based solutions.

Finally, I would like to express my gratitude to the authors of these works who accepted the unreasonable demand for a significant adjustment in the length of their articles, so this book could be published. Also, thanks to the help and hard work of intern Kim Chaeyun, who translated the difficult texts of Korean into English, and Professors Allison Kennedy, Bogue Hermsmeyer and John Dawber, who reviewed the draft - this work is possible because of their efforts, so I take this opportunity to thank you.

2021.01.

Director The Institute of International Maritime Affairs

Jeong, Moon-Soo

CONTENTS

<table>
Chapter 4 | **Discourse on Sea and Seaport Cities**
</table>

Chapter

1

What is Bada Humanities?

Studies on the Relationship between Maritime / Marine Studies and Humanities

Jeong, Moon-Soo
Chung, Chin-Sung

Ⅰ. Prologue

The Institute of International Maritime Affairs is going to undertake about an Research Agenda for Human Korea Plus Project of the called "Bada Humanities" from September 2018 to August 2025. The purpose of this paper is to describe the blueprint of "Bada Humanities."

Humans did not have a particular interest in the effects of oceans and seas on human life for a long time because land was the main living base for humans, who are mammals. However, humanities scholars have begun to pay attention to the relationship between humans and oceans and seas based on recent research outcomes in various disciplines, such as astronomical cosmology, earth science, geology, oceanography, climatology, and biology. That is, current outcomes of various disciplines show that the principle of oceans (maritime/marine studies) and the principle of humans (humanities) have evolved, interacting with one another.

In the second chapter, "the relation between seas and human beings," authors suggest that physical movements of oceans have profoundly affected humans' social economy and culture since time immemorial. In contrast, it is only recently that humans have begun to understand the physical movements of oceans in a scientific manner and have even affected oceans. As seen here, the relationship between humans and oceans has dynamically evolved from the time human activities began up to the present time. Therefore, the research on the physical movement of seas and the study on the humans require mutual academic communication and interdisciplinary analysis.

In the third chapter, "restoration and creation of the interdisciplinary research," authors explore that the maritime/marine studies and humanities have been researched until now separately. and then suggest the creation of the interdisciplinary studies between maritime/marine field and humanities. Authors suggest with "Bada Humanities" the interdisciplinary research between heaven and earth including the maritime/marine studies and humanities(天地海人), while restoring the rethought of heaven, earth and human-being(天地人), which is emphasized in the traditional Asian scholarship.

In the forth chapter, "Bada Humanities," authors explain that 'Bada' has a dual meaning. First 'Bada' means a sea, natural world independently of human intention, in which the physical movement of the sea itself, which operates and develops. Another meaning of 'Bada' is to accept (Korean word bada means to accept all the waters) of all the research results of all the disciplines as means of communicating with other scholars outside of the humanities like oceans and sea accept all the small rivers and waters.

Finally in the epilogue, the "Bada Humanities" denominates the "Impeding Issue Solving Humanities" in the sense of presenting solutions for the issues that are revealed in the relationship between the sea and human-beings. Authors suggest seven issues for seven years to deal with.

II. The Relationship between Seas and Human Beings

1. The Scientific Discovery of the Sea

1) The Sea, Mother of Life

All living organisms on the Earth originated in the oceans, as connoted in the expression, "great mother of life, the sea," said by Rachel Carson. Oceans are the source of life on the Earth.[1] Cosmic history began 13.8 billion years ago, and the Earth, a planet in the solar system, came into being 4.6 billion years ago. The first living organism on the Earth, prokaryotes, appeared from hydrothermal vents on the seabed 3.5 billion years ago. In the early days of the Earth, the ozone layer did not exist in the atmosphere and there was no way to block ultraviolet radiation emitted from the sun, which is harmful to life. At such a time, the oceans were the only place to avoid ultraviolet radiation.[2] Prokaryotes evolved into eukaryotes around 2.5 billion years ago. Around 1.5 billion years later, multicellular organisms appeared, and organisms began to

---

[1] Rachel Carson, (Lee, Chung-Ho, trans.) (2003). *The Sea Around Us*, Seoul: Tindrum Publishing (Original work published 1951). pp.22-42.

[2] There is solid evidence proving that organisms lived in oceans around 3.5 billion years ago. Stromatolites found in Shark Bay, Western Australia, are the evidence. Stromatolites are dark red rocks with a pattern reminiscent of the growth rings of trees. They were formed by green algae living in clusters, a type of prokaryotes, which did not have a nucleus. These green algae had chlorophyll to photosynthesize. David Christian, (Lee, Gun-Young, trans) (2013), *Maps of Time*, Seoul: Simsan, (Original work published 2003), pp.187-188.

move onto the land around 475 million years ago.

The moving process of organisms from sea to land was in line with the emergence of amphibians, reptiles, and mammals. The first animal that lived on the land is considered to have been similar to the lungfish (fish that breathe air through the lungs that evolved from swim bladders). The lungfish had to return to the water for reproduction. However, amphibians continued to evolve. The emergence of amphibians was followed by that of reptiles, such as crocodiles and dinosaurs. Reptiles laid large and strong eggs that would help ensure a higher probability of survival to overcome the farther distance from the water. Afterward, around 250 million years ago, the first mammal appeared on the Earth. The mammal had evolved from a type of reptile which resembled birds. Mammals were warm-blooded, had hair, and did not lay eggs.[3]

Homo sapiens, among mammals, appeared about one to two hundred thousand years ago. The ancestors of modern humans began to migrate from the African continent to other continents about 70,000 years ago. Humans transitioned into the agriculture society 10,000 years ago. As seen here, the ocean is the great mother of all organisms existing on the Earth, including humans. Therefore, it can be said that without oceans, humans would not have existed.

2) The Seas and Oceanic Crust Covering the Earth

Over 70% of the Earth's surface is covered with seas and oceans. The five oceans (the Pacific, Atlantic, Indian, Arctic, and Southern Oceans), along with smaller seas, are connected with one another. Under the surface of oceans lie geographical features that have continued to evolve in a considerably similar

---

3 Ibid., pp.181-223.

manner to those of the continents. In general, the movement of oceanic plates is explained through plate tectonics.

Plate tectonics is a scientific theory describing the large-scale motion of seven large plates and the movements of a larger number of smaller plates of the Earth's lithosphere, since tectonic processes began on Earth between 3 and 3.5 billion years ago. The model builds on the concept of continental drift, an idea developed during the first decades of the 20th century. The geoscientific community accepted plate-tectonic theory after seafloor spreading was validated in the late 1950s and early 1960s.[4]

The process of plate tectonics results from the splitting and moving of the Earth's crust. Around 250 million years ago, all the continents were connected together, constituting one continent known as the supercontinent Pangaea. The water surrounding the supercontinent later constituted the body of water known presently as the Pacific Ocean. Around 200 million years ago, Pangaea broke into two continents: Laurasia in the Northern Hemisphere and Gondwana in the Southern Hemisphere. These two continents continued to break into smaller land masses over the following period of 50 million years. The Central Atlantic Ocean began to be formed during the age of dinosaurs, specifically, the late Jurassic period. The Southern Atlantic Ocean was formed around 135 million years ago as the South American plate and the African plate broke away from one another. Immediately after the breakaway, the Northern and Southern Atlantic Oceans were connected around 100 million years ago. The last major ocean that was formed was the Indian Ocean, which appeared around 60 million years ago. The Red Sea was formed around 20 million years ago as the Arabian plate broke away from the African plate.

---

4 W. Little; H.W. Fowler; J. Coulson (1990). C.T. Onions (ed.) *The Shorter Oxford English Dictionary: on historical principles. II* (3 ed.). Oxford: Clarendon Press.

The continents on the Earth have continuously changed in shape and position, while converging and splitting because the Earth's plates have moved due to the splitting and moving of the two types of the Earth's crust. One type of crust is the continental crust on which people walk and the other is the oceanic crust on the seabed. Generally, the oceanic crust consisting of basalt is denser than the continental crust consisting of granite. When the two types of crust collide, the denser oceanic crust is subducted beneath the continental crust, and the continental crust is crushed by the oceanic crust. As enormous friction and heat are generated, some parts of continental crust melts and a mountain range rises in the form of chains. A mountain range is also formed when parts of the continental crust collide with one another. When two plates of the continental crust have the same density, one is not subducted beneath the other. Instead, the crust breaks, and an enormous mountain range is formed. Conversely, two plates sometimes move in different directions, sliding along against each other. As the two plates are pulled toward one another through friction and the pressure increases, they suddenly split apart. This is how earthquakes occur.

The above is the basic idea of plate tectonics. Plate tectonics explains not only the formation process of mountain ranges and the cause of continental drift but also the reasons for a string of volcanoes and earthquakes around the edges of the Pacific Ocean.[5] Plate tectonics explains why the Earth's continents are dispersed like a broken eggshell and why violent activities, like volcanoes

---

5 The Ring of Fire is a 25,000 mile (40,000 km) horseshoe-shaped area of intense volcanic and seismic (earthquake) activity that follows the edges of the Pacific Ocean. Receiving its fiery name from the 452 dormant and active volcanoes that lie within it, the Ring of Fire includes 75% of the world's active volcanoes and is also responsible for 90% of the world's earthquakes. https://www.thoughtco.com/ring-of-fire-1433460, Retrieved 2020-10-01.

and earthquakes, occur around the edges of the plate. The core idea of plate tectonics is that the splitting and moving of the continental crust humans have experienced are significantly affected by the splitting and moving of the oceanic crust under the ocean surface, given that over 70% of the Earth's surface is covered with oceans.

3) The Sea, Engine of Weather System

Oceans act as a giant thermostat by absorbing heat from the surface of the adjacent land and slowly transferring heat to the adjacent land. This role of oceans has an important effect on the global climate, providing cooler summer and warmer winter seasons in the coastal and surrounding areas. The interaction among oceans, continents, and the Earth's climate has a significant effect on the development of ocean currents, which in turn affects the entire Earth and human activities.

The sea is so big, so huge the great part of the biosphere, that no region is uninfluenced by its effect. It is the engine of weather systems that help to forge the environment even in lands remote from it. The Southern Oscillation is a "major oscillation" of air pressure that moves forward and backward between the Indian and Pacific Oceans and is one of the most impactful weather determiners. El Niño-Southern Oscillation (ENSO) is an irregularly periodic variation in winds and sea surface temperatures over the tropical eastern Pacific Ocean, affecting climate of much of the tropics and subtropics. The warming phase of the sea temperature is known as El Niño and the cooling phase as La Niña. Southern Oscillation is the accompanying atmospheric component, coupled with the sea temperature change. El Niño is accompanied with high, and La Niña with low air surface pressure in the tropical western Pacific. The two periods last several months each (typically occurring every few years) and their effects vary in intensity.[6] The Pacific Countercurrent, known as El Niño, is the cause of drought and flood in Africa and North America.

The North Atlantic Oscillation (NAO) is a weather phenomenon in the North Atlantic Ocean of fluctuations in the difference of atmospheric pressure at sea level (SLP) between the Icelandic low and the Azores high. Through fluctuations in the strength of the Icelandic low and the Azores high, it controls the strength and direction of westerly winds and location of storm tracks across the North Atlantic. It is part of the Arctic Oscillation, and varies over time with no particular periodicity. Unlike the El Niño-Southern Oscillation phenomenon in the Pacific Ocean, the NAO is a largely atmospheric mode. It is one of the most important manifestations of climate fluctuations in the North Atlantic and surrounding humid climates.[7] The North Atlantic Oscillation affects the severe winter weather in central Russia, a continent far from the Atlantic Ocean.[8]

2. Exploring the Sea and Ocean

1) Sea Route: Exchange of People, Goods, Culture, and Species

While continents are described as a lively space on maps, seas are

---

6 "El Niño, La Niña and the Southern Oscillation". https://www.metoffice.gov.uk/research/climate/seasonal-to-decadal/gpc-outlooks/el-nino-la-nina/enso-description. Retrieved 2020-10-18.

7 D.B Stephenson, H. Wanner, S. Brönnimann, and J. Luterbacher (2003), *The History of Scientific Research on the North Atlantic Oscillation, in The North Atlantic Oscillation: Climatic Significance and Environmental Impact,* edited by J.W. Hurrell, Y. Kushnir, G. Ottersen, and M. Visbeck, pp.37-50, Washington, DC : American Geophysical Union.

8 Felipe Ferdinández-Amesto (2004), "Maritime History and World History," Daniel Finamore (eds., 2004), *History as World History*, Florida: University of Florida, p.9.

represented as a vacant space. That is, geographic features, such as mountains and canyons dotting continents, are not described on maps in the case of seas. Maps drawn this way distort the actual appearance of seas. The reason is that large oceans and small seas include the highest mountains and the deepest oceanic trenches on the Earth.

Seas, like continents, are a dynamic space. Scientists and, recently, humanities scholars argue that ocean currents are similar to rivers. Aided by wind directions, ocean currents would provide major connecting routes in the days of sail just as rivers traversing a continent acted as the main artery for exploration and exchange before the adoption of the steam engine and railway. In addition, ocean currents and winds have played an important role in human labor and economic cycles. Humans recognized at some point that the trade conducted across rivers, seas, and oceans was far more economical than overland trade.

Ships could transport more loads than animals, such as the horses and camels that were used for carrying loads. Moreover, ships were faster. Unfortunately, shipwrecks often occurred, but the potential risk was offset by the fast speed and loading capacity of the ships. Although it might have taken hundreds of years to develop a complete understanding, sea routes became highways as humans began to understand the seasonal winds in the Indian Ocean, trade winds in the Atlantic Ocean, the Roaring Forties, and ocean currents. Mastering the movement of seas provided an important stimulus for technological advances related to vessel structures, forms of sails, and nautical instruments.

Long distance trade not only had considerable cultural effects on societies along the coasts across the world but also caused the global exchange of species. Long distance trade began to be invigorated in the Afro-Eurasia region in the 8th and 9th centuries, and later in the 15th century, expanded into the trade between the Old Continents and the Americas. This sea route eventually came to be connected to the route between Acapulco and Manila in the Pacific in the 16th century. Its connection further extended to the route in Australasia beyond "the Roaring Forties" in the 17th century, which then created a global network of sea routes.

As humans sailed across the sea, the two-way exchange of commodities, flora and fauna, and pathogenic bacteria, as well as people and their ideology, religion, and information, occurred. The invigoration of the sea route between the Old Continents and the Americas, which triggered the global network of sea routes, facilitated what would later be known as the "Columbian Exchange." What was brought into the Americas from the World Old included crops and livestock, such as tangerines, apples, bananas, mangos, onions, coffee, wheat, and rice, and horses, pigs, chickens, sheep, lambs, and bees. African slaves and immigrants were also brought into the Americas, along with the Christian religion, and viruses such as smallpox and yellow fever. Conversely, what was brought into the Old Continents from the Americas included other types of crops and livestock, such as corn, tomatoes, potatoes, vanilla, rubber, cacao, and tobacco, and turkeys, alpacas, and llamas. Pinta (tropical skin disease) and nonvenereal syphilis were also introduced to the Old Continents.[9] The exchange of pathogenic bacteria, that is, diseases, was also important. The diseases imported to certain regions around the world annihilated some indigenous peoples who had no immunity to such diseases.[10]

---

9 Alfred W. Crosby Jr. (2002), *The Columbian Exchange: Biological and Cultural Cionsequences of 1492*, London: Parager, pp.208-219.

10 For example, between 1871 and 1947, the total number of natives of Tierra del Fuego dropped from between 7,000 and 9,000 to 150, many of them vitims of a malady which is even now one of the chief killers of the aborigines of the Chaco: maeales. Ibid., p.208.

2) Global Connectivity of Sea Route: Globalization

After the 1800s, the seas were integrated around the world. Further, ocean sailing appeared and new technologies to facilitate the connection of oceans were developed. The development of nautical technology intensified the connection among the Atlantic, Indian, and Pacific Oceans. The development of steam engines, in particular, led to the gradual disappearance of seasonal cycles of labor and trade, which depended on the physical environment of the seas. It also greatly reduced the time expended sailing across oceans. The network of seas around the world was further strengthened by the development of communications technology (submarine cable and telegraph) and the construction of the Suez and Panama Canals. European powers could expand into the world due to these advancements in science and technology. In a short time, warship fleets of other powers were added to those of European powers that sought to develop and solidify their sea power. As a result, empires whose ships sailed across oceans appeared and a complex scheme of the seas was created that boosted human migration.

The emergence of steamships was encouraged by the introduction of the steel hull and the following series of scientific innovations. For example, the development of steamships went through a series of successive inventions, which included Robert Fulton's steam paddle-boats, hybrid ships that were powered by both wind and steam, and screw propellers and compound engines. This enabled the development from tramp ships to regular liners and paved the way for the introduction of a shipping timetable and the establishment of the global standard time. Over several centuries, sea routes were used to transport humans and goods. Ocean liners were the major means of passenger transport, before the advent of jet aircraft. In the 1800s, large-scale human migration, voluntary and forced, took place from Africa to Europe and the Americas across the Atlantic as well as from Asia to the Americas and Oceania across the Pacific. Summarily, global human immigration took place through sea routes, although, in the 1960s, ships as a means of human transport were replaced by jets.[11]

While air transport has been the major means of human transport since the 1960s, large-scale freight is still transported through marine transport. The characteristics of marine transport for the last 25 years of the 20th century can be summarized as containerization. Containerization began with the simple process of putting packed freight into metal boxes known as containers. The system was as simple as attaching wheels to a suitcase. However, a standardized unit in one or two basic sizes made it possible to process the containers faster and at lower port costs than before. The loading process also became simpler. Containers can be transported across lands and seas through a minimum exchange and work or a process called intermodality. Containers and intermodality have made it possible to transport a large amount of freight faster, more regularly, and at lower costs than in the past. Today's global connectivity has been made possible through computerization, air travel, and unbridled capital flow, while containers have realized the global connectivity in terms of the distribution of finished goods, semi-manufactured goods, and unfinished goods, thus accelerating globalization.

Containerization made ports and ships designed to be suitable for the transportation and the carrying devices for the exclusive use of containers. The reason is that containers could be proven to be of optimal value only when all aspects of a transport chain are designed to systematically integrate

---

11 Michael B. Miller (2012), *Europe and Maritime World*, Cambridge: Cambridge University Press, pp.322-332.

containers.[12] IT technology has further made it possible to track the locations of millions of containers moving around the world and to develop systems to distribute and retrieve them. Achieving intermodality required the standardization among three different types of transport: ships, railways, and trucks. Above all, containerization has enabled the practice of "global sourcing." Containerization could reduce marine freight charges by virtue of the reductions in the risk of being stolen, loading and unloading time, and non-operation expenses. Now, freight charges have dropped to a level so low that it is practically no longer a consideration when making a decision regarding sourcing (overseas purchase) and sales. The Barbie doll is cited as a good example of a global purchase. Barbie dolls' hair is manufactured in Japan, plastics in Taiwan, clothes in China, and molds in the United States or Europe. The components are assembled in Indonesia, Malaysia, and China. Completely assembled finished goods are transported by sea to Hong Kong, and dolls collected there are finally transported to the United States.[13]Containerization is the outcome of globalization, and, at the same time, has facilitated globalization.

3) Discourses on the Oceanic Space

Human activities in the sea have been sustained for thousands of years, but humans rarely declared exclusive rights to the seas. The Treaty of Tordesillas and the Treaty of Zaragoza, signed between Spain and Portugal in 1494 and 1529, respectively, were the first agreements that had disrupted the concept of international waters: seas were common to all by natural law

---

12 Marc Levinson, (Lee, Kyeong Sik, trans., 2017) *The Box*, Seoul: Chungrim Publishing, pp.18-28.

13 Michael B. Miller (2012), op. cit., p.343.

and the use of seas, like air, was freely open to all. Spain and Portugal, which led the pioneering of the sea route connecting the Old Continents with the Americas, divided the seas around the world exclusively between themselves and declared their exclusive rights to seas. Meanwhile, the Netherlands and England, countries that challenged the rule of seas by Spain and Portugal, argued for the freedom to the seas in an effort to reorganize the existing maritime order. Hugo Grotius, a Dutch jurist, argued in his book The *Freedoms of the Seas*, that seas should be free to all people so as to deny Portugal's domination of the sea in the Moluccas.[14] A century later, Dutch jurist Cornelis van Bijnkershoek, agreed with the idea that international waters should be a free space but argued for a country's right to maritime space, that is, territorial waters. He suggested 3 nautical miles as the measure of the width of territorial waters. This distance is the range of coastal defense cannons. The discourse on the freedom of navigation prevailed under the slogan, "Free ships make free goods," in the 18th century. Entering the 19th century, nation-states in Europe competed in the debate about oceans, and the seas turned into a political space on which the sovereignty of nation-states is projected. During this period, the concept of 'imperium' regarding maritime space was replaced by that of 'dominion'.[15] Until the mid-20th century, the discourse on maritime space was focused mostly on matters related to navigation rights for trade and fishing rights in coastal waters.

In the 1950s, the seas were no longer a space with transport routes to deliver materials and goods regularly between continents. Humans shifted

---

14 Hugo Grotius (2015), *The Freedom of the Seas Or the Right Which Belongs to the Dutch to Take Part in the East Indian Trade*, London: Forgotten Books.

15 Elizabeth Mancke (2004), "Oceanic Space and rthe Creatio of a Global International System, 1450-1800," in Daniel Finamore (eds., 2004), op. cit., pp.157-162.

their attention from fishing rights to the source of wealth in the seas. The discourse on maritime space became even more complex as marine mineral resources were discovered. Humans had long been interested in marine mineral resources. A full-fledged development was triggered by the discovery of oil deposits in ocean basins. In September 1945, President Truman declared the United States' exclusive right to exploit resources contained in the continental shelf off the coast of the country. His declaration was soon followed by the declarations of exclusive rights by Mexico and countries in Central and South Americas. It became evident that an international discussion was necessary to solve this problem, and the newly created United Nations carefully examined the maritime law in the 1950s.

What made matters more complex was the location of manganese nodules on the ocean floor. More research on the ocean floor was conducted as antisubmarine warfare methods were concurrently developed. Scientists found that such nodules lie scattered on the ocean floor. Those nodules were analyzed and found to contain not only manganese but also other minerals such as copper, iron, and nickel. Scientists discovered that these minerals lie in abundance on the ocean floor compared to the land surface of continents.

As the possibility of seabed resources development was realized, cautious dialogs led to public meetings. Among these public meetings, the United Nations Convention of Law of the Sea of 1982 was of the most importance.[16] This convention was ratified by most countries, and as a result of the convention, the width of territorial waters was extended, at most, to 12 nautical

---

16 "The United Nations Convention on the Law of the Sea (A historical perspective)". United Nations Division for Ocean Affairs and the Law of the Sea. https://www.un.org/ Depts/los/convention_agreements/convention_historical_perspective.htm, Retrieved 2020-10-30.

miles and an exclusive economic zone (EEZ) of up to 200 nautical miles was newly established. The convention also defined seabed mineral resources as that of humans' common heritage, and stipulated nations' rights and obligations to prevent marine pollution. The assembly also established regulations on the approval of marine scientific research in the waters under the jurisdiction of coastal states. As a result of the convention, however, a third of the seas around the world fell under the control of nation-states. Before the mid-20th century, the seas functioned only as routes to transport goods. In such a condition, the discourse on maritime space supported the freedom of navigation as can be seen in the short width of territorial seas of only 3 nautical miles. In contrast, after the mid-20th century, seabed resources development has emerged as a key issue and the discourse on maritime space tended to support less high seas as can be seen in the extension of the width of territorial sea up to 12 nautical miles and the establishment of an EEZ of up to 200 nautical miles.

3. Reversal of the Relationship between Humans and Oceans

The location and use of marine resources (animals and minerals) have triggered human interest in the environment. Some scientists and, recently, some historians are aware that the relationship between humans and oceans has been reversed. Until as recently as the 1900s, humans regarded small and large seas as major threats to their life and property. However, over the last century, humans have emerged as one of the major threats to the seas.

Fishery was one of the industries that first showed the change in this relationship. The whaling industry drove many whales to near extinction in the 1800s, and various smaller marine organisms sustained other forms of devastation in the following century. Around 1950, powerful trawlers were introduced to the fishery industry and these vessels used cutting-edge technology that not only helped to catch fish but also identify the location of a school of fish. Subsequently, catches of fish increased while the global fish stock began to be greatly depleted. The results of such overfishing can aggravate the long-term damage to the food chain of the ecosystem, affecting humans around the world for several generations.

Other factors that have significantly impacted the global seas are marine pollution and eutrophication. Chemical pollutants, plastics, wastewater, agricultural leachate, etc. can have harmful effects on the global seas. In moderate cases, such pollutants can enter the food chain and, ultimately, the human body through the consumption of fish. When consumed by humans, such pollutants can cause cancer or, in women, stillbirth. In the worst case, all species of fish, would one by one gradually become extinct and thus, famine would spread around the globe. Marine pollution can also contribute to the long-term algal bloom along coastal areas. Although regular algal bloom was not a rare phenomenon, in some waters, such as the North Sea, around 15 percent of the sea surface is covered with algae. This clearly shows change in the ecosystem. The transport of hazardous material fuels environmental aggravation. Oil tankers and oil drilling ships are other sources of major threats. In the event of an oil spill in the sea or a similar accident, oil covers hundreds of or even thousands of square miles of an area on seas and beaches (as shown in the well-known distressing image of a seabird covered in oil slick), suffocating animals and having fatal effects on fishery and aquaculture.

A recent threat to the seas, and subsequently, human life, is the greenhouse effect. The greenhouse effect leads to the increasing temperature of the Earth's atmosphere, which in turn slowly melts the ice caps in polar regions and raises sea level. There is a considerable controversy as to whether such a rise in temperature has been caused by human activities. However, many scientists now agree that the accumulation of carbon dioxide in the Earth's atmosphere is related to the increase in the use of fossil fuels since the Industrial Revolution and the accompanied deforestation activities that have had harmful effects on the last tropical rainforest sanctuaries on the Earth. An increasing amount of carbon dioxide in the atmosphere holds a greater amount of solar heat and ultimately melts ice caps.

In early human history, the seas threatened humans who explored and lived in the seas. Today, however, humans threaten marine ecosystems and search for measures to recover marine ecosystems. Humans are warned of the reversal of the relationship between humans and oceans, which is named Anthropocene, a period characterized by the global warming caused by humans and humans' intrusion into the ecosystem.[17] The relationship between humans and seas has recently undergone a dramatic change. Humans no longer regard the seas with awe and have instead rapidly emerged as its major threat. However, it is not the seas but humans that face danger in the long-term.

---

[17] One of Crutzen's research interests is the Anthropocene. In 2000, in IGBP Newsletter 41, Crutzen and Eugene F. Stoermer, to emphasize the central role of mankind in geology and ecology, proposed using the term anthropocene for the current geological epoch. "Opinion: Have we entered the "Anthropocene"?" IGBP.net. Retrieved 2020-10-24. http://www.igbp.net/news/opinion/opinion/haveweenteredtheanthropocene.5.d8b4c3c12bf3be638a8000578.html

III. Restoration and Creation of the Interdisciplinary Research

As seen above, humanities that associate the relationship between humans and oceans demand efforts to communicate with outcomes of several disciplines related to seas, that is, interdisciplinary research. In premodern periods, people in the humanities regarded interdisciplinary research as natural. In the West, the scientific revolution brought about the subdivision into natural science, social science, and humanities, as well as the change in the meaning of "science," from disciplines at large to a more specific discipline, that is "natural science."[18] The methodology of natural science was established as the classic model for academic methodologies.[19] Therefore, natural science became the classic model of disciplines, and social science and humanities showed a tendency to imitate the academic methodology of natural science or introduce academic methodologies differentiated from that of natural science. As a result, today's disciplines are largely categorized into natural science, social science, and humanities with distinctly delineated boundaries, and each discipline has its sub-disciplines. This tendency of subdivision has since deepened. Against this backdrop, today's academic innovations are closely related to interdisciplinary and trans-disciplinary research, which argue for communication among disciplines.

---

18 The meaning of science is in mid-14c., "what is known, knowledge (of something) acquired by study; information;" also "assurance of knowledge, certitude, certainty," but from c. 1400 science means as "experiential knowledge." *Online Etymology Dictionary*, retrieved 2020-10-28.

19 Scientific method means a method of procedure that has characterized natural science since the 17th century, consisting in systematic observation, measurement, and experiment, and the formulation, testing, and modification of hypotheses.https://www. lexico.com/definition/scientific_methods, retrieved 2020-10-28.

In the East Asia, there was a strong tradition of "reaching generality (不器) beyond specialities" with the goal of self-cultivating and people-governing rather than the subdivision into natural science, social science, and humanities resulting from the outcomes and advancement of scientific revolution. In such a tradition, there was a pronounced tendency to incorporate disciplines of specialities (器) after the contact with Western learning and due to the internal growth of the study of disciplines. That is, a tradition of incorporative disciplines was relatively strong. However, since the 19th century, the Western power was dominant in the East and the study of disciplines from the West became mainstream in the modern age. The school system of universities, modeled after Western universities, also became common. Consequently, the communication among disciplines, a task for the Western study of disciplines, is currently a key issue in the East as well.

Like ancient futures, the interrelation between natural world studies and human world studies was regarded as important in the study of disciplines in the premodern ages both the East and the West, and especially in the Eastern study of disciplines. For example, the content of 3 principals and 8 steps to achieve the principals of *The Great Learning* (『大學』) appears to define methodologies of disciplines in the human world but it stresses the interrelation between the natural world and the human world.

The 3 principals are:

What the Great Learning teaches, is to illustrate illustrious virtue; to renovate the people; and to rest in the highest excellence[20]

---

20 Lee, Ki-Dong (annotator, 2010). *The Great Learning*, Seoul: Sungkyunkwan University Press, p.21.

The 8 steps are:

The ancients who wished to illustrate illustrious virtue throughout the world, first ordered well their own states. Wishing to order well their states, they first regulated their families. Wishing to regulate their families, they first cultivated themselves. Wishing to cultivate themselves, they first rectified their hearts. Wishing to rectify their hearts, they first sought to be sincere in their thoughts. Wishing to be sincere in their thoughts, they first extended to the utmost their knowledge. Such extension of knowledge lay in the investigation of things. Things being investigated, knowledge became complete.[21]

According to 3 principals and 8 steps to achieve the principals of *The Great Learning*, the principles of the human world begin with the investigation of things, and the extension of knowledge and the investigation of things appear to be an understanding of the laws and principle of the natural world.

Another example is *The I Ching*(『易經』). Some phrases in *The I Ching* suggest the interrelation between the laws of the natural world and the laws of the human world. Those phrases include "One discovers changes by examining the study of heaven(天文), and achieves the world at peace by examining the study of humans(人文),"[22] "One looks upward to observe the principle of heaven and looks downward to discover the principle of the earth (地文)"[23] and "There is the principle of the heaven(天道), the principle of the earth(地道), and the principle of humans(人道)."[24] The phrases specifically define the Eastern thought of heaven, earth, and humans, or three composites, as well as

---

21 Ibid., p.31.
22 Lee, Ki-Dong (annotator, 2010). *The The I Ching* Seoul: Sungkyunkwan University Press, p.341.
23 Ibid. p.865.
24 Ibid., p.979.

the interrelation among the principle of heaven, the principle of earth, and the principle of humans.

Jeong do-jeon(鄭道傳), a prominent Joseon Dynasty scholar, more clearly summarized the interrelation of heaven, earth, and humans. He explained, "The sun, the moon, and the stars are the study of heaven; mountains and streams, plants and grass are the study of earth; and poetry, prose, manners, and music are the study of humans. Heaven originates from energy, earth from forms, and humans from principle." He went further to stress the study of humans when he said, "A principle is the container that carries nature. As for the principle of humans, if one understand the principle which is enlightened by the teachings of poetry, prose, manners, and music, and the principle of humans follows the operation of three lights of the sun, the moon, and the stars, and rules the world with the suitableness of all things, then a study reaches grandness and, subsequently, the utmost."[25] The explanation that the principles of the study of humans accord with the principles of the study of heaven and the study of the earth is an explanation of academic interdisciplinarity and academic interdisciplinary methodologies.

Interdisciplinary research itself is not new, and it may be a simple task to restore the academic tradition from the time before the scientific revolution. However, the principles and the laws of the seas (海道, 海文) were also neglected in the academic tradition of the East. Authors believe that disciplines that pertain to the relationship between humans and oceans should pursue the goal of adding the principles of seas to the principles of heaven and earth, so that the principles of heaven, earth, seas, and humans can interact with academic outcomes for the advancement in the discipline. In this context,

---

25 Chung, Do-Jeon (1997), *Sambongjip*, Seoul: Sol, pp.242-243.

interacting with the principle of seas and the movement of oceans is required in "Bada Humanities" by the Institute of International Maritime Affairs, Korea Maritime and Ocean University, which is concerned with the interrelationship between humans and oceans. Of course, this study pursues the restoration of the tradition of interdisciplinary research in premodern periods, while making an attempt to transcend the tradition. This can be said because "Bada Humanities" has a meaning that is more significant than merely breaking boundaries. This is in consideration of the Eastern study of discipline in which the heaven-earth-humans relationship was regarded as important but the relevance between the principle of seas and the principle of humans or the relevance between maritime/marine studies and the study of humans have largely remained unexamined.

IV. "Bada Humanities"

"Bada" has a dual meaning. as described in the chapter II, "Bada" means a sea, natural world operates and develops itself regardlessly of human intention. Another meaning is to accept(korean word bada means to accept) all the research outcomes of various disciplines, like big and deep oceans and seas accept all the rivers and waters.

Disciplines pertaining to the relationship between humans and oceans is a study of the interrelationship of how physical movements of oceans have profoundly affected humans' social economy and how humans understand physical movements of oceans and have even affected oceans. To some extent, the academic methodology of disciplines regarding the relationship between humans and oceans pursues interdisciplinary research to overcome the harmful effect of modern projects that severed the communication between disciplines. The academic methodology is novel because it combines humanities with academic outcomes related to the seas that were not recognized in traditional academic methodologies.

The modern discourse on the seas has contributed to progress and evolution, which are goals of modern projects that include polarization into the center and periphery of the world, the unification and homogenization of values, and domination and subordination. In contrast, the discourse on the seas of the 21st century that are addressed in this study presents post-modern prospects, including reflections on progress and evolution, encouragement of tolerance and coexistence, and prospects on diversalité

Lao-tzu(老子), an ancient Chinese philosopher, said that the highest good is like water(上善若水). That is because "water benefits everything without striving. It stays in places that society despises. Here, reverently, it approaches dao (道)." Water that stays in the lowest place in the world is the "seas." The seas stay in the lowest place but they are the largest bodies of water in the world.[26] The reason is that all waters belong to the seas. A similar phrase is found in *Sagi*(『史記』「李斯傳通」). Li Si(李斯), from a border area of the Qin(秦) state, proposed to Qin Shi Huang(始皇帝) that offices be generously opened to talent, saying, "Rivers and seas reach deep down because they accept small streams." Moreover, Chinese intellectuals of the following ages have cherished the phrase "Seas accept all waters and their generosity is immense."

The word "ocean," which originates from a Greek mythology, has a connotation similar to that of the corresponding Chinese word. The English word "ocean" originates from the Greek mythology of Oceanus. A son of

---

26 Bang-Woong (2003). *Chogan Lao-tzu*, Seoul: Yekyong Publishing, p.95.

Uranus and Gaia, Oceanus, married his sister Tethys and this union produced as many as 3,000 rivers. Oceans are the source of all rivers. Ancient Greeks thought all rivers flow into the seas and regarded the seas as the largest river that surrounds the earth.[27] In this sense, the Korean word "bada" (meaning "sea") is far clearer and implicative. The seas accept("badadeurida") all waters, hence the name "bada."[28] Authors believe that the teaching of Lao-tzu can be extended to suggest the philosophy and vision of "sangseonyakhae(上善若海)," which means "The highest good is like the seas." According to this philosophy and vision, in the 21st century, the seas are the highest good as it is the source of everything and contains a vision of new order for coexistence and communication. The discourse on the seas of the 21st century should pursue the highest good represented by sangseonyakhae. This vision can replace the theory of progress and evolution. Based on this vision, one can reflect on the individual to individual, society to society and human to nature relationships in a relational and organic manner within the framework of awareness that they all constitute one system.

Many academic factors related to the seas can provide an analysis framework for a new understanding of humans in and of themselves. Authors can confirm this, although to a slight extent, through the examination of studies on the relationship between sea and human. This may present what to focus on in terms of future research directions. In this sense, authors think that disciplines pertaining to the relationship between humans and oceans will contribute in the development of a new understanding and a reconstruction to include into the concept and category of humanities the outcomes of natural

---

27 N.G.L. Hammond and H. H. Scullard (ed. 1970), *The Oxford Classical Dictionary*, Oxford: Oxford University Pree, p.744.

28 Shin, Young-Bok (2008), *Lecture*, Seoul: Dolbegae, p.289.

science studies related to the movement of oceans (such as cosmology, life science, earth science, geology, climatology, oceanography. and ecology), as well as the many other factors that have traditionally been considered to be inside the boundary of humanities. This way, disciplines pertaining to the relationship between humans and oceans will establish the framework to understand humans and analyze the world more profoundly. Pursuing this endeavor is novel because it may suggest a need for a new discipline of humanities that address the relationship between humans and oceans.

Mencius(孟子) said the following in Chapter 24, Jin Xin, Part I (盡心章句上) of The Mencius about the art of observing the seas.

> One who has looked upon the sea finds small other waters difficult with which to describe or define. (That is because a small body of water is nothing compared to a large body of water.) … The art of viewing seas is to observe the waves. (That is because the waves change according to the volume and depth of water.) The light of the sun and moon always reflects upon them. The nature of flowing water is that it does not move forward until it has filled each depression in the ground.[29]

An art of observing the seas suggested by Mencius can be explained by and in line with the principles of gravity and optics. The tidal phenomenon, or the periodic rise and fall of sea level, can be explained through Newton's principle of universal gravitation. It occurs because the gravitational pull of the moon can draw sea waters but cannot draw the Earth, which is heavier than the Moon. Waves occur due to the difference in the force of the moon, drawing

---

29 Lee, Ki-dong (annotator, 2010). *Lecture on The Mencius*, Seoul: Sungkyunkwan University Press, pp.646-648.

sea waters between the waters closer to it and the waters farther away.[30] Visible light is a range of wavelengths perceived by humans' naked eye. The colors of visible light are red, orange, yellow, green, blue, indigo, and violet. What is the reason the seas, namely the largest and deepest waters, are perceived as blue? The colors red and yellow, having long wavelengths, are absorbed usually 5m or less below sea level. The color blue, with a short wavelength, advances deeper into the waters and some particles of blue collide with water particles and bounce off.[31] That is why large and deep sea waters are perceived as deep blue while shallow stream waters are perceived as light blue or white.

As seen above, disciplines pertaining to the relationship between humans and oceans deserve to be named "bada" humanities. This is because they can accept ("badadeurida") outcomes of all disciplines as an attempt to cross the boundary between natural science and humanities while pursuing tolerance and diversalité, which are values demanded in the 21st century. The world view of such disciplines stresses an uncertainty that is ruled by accident and probability rather than determinism and mechanism. As with all organisms, this is not about a static system in which man and nature perform regular operations but about an irregular yet flexible, dynamic system in which they adapt to a fast-changing environment within a chaotic state.

---

30 Isaac Newton (1729), *Mathematical Principles of Natural Philosophy, to which are added The Laws of Moon's Motion according to Gravity.* by Jhon Machin, *Tides are the rise and fall of sea levels caused by the combined effects of the gravitational forces exerted by the Moon and the Sun, and the rotation of Earth.* https://books.google.co.kr/books?id=Tm0FAAAAQAAJ&pg=PA1&redir_esc=y#v=onepage&q&f=true, retrieved 2020-11-09.

31 Newton, Isaac (1998). *Opticks: or, a treatise of the reflexions, refractions, inflexions and colours of light.* Also two treatises of the species and magnitude of curvilinear figures. Commentary by Nicholas Humez (Octavo ed.). *Palo Alto, Calif.: Octavo.* (Opticks was originally published in 1704).

V. Epilogue

The Cultural Interaction Studies of Seaport Cities from 2008 to 2018 have been aimed at the interdisciplinary research required by the 21st century science and the accomplishments and communication of the ocean (sea) related studies that have been neglected in the field of the Humanities.[32] The "Bada Humanities", which was designed based on the achievements of the cultural Interaction Studies of the Seaport Cities for the next seven years, deepens the study of cultural interaction in the maritime cities. At the same time it points out the relative weakness of Humanities, which was actively criticized due to the lack of communications with the society. In other words, Humanities need to cope with social demands more quickly, and based on existing achievements "Bada Humanities" aims at "Impending Issue Solving Humanities" that present solutions to the problems which in the relationship between the oceans and seas and human beings.

What is required in the 21st century science is dialogue and communication between different scholars. In the case of Humanities, we need a specific technique of "Bada(to accept)" Humanities which is a rhetoric in the sense of accepting and communicating various academic achievements. Therefore, in the "Bada Humanities", the ocean and sea(Bada) not only implies the meaning of "the ocean" as a physical object, but also the meaning of accept research outcomes of various disciplines as a research method.

The relation between man and nature has been in the defensive position of mankind for a long time since the appearance of humans, but since the modern

---

32 Jeong, Moon-Soo (2010), "Roadmap for the Cultural Interaction Studies of Seaport Cities in the Global Age," *Cultural Interaction Studies of Sea Port Cities*, (April, 2014), Institute of International Maritime Affairs, pp.265-298.

era, this relationship has begun to reverse, and humans have become an offensive position against the nature. This flow of the human history is applied to the relationship between human and sea. The reversal of the relationship between the seas and humans as seen from global warming, rising sea level, environmental pollution, disturbance of ecosystem, and frequent occurrence of unpredictable natural disasters which can not cope with accumulation data by human, it is not the sea but the human being that is at risk.

This relationship is caused by the encounter between man and the sea in the ocean and the sea region. In this process, the ocean and the sea have not been obstacles and boundaries, but as transportation routes, communication and exchange of people and culture has been proceeded. The human community has been formed around the oceans and the waters due to these contacts and exchanges. Understanding the crisis and problem of the maritime community around the ocean and the sea today through a long-term search will ensure the contents of a complex and practical humanities that can predict the possibility of a sustainable human society.

In this context, "Bada Humanities" can be called as "Impending Issue Solving Humanities" that seeks solutions to the problems revealed in the relationship between the sea and humans. The study process of "Bada Humanities" is a research theme that leads to various problems at the academic level for the research agenda implementation. It also focuses on solving the problems that arise in the encounter between humans and the sea. We will select the topics and draw out the results.

The theme of the study of the research topics and issues of the first phase (2018-2021) and the second phase (2021-2025) of the "Bada Humanities" and "Impending Issue Solving Humanities," which will be held for seven years from 2018.[33] Here is the main proposal:

The first step of the study Topic: Encounter of humans and sea in the sea regions.

The first year is the relationship between humans and sea in the oceans and seas,

The second year is a longitudinal comparison of encounters between humans and seas,

The third year is the horizontal comparison of encounters between humans and seas.

The second phase of the research theme is the formation and development of the maritime community through resolution of issues arising from the relationship between the maritime/marine and the human.

The main themes for solving the problems that arise from the relationship between the texts and humanities are as follows

Year 1: Past, present, future in the maritime territorial and marine conflicts,

Year 2: Comparative study of redevelopment of the old harbors,

Year 3: China's One Belt One Road Policy and Korea's Northern and New Southern Policies - Between antagonism and cooperation,

Year 4: Drifting and refugees - Historical experience and current problems,

Year 5: Seamanship and ship officer-ship

Year 6: Comparative study on the use of cultural heritage

Year 7: Anthropocene - Towards a new future vision

---

33 For the details see Jeong, Moon Soo (2018), *The Research Proposal for the 2018 Human Korea Plus (Type 2) of Institute of International Maritime Affairs: Bads Humanities.*

Chapter

2

Open Sea,
Closed Border

The Drift and Sea Area of Gyeongsang-Province and Ryukyu Drifters during the Joseon Dynasty

Kim, Kang-Sik

Ⅰ. Introduction

On the stage of history, the ocean has also been the main stage of human activity. However, human maritime activities have also led to unexpected accidents. Drifting, which was a common maritime incident during the pre-modern period, has occurred since the beginning of human maritime activities. During the pre-modern period, the number of drifts increased as marine activities increased. These drifts were a complex problem at both the national and individual level, and naturally occurring drifts were applied to the base of tributaries of government offices in East Asia and continued to influence the sea area.[1]

During the Joseon Dynasty, there were also many people who drifted

---

[1] Yasunori Arano (1988), *Modern Japan and East Asia*, Tokyo University Press, 1988; compiled by Momoki, translated by Choi Yeonsik (2012), *Introduction to Research on Asian Sea area History*, Minsokwon.

between Joseon and Ryukyu, though only a small number of them were recorded. Joseon and Ryukyu were friendly and maintained a direct relationship[2] with each other at first. However, after the Imjin War, the Satsuma-domain of Japan invaded Ryukyu. After that, the relationship became indirect. As a result, the existing China-centered tributary trade system changed, and the way drifting people were repatriated also changed. So far, studies of drifts between Joseon and Ryukyu have centered on drifts between Jeju-Province and Ryukyu, and between Jeolla-Province and Ryukyu.[3] Through a case study of drift and drifting ashore between Gyeongsang-Province and Ryukyu during the Joseon Dynasty, this article examines the process and cause of drift between Gyeongsang-Province of Joseon and Ryukyu, contact and exchange due to drifting, the repatriation process and system of drifters (the people are drifters, they drift, or drifted, drifted to and drifted from), and the shipping routes and problems of the sea area in Joseon and Ryukyu.

---

2 Ha Woobong (2016), *Exchange through the Sea in the Joseon Dynasty*, Kyungin; Ha Woobong et al. (1999), *Joseon and Ryukyu*, The Korea-Japan Historical Society, Arche; (2001), *Research on Korean-Japanese Drifters in Joseon Dynasty*. Kookhak.

3 Lee Hoon (1994), "Relations between Joseon and Ryukyu through the repatriation of the drifter of the late Joseon Dynasty", *Journal of Historical Studies* 27; Kim Kyungok (2012), "The Real Condition of Casting away on Chosun and Repatriation of Ryukyu-People : Focusing on Chosunwangjoshilok (朝鮮王朝實錄)", *Local History and Local Culture* 15-1; Lee Soojin (2015), "The Ryukyu Drift and Repatriation by Joseon people", *Yeol-sang Journal of Classical Studies* 48; Jeong Hami (2015), "Identification of the Joseon people and Response of the Ryukyu Kingdom : in the case of Kerama Islands in 1733", *The Korean Journal of Japanology* 104.

II. The Ryukyu Drift and Repatriation by Joseon people

1. Cases of Ryukyu Drift by Joseon People

Forty-eight cases of drift were found to have occurred between Joseon and Ryukyu, which had a friendly relationship during the early Joseon Dynasty. Ryukyu drift of people from Joseon was more frequent in the late Joseon Dynasty, than in the early Joseon Dynasty. The area where drifts most often occurred in Joseon were Jeju Island and Jeolla Province. Many drifts occurred from Jeju Island as it is geographically close to Ryukyu, and from Jeolla Province due to the large number of active maritime activities taking place during the Joseon period. However, there were also three cases where drifting from Gyeongsang Province to Ryukyu, which was not common. Table 1 includes all known cases of Ryukyu drifts during the Joseon Dynasty.

<Table 1> Cases of Ryukyu drift by Joseon people[4]

Date of Drift	Date of Repatriation	Drifting site	Outport	Number of Drifting People	Reason for Drift	Way of Repatriation	Repatriated by	
							Document	Repatriation Mission
	1397		Unknown	9		Along with delegation	King Zhongshan	Not clear
1450.12	1453	Gajatoshima		6		Along with delegation	King Zhongshan	Doan (道安)
	1455		Unknown	Unknown		Along with delegation	King Zhongshan	Doan

---

4 <Table 1> was created and complimented by compiling data from Lee Hoon (1994), "The Choson-Ryukyu Relations as seen by Drifter's Repatriation in the Latter Half of Choson Dynasty", *Journal of Historical Studies* 27, pp.123-124; The Korea-Japan Historical Society (2001), *Research on Korean-Japanese Drifters in Joseon Dynasty*, Kookhak, p.21; Shigeru Kobayashi·Takatoshi Matsubara·Yutaka Rokanda editor (1998), "Timeline of drifts from Ryuku to Joseon in Joseon", *Research on the Diplomatic Records of Ryukyu (Rekidai Hoan)* 9, Okinawa Prefecture Education Research Society, pp.86-117.

Date of Drift	Date of Repatriation	Drifting site	Outport	Number of Drifting People	Reason for Drift	Way of Repatriation	Repatriated by	
							Document	Repatriation Mission
	1457		Jeju	5		Along with delegation	King Ryukyu	Doan
	1458		Jeju	3		Along with delegation	King Ryukyu	
	1458			1		Along with delegation	King Ryukyu	
	1458		Jeju	2		Along with delegation	King Ryukyu	Munehisa (宗久)
	1461			2		Along with delegation	King Ryukyu	
1456.2.2	1461	Kumejima	Naju (Jeju)	more than 2		Along with delegation	King Zhongshan	
1461.1.24	1461.2.4	Miyakojima	Naju	8	Conferment of a Buddhist scriptures			
1477.2.14	1479	Yonaguni	Jeju (Yeompo)	3	A public payment, a wooden surface	Along with delegation	King Zhongshan	Shinsira
	1480			23	A wooden surface	Along with delegation	King Zhongshan	
1542	1546		Jeju	12		via Ming	King Zhongshan	Ryukyu, an envoy of tributes
	1594.3	Ryukyu	Joseon			via Ming	King Ryukyu	(Dongji envoy)
1661.8.13	1662.6	Ryukyu	Jeolla	18	A yellow horn, collection	Satsuma-Nagamine-Tsushima	Lord of Tsushima	
1662.6	1663.6	Ryukyu	Jeolla Haenam	28 (4 Fatalities)	Trade, return	Satsuma-Nagamine-Tsushima	Lord of Tsushima	
1669.3.15	1669.7	Irabushima	Jeolla Haenam	21	Fishing	Satsuma-Nagamine-Tsushima	Lord of Tsushima	
1697.9.8.	1698	Mount Kumei	Jeolla Yeongam	8	Fishing	Fujian-Beijing (Ryukyu's tribute Ship)	Qing Ceremonies Board	Lee Heungseo
1704.1.27		Irabushima	Jeolla Yeongam, Jeju	39 (death by drowning 2, Child 1)	Grain and rice, purchase			
1714.8.19 (1715)	1716	Yasudaura	Jeolla Jindo	9		Fujian-Beijing (Ryukyu, an envoy of tributes)	Qing Ceremonies Board	

Date of Drift	Date of Repatriation	Drifting site	Outport	Number of Drifting People	Reason for Drift	Way of Repatriation	Repatriated by	
							Document	Repatriation Mission
1726.3.28	1728		Jeolla Jeju	9	Purchase	(Ryukyu, an envoy of tributes)	Qing Ceremonies Board	(An envoy of tributes)
1733.11	1735	Gyeongrama	Gyeongsang, Geoje	12 (1 Pregnant woman)	Fishing	Fujian-Beijing-Uiju (Ryukyu 馬艦船)	Qing Ceremonies Board	(Second interpreter)
1739	1741	Tokunnoshima	Jeolla Yeongam	20		Fujian-Beijing (Ryukyu's tribute ship)	Qing Ceremonies Board	(Hansoojeog)
1770	1771	Torayama		29	Public affairs			
1779	1780	Oshima	Jeolla Yeongam*	12		Fujian-Beijing (Ryukyu's tribute ship)	Qing Ceremonies Board	
1794.1.29	1795	Yamakima	Jeolla Gangjin	10		Fujian-Beijing-Uiju (Ryukyu's tribute ship)	Qing Ceremonies Board	
	1796	Ryukyu	Hwanghaedo	7		Fujian-Beijing (Ryukyu's tribute ship)	Qing Ceremonies Board	(Annual envoy of tribute)
1796	1797	Oshima	Jeolla Gangjin (Jeju)	10 (4 Fatalities)		Fujian-Beijing (Ryukyu's tribute ship)	Qing Ceremonies Board	
1802	1804	Oshima	Jeolla	4 (6)	Commercial sales	Fujian-Beijing (a chief interpreter)	Qing Ceremonies Board	(Annual envoy of tribute)
1814	1816	Taiping Mountain	Jeolla	7 (1 Fatality)		Fujian-Beijing-Uiju	Qing Ceremonies Board	(Second interpreter)
1814		Miyako Tarama						
1825	1826	Oshima	Jeolla Haenam	5		Fujian-Beijing	Qing Ceremonies Board	(Seasonal envoys)
1827	1829	Kurenzu	Jeolla Jeju (Haenam)	12 (12)		Fujian-Beijing	Qing Ceremonies Board	(Seasonal envoys)
1831.12	1833	Ie	Jeolla Jeju	26 (7 Fatalities)	Commercial sales	Fujian-Beijing	Qing Ceremonies Board	(Seasonal envoys)
1832	1834	Yaeyama	Jeolla	12 (9 Fatalities)		Fujian-Beijing-Uiju	Qing Ceremonies Board	(Second interpreter)

Date of Drift	Date of Repatriation	Drifting site	Outport	Number of Drifting People	Reason for Drift	Way of Repatriation	Repatriated by	
							Document	Repatriation Mission
1832		Yaeyama	Jeolla Haenam	8 (2 Fatalities)				
1833	1837	Yaeyama	Jeolla Haenam	9 (3 Fatalities)		Fujian-Beijing-Uiju	Qing Ceremonies Board	(Second interpreter)
1835	1837	Kumejima	Jeolla Gangjin	10 (6 Fatalities)		(Annual envoy of tribute)		
1836				1				
1841		Mount Yeomwol	Jeolla	11 (3 Fatalities)				
1849	1851	Not clear	Jeolla Gangjin	7				
1853		Taiwan	Jeolla Gangjin	1				
1854	1855	Not clear	Jeolla Gangjin	47 (41 Fatalities)				
1855	1857	Not clear	Jeolla	3				
1856.9.23	1859	Not clear	Jeolla Gangjin	6	Fishing	Fujian-Beijing		
1860	1861	Not clear	Jeolla Gangjin	9				
1865	1866	Not clear	Jeolla Haenam	15				
1868		Kumejima	Joseon 6 persons					

During the Joseon Dynasty, the reasons for the drift of Joseon people in Ryukyu were mostly due to being caught in a storm off the coast while engaging in activities such as fishing and commerce. This can be understood in conjunction with the large number of people who drifted from Jeolla Province to Ryukyu, on account of the many islands in Jeolla Province where many maritime activities took place.

2. Change in the Way Joseon Drifters Repatriate

What is noteworthy about the case of the Joseon people who settled in Ryukyu during the Joseon Dynasty is that the method of repatriation changed greatly between the early and late days of the Joseon Dynasty. First of all, the process of repatriation of the drifters was not easy because in East Asia during the pre-modern era[5] the practice of occupation of the drifting site took precedence before the mutual repatriation of the drifters. The Joseon people who drifted into Ryukyu were sometimes rescued by the residents of the drifting site, but were also enslaved or sold. Even if they were rescued, it can be assumed that the degree of restrictions on them was severe, both physically and economically. However, after the character of the Japanese pirates at the end of the Koryo Dynasty and early Joseon Dynasty changed, Ryukyu decided to recognize the Joseon drifters as a chance to have friendly relations with the Joseon Dynasty. They first repatriated drifters in 1453[6] although no guidelines are provided for the repatriation.

During the early Joseon Dynasty, Ryukyu's method of repatriating Joseon people was deeply related to the Japanese integration process and the issue of history fabrication[7] due to changes in activities of Japanese pirates. It had been a while since Ryukyu had last been able to send an envoy to Joseon in 1410, and so no one among the Ryukyu people were familiar with the passage to Joseon. Therefore, in 1431, when an envoy of Ryukyu visited Joseon, they barely managed to get to Joseon by way of the Tsushima merchant, Hyolangcharang's (穴郎次郎) boat. After that, Ryukyu decided to use Japanese

---

5 Yasunori Arano (1988), *Modern Japan and East Asia*, Tokyo University Press, pp.119-120.

6 *The Annals of King Danjong* 24 April, in the first year of King Danjong's reign.

7 The Korea-Japan Historical Society (2001), op. cit., pp.20-21.

ships or hired Japanese envoys to send their envoys to Joseon. The drifters were no exception, so during their repatriation, they travelled with Japanese Buddhist monks or merchants in Hakada, acting as deputy envoys. However, due to the prevalence of fabricating history the relationship between Joseon and Ryukyu became worse and Joseon's drifters instead began to travel through Ming China in 1546 (the first year of King Myeongjong's reign). When Dongji's envoy (冬至使) from Joseon went to Beijing, 12 people, including Park Son (朴孫) from Jeju Island, met with Ryukyu envoys at Hoedonggwan, a government office, that had jurisdiction over the reception of foreign envoys during the Yuan, Ming and Qing Dynasties on a China tribute ship (進貢使), and then returned home.[8] However, except during King Myeongjong's reign - Ryukyu asked a Japanese envoy to repatriate the Joseon drifters. During the early Joseon Dynasty, Joseon and Ryukyu traded directly, documents on the repatriation of the drifters were brought with them in the name of King Ryukyu.[9]

The specific route for repatriation of Joseon people who settled in Ryukyu during the early Joseon Dynasty is based on the Journal of Kim Bieui (金非依) in 1479. They were repatriated along with the Hakata merchant Shinsira (新時羅). The route followed was the drifting sites (琉球, 与都國島) → Naha (郡屬) → Satsuma (摩) → Hakata (博多) → Iki (壹岐) → Tsushima (對馬島) → Yeompo (鹽浦). At this time, the reason for the layover in Tsushima was to obtain a certificate allowing one to sail out of the country. It took nearly a year for the drifters to return to Joseon via a detour.[10] This was because they

---

8 *The Annals of King Myeongjong* Day of Muja February, in the first year of King Myeongjong's reign.

9 *The Annals of King Seongjong* Day of Eulmi June, in the tenth year of King Seongjong's reign.

10 Ha Woobong et al. (1999), *Joseon and Ryukyu*, Arche, p.241.

were not repatriated directly from the drifting site to Naha but traveled to several islands waiting for favorable weather conditions. As a result, Ryukyu had to pay a lot of expenses. Nevertheless, Ryukyu spent the time and money to repatriate the drifters to Joseon because of the need to expand opportunities for communication and trade with Joseon. Through the repatriation, Ryukyu was able to obtain many rare return presents from Joseon, such as cotton and Buddhist scriptures.[11]

Next, it was in 1594 that Ryukyu repatriated Joseon drifters for the first time after the Imjin War. They repatriated drifters with the Dongji envoy who had been dispatched to Ming China from Joseon. Ryukyu did not directly repatriate the drifters to Joseon with their envoys though but repatriated them to Joseon via Ming China. During the early Joseon Dynasty, the drifters were repatriated through a complicated process.

However, after the Imjin War, the features of the repatriation route of Joseon drifters can be summarized in two ways. First of all, the repatriation route changed greatly on account of the subjugation of Ryukyu to Satsuma in 1609, and the change in the repatriation policy, following changes in Tokugawa's foreign policy in 1696.[12] They repatriated by way of Ming China before 1609, through Japan between 1609 and 1695, and Qing China after 1696. During this period, the method of repatriation also differed depending on which country they were returned by. From the Imjin War to 1609, in the case of Ming China, they were sent back to Joseon along with diplomatic delegations. From 1609 to 1695, when Ryukyu was subjugated by Satsuma, Japan's envoys repatriated the drifters.

---

11 *The Annals of King Sejo* Day of Imshinjo leap February, in the fourth year of King Sejo's reign.

12 Lee Hoon (1999), op. cit., pp.121-123.

In the late Joseon Dynasty, the repatriation of Joseon people from Ryukyu was again based on the principle of layover in China, as before the 17th century. However, in 1638, Joseon and Ryukyu stopped all trade. The drifters were interrogated in Nagasaki and repatriated to Joseon via Tsushima. Since Qing integrated Beijing in 1636, Joseon sent a delegation and received investiture from Qing as a result of the Manchu Invasion. In the case of Ryukyu, they returned the investiture received from Ming China in 1651, and from 1663 they were under Qing's investiture. However, no direct contact between Joseon and Ryukyu took place such as in the early Joseon Dynasty even during the period when both countries were under Qing's investiture. The occasional repatriation of drifters were, however, done in a simple manner between the two countries. Of the 20 cases of Joseon drifters in Ryukyu after the Imjin War, seventeen cases between 1698 and 1856, were repatriated by land, via Fujian.[13] As such, the indirect repatriation of the drifting people continued between Joseon and Ryukyu.

Secondly, after 1696, when the repatriation took place through Qing China, there were no envoys although Joseon's diplomatic corps who were dispatched to Qing, took over the drifters. King Zhongshan (中山王) asked the Tokugawa shogunate about his intent through Satsuma's noble Matsudaira. He asked that in 1696, a Namman ship (a foreign ship carrying Westerners) or ship which has been suspected of having Christians onboard among the foreign ships in Ryukyu, was sent to Nagasaki, while other ships were immediately returned from Ryukyu to Fujian Province without going through Nagasaki. In response, the Tokugawa ministry instructed Satsuma's noble to allow the repatriation of foreign ships directly from Ryukyu to Fujian Province in Qing in 1696 as

---

13 Ibid, pp.121-160.

requested. These measures were made to escape the repatriation process of the Tokugawa feudal system. Ryukyu was able to cover up the subjugation relationship between Ryukyu and Japan to Qing, and externally, it was able to keep a tributary and appointment relationship with Qing as an independent kingdom. Following this measure, the drifters were first repatriated to Joseon through Qing in 1698. After this, changes were made in diplomatic documents and costs of repatriation. Ryukyu first brought the drifting people to Fujian with a tribute ship. Then they handed over the drifting people to the officials of Fujian Province to have them repatriated to Joseon. At this time, diplomatic documents on repatriation were written in the name of the Ceremonies Board (禮部) of Qing. By the 19th century, Ryukyu was once again under the control of the Satsuma, so they repatriated drifters via China.

III. Ryukyu Drift by People of Gyeongsang-Province and the Ryukyu Sea Area

1. The Case of Kim Bieui (金非衣) in 1479

There are not many cases of drifting from Gyeongsang-Province of Joseon to Ryukyu during the Joseon Dynasty. However, we would like to examine the sea area issue through the relationship between Gyeongsang-Province and Ryukyu, the negotiation and repatriation procedures for the drifting people, and the repatriation route.

First of all, there are no official cases of direct Ryukyu drift from Gyeongsang-Province of Joseon during the early Joseon period. It can be assumed, however, that drifting at this time did occur, as noted in the journal of Kim Bieui, who was repatriated to Yeompo, Ulsan in 1479 (the 10th year of King Seongjong's reign). Kim Bieui, a resident of Jeju Island, who returned to Joseon in June 1479, drifted because of a maritime accident near Chuja Island. In February 1479, Kim Bieui's party set sail for Jeolla Province with citrus fruits, a tribute from Jeju Island. They were pushed west by the east wind near Chujado Island. After seven to eight days of drift, they passed through the Yellow Sea and were pushed back south by the west wind. They were cast away on Yuni Island (presumed to be Yonagunijima) in the Ryukyu Islands.[14] At that time, most maritime accidents experienced by Joseon people, between Jeju Island and Jeolla Province, occurred in the winter months.

During the Joseon Dynasty, maritime accidents frequently occurred in the area near Chuja Island.[15] Chuja Island was one of the sea areas where Jeolla Province residents frequently had accidents during sailing or fishing. If there was a marine accident near Chuja Island, many of them often drifted to southern states such as Tsushima and Satsuma in Japan, or Ryukyu. These accidents also occurred mainly in winter. The detail of Kim Bieui's 1479 drift is described in relative detail. The east wind in February was generated by changes in wind direction caused by low pressure that passes through the vicinity of Japan in the winter. In other words, there was a seasonal wind blowing from the east or south before the low pressure passed, and then, it turned back into a strong northwest wind. This contrasts, however, with the Joseon drift by Ryukyu people which occurred in the summer when a typhoon blew.

---

14 *The Annals of King Seongjong* 16 May, 10 June, in the tenth year of King Seongjong's reign.

15 Lee Hoon (2000), *The drifter in the late Joseon Dynasty and Relations between Korea and Japan*, Kookhak.

Shinsira, a senior official of King Ryukyu Sangdeok, and Sammoksambora, a deputy official, who came to Joseon in 1479 to make a private act regarding a problem of authenticity. There were 219 people in the group, and they entered Yeompo, Ulsan on three ships.[16] They were accompanied by three Koreans who had been in Ryukyu (Kim Bi-eulgae 金非乙介; also known as Kim Bieui 金非衣, Kang Moo 姜武 and Lee Jung 李正) at the order of the King of Ryukyu. The three Ryukyu-drifted Joseon people left Jeju Island earlier with tributes of tangerines along with four others. Due to the windstorm, only three of them drifted to several islands near Ryukyu and finally reached Ryukyu. From then on, they were given King Ryukyu's generous help and luckily returned to Joseon on board a Japanese merchant ship. Detailed reports of their drifting situation and information about Ryukyu are written in detail, in the Annals of the King.[17] Shinsira (reported as Shinsira 新時羅, Shinsarang 新四郎, and Shinisarang 新伊四郎) went to Ryukyu for trade and was accompanied by the Ryukyu drifters, as a favor, for the King of Ryukyu. One can see here that there was an exchange between Joseon and Ryukyu during the early Joseon Dynasty, the repatriation of the drifting people was completed indirectly, using Japanese merchants.

It took nearly a year for the drifters to return to Joseon, via some detours. Because of this, Joseon's drifting people could experience Ryukyu's natural environment, agriculture and products, social systems, customs and international relations. The case of Kim Bieui, who drifted during the early Joseon Dynasty, contains the most detailed and abundant information about Ryukyu. Kim Bieui's drift is shown in the following two log entries:

---

16 *The Annals of King Seongjong* 16 May, in the tenth year of King Seongjong's reign.
17 *The Annals of King Seongjong* 105. 10 June, in the tenth year of King Seongjong's reign.

A. On February 1st in the year of Jeongyu, we took a boat with Hyun Sesoo, Kim Deuksan, Lee Chungmin, Yang Seongdol, and Jo Gwibong to the sea with potatoes for tributes and headed for Chuja Island. Then we drifted westward in the face of a sudden east wind. From the first day of departure until the 6th, the sea was clear and blue, and when a week had passed on the 7th to the 8th, the sea was murky as used water from washing rice. I met a west wind again on the 9th, I drifted toward the south where the sea was clear and blue. On the 14th day, I was looking at a small island. All the rest of us were drowned and all the equipment was lost since we were unable to bring the boat to the shore. Only three of us were left sitting on board. There were two fishing boats where four people sat, and when they found us, they took us and carried us to the shore of the island.

B. Kim Bieui, Gangmu, and Lee Jeongeun said, "We received potatoes from people in Jeju on February 1, in the year of Jeongyu, and rode the boat with Hyun Sesoo, Kim Deuksan, Lee Chungmin, Yang Seongdol, and Jo Gwibong. We met a wind on Chuja Island and headed westward. On the 7th, we drifted southward. Kim Deuksan died of illness and hunger on the 11th. On the morning of the 14th, our boat was wrecked since we failed to bring the boat to the shore. Hyun Sesoo, Yang Seongdol, Lee Chungmin, and Jo Gwibong drowned, and we did not die thanks to a sandbar.[18]

The two journal entries above, show that Kim and his eight companions

---

[18] *The Annals of King Seongjong* 105. 10 June, in the tenth year of King Seongjong's reign.

were drifting because they met strong winds near Chuja Island. It can be seen that the drifting period of Kim Bieui's party was 14 days, from when they left Jeju Island on February 1, 1477.

What is certain from Kim Bieui's drift is that they had to layover at all the Ryukyu Islands after their arrival at Ryukyu. They arrived in the Ryukyu kingdom via Yonaguni (閏伊是麿; 与那國島), Iriomote (所乃是麿; 西表島), Hateruma (捕月老麻伊是麿; 波照間島), Aragusuku (捕刺伊是麻, 新城島), Kuroshima (欻尹是麻, 黑島), Tarama (他羅馬是麿, 多良間島), Irabu (伊羅夫是麿; 伊良部島), and Miyakojima (覓高是麿, 宮古島). However, it took about a year for Kim's party to return to Yeompo in Joseon, in May 1478 via Naha-Satsuma-Hakada-Iki-Tsushima from the time of his first Ryukyu encounter at Yonaguni (与那國島).[19]

After spending six months in Yonaguni, Kim Bieui's repatriation process and overall schedule included five months in Iriomotejima, one month in Hateruma, and one month respectively in Aragusuku, Kuroshima, Tarama, and Miyakojima. In May 1478, they were transported to Okinawa and stayed there for three months. The reason for this was related to the periodic wind in the East China Sea.[20] After this, more than 100 people, including Shinisarang (新伊四郎), took them to Satsuma on August 1 to stay for a month. They reached Tagaseopo (打家西浦) in three weeks where they waited for the winds of September. They stayed here for six months to wait for the suppression of the Manchu war. Then, they arrived at Shika (軾駕) in February 1497 and arrived in Iki the next day. After staying here for three days and two months at Tsushima Chonapo (草那浦), they met the easterly winds of April and reached

---

19 *The Annals of King Seongjong* 105. 10 June, in the tenth year of King Seongjong's reign.

20 Michitaka Uta (1941), *History of Exploration of the Sea*, pp.202-207.

Sapo (沙浦). After two days here, they arrived in Doisajipo (都伊沙只浦) in Tsushima and stayed for three days. They left early the next morning and arrived at Yeompo on an evening in April, 1479. As such, Kim's repatriation was an indirect method through Tsushima, together with Japanese merchants.

Looking at Kim's relief and repatriation route, after arriving in Ryukyu, we see evidence that Kim's group received an interrogation. They then received relief measures, which were as follows.

King Ryukyu rewarded the Joseon people and bestowed them with blue and red cotton cloth. They were drunk all day long with a generous supply of rice and wine. They made clothes with a cotton cloth and stayed for a month before returning to the main island. The people of the country and a tongsa (interpreter) came to us and asked, "What country are you from?" We answered, "We are from Joseon." "Did you drift away from fishing and come all the way here?" they asked. So we discussed among ourselves and said, "We are from the south of Joseon, and we were on the way to Kyoto (京都) with some tributes." The tongsa wrote what we said and reported it to the king of the land. Later, a couple of government officials came to us and led us to a residence.[21]

Kim's group stayed here for three months and told the governor to let them return to their homeland. When the tongsa told the king, the king replied that, "The Japanese have a bad temper and you may not be able to bear them, so I want to send you to south of the Yangze River (江南)." Kim's group asked the tongsa earlier if they could go to Japan because they knew that Japan was

---

21 *The Annals of King Seongjong* 105.

closer and south of the Yangze River was far away. Shinisarang, a member of the Japanese Paegadae (覇家臺), and others who wanted to do business in Ryukyu came to the king and asked him, "Our country pledged an intimacy with Joseon, so please let us take these people and protect them and send them back." Then the king said, "Let them be well-treated and sent back." He then gave us 15,000 pieces of money, 90 kgs of black pepper, three pieces of blue-dyed cotton clothes and Tang cotton clothes, and 300 hundred kgs of white rice for three months, salt, jeotgal (salted seafood), rush mats, woodenware, and a dining table.

Kim Bieui's group spent about a year and a half in Ryukyu, where they had the unique experience of passing through nine islands, introducing 105 surveys of each island made by themselves, and providing good information about Ryukyu to Joseon. During the pre-modern period, when ship construction and navigation techniques were not developed properly, the drift became an opportunity to experience and introduce foreign cultures.[22] Kim's party experienced various customs and information during their stay, which lasted about a year before returning to Korea. This information was a valuable opportunity to promote Ryukyu to Joseon. Some representative examples are as follows.

A. They were pierced with blue earrings and threaded with small beads, which hung two or three Chi (6.66cm~9.99cm). They wore three or four layers of beads around their neck. Both men and women did it together, although the old did not do it.

---

22 Liu Hsiu-feng (2012), "Drift, Drifting records, Sea risks", *Introduction to Research on Asian Sea area History*, Minsokwon.

B. The men twisted their hair together, tied it with a hemp cord, and put a topknot behind their neck, though they did not wear a horsehair-woven headband. The beards were long enough to pass beyond the navel or were twisted in two layers into a topknot. Women's hair was long enough to reach their heels, and in the case of short hair, it reached their knees. They put their hair up around their head and put a wooden comb in under their ears to the side.

C. The rice is placed in a bamboo box. They make rice balls, which are the size of a fist. Each is placed in front of a person using a small wooden ark without a table. When we ate a meal, a woman took care of the box and distributed it to each person. First, they put the leaves in the middle of their palms and put the rice ball on top of the leaves, and the leaves were like lotus petals. When I ate one whole loaf, they gave me another one but limited it to three, however, they continued to give it anyone who wanted to eat more according to how many pieces a person could eat without counting them.

D. There was raw rice wine even though there was no refined rice wine. The rice soaked in water was made into a porridge by a woman who chewed it. They brewed the wine in wooden barrels but did not use yeast. We got a little tipsy after a heavy drink. You drink with a basket as a glass although there was no liquor etiquette. They drink according to their alcohol tolerance, and they add more alcohol to the good drinker. The liquor has a very plain taste. It ripens after three to four days but after more than three to four days, it goes bad. It is normally served with a piece of vegetable as snack. Sometimes dried fish is served, or fresh fish is cut into small pieces with garlic and vegetables.

E. There is no hemp, cotton, or silk. They only weave and make clothes with ramie. It looks like a Jikryeong (one of the wide-sleeved and stiff coats worn by military officers during the Joseon Dynasty). It has no collar and wrinkles but has short and wide sleeves. They were dyed dark blue with the clothes and hung the underwear near the hip using a white cloth with three widths. Women's clothes were mostly the same but there was no underwear, rather they wore an underskirt. They were dyed light blue as with the skirts.

F. While there is a smithy, they do not produce plows. Instead, they use small shovels to dig up fields and remove grass to plant rice. In December, they sow rice seed in paddy fields using oxen. They planted rice over the first month of the year without cutting the grass. In February, rice is thick and about a cubit high, and ripens in April. Early rice is harvested in April and late rice is harvested in May. After cutting the crop, it grows back from its roots and is thicker than the first, and it is harvested in July or August. During the harvest season, all the people behaved themselves. When they spoke, they did not speak loudly or whistle with their mouths. When they rolled up the leaves of the grass and blew them, they fanned them with sticks. Only after the harvest, were they allowed to whistle though the sound was very soft. Once harvested, the ears of rice were tied up in a row and placed in a warehouse. They threshed the rice with a bamboo stick and ground it using a treadmill.

G. There was no chief, no text, and we could not communicate and make them understood. However, since I have been in the land for a long time, I have learned a little bit about their language. We were always crying over our hometown, and the islander pulled out the stalks of the new rice and compared them with the old one and blew toward the east. It usually means that when new rice is ripe like old rice, it will depart and return.

H. There were Chinese men who came to trade and continued to live here. All their houses were covered with tiles, large and colorful. The fine and vivid reddish soil was painted inside, and chairs were all set up in the hall. They all wore gamtoo, a horsehair cap formerly worn by gentry or officials, and wore the same clothes as Ryukyu people. When they saw us without a gamtoo, they gave us some.

I. People from south of the Yangz River (江南人) and from Nammanguk (南蠻國) (now the area of Philippines and Indonesia) all came to do business, and we saw all of them. People from Nammanguk had their hair in a topknot, which was more unusual than ordinary people because the hair color was very dark. The garment was like those of Ryukyu although they didn't wrap the head with silk.[23]

The sea area and repatriation routes where Kim Bieui's party drifted from Joseon to Ryukyu is just like that in Figure 1 below. It was the wind near Chuja Island that affected the drift. However, there are also the factors of ocean surface water flow such as the ocean, tidal, wind-driven, and longshore

---

23 *The Annals of King Seongjong* 105.

currents. Among them, the ocean current is the flow of water on a global scale, flowing from the ocean, and the tidal current is the periodic flow of the seawater produced by the tides generated by the gravitational pull of the moon, and to a lesser degree, the sun. In coastal sea areas, tidal currents usually account for most of the coastal sea flow, as they are stronger than sea currents. Wind-driven current are the flow of seawater caused by the wind blowing on the surface of the sea, and the longshore current is the flow of water flowing parallel to the shoreline after the wave entering the coast enters and breaks into the surf zone.[24]

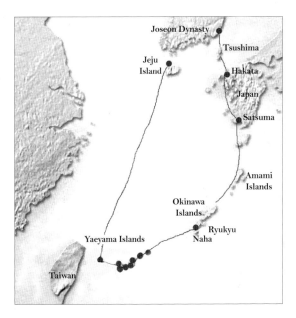

<Figure 1> Sea area of repatriation after the drift to Ryukyu by Kim Bieui's party in 1479 East Sea The sketches of this map are from Tamra and the Kingdom of Ryukyu (Jeju Museum, 2007)

Arguably, ocean currents were the main factor in terms of navigation

---

24 Lee Changhee · Cho Iksoon (2020), *Modern Reinterpretation of Daegaya Okinawa Route*, pp.16-30.

between Gaya in Gyeongsang-Province of the Joseon Dynasty and Okinawa in Ryukyu. The Kuroshio Current, which has close ties here, is the second-largest current after the world's largest turbulence, the Antarctic circumpolar current. It originates from the low latitudes of the western tip of the Pacific Ocean, passing through the Okinawa Sea and moving north and south of the Korean Peninsula along Japan's eastern coast.[25] Additionally, a tributary of the Kuroshio Current flows into the Yellow Sea and Korea's East Sea, centering below the south of Jeju in winter, forming the Yellow Sea Warm Current and the Tsushima Warm Current. Meanwhile, the Ryukyu Current would have played an important role in determining the return route because it is a current that flows along the Ryukyu Islands in the east. Moreover, the Ryukyu Current has its center below the ocean surface layer as it moves from southern Okinawa to southern Kyushu. Noting that as it is present in the surface layer, it is expected that the small vessels of the Daegaya era could have used this surface layer current as the main means of moving to Kyushu, the southern part of the Japanese archipelago.

Looking at the winter wind direction distribution from the perspective of the navigators in the Daegaya era, north/northwest wind was would have been used the most in Korea's South Sea. In the northern part of Taiwan, with the destination of drift and landing, it can be confirmed that the north or northeast winds are the main winds. With regard to the summer wind distribution from the point of view of the navigators of the Daegaya era, it is said that around the Korean Peninsula and the Japanese archipelago, the south wind was predominant, while in northeastern Taiwan, the southwest wind was significant.[26] During the Joseon Dynasty, the natural conditions of the

25 Michitaka Uta (1941), op. cit., pp.202-207.
26 Lee Changhee · Cho Iksoon (2020), op. cit., pp.16-30.

current and wind direction changed little, and those who drifted from Joseon to Ryukyu during the early Joseon Dynasty were also affected by the current and wind directions.

2. The Case of Seo Hujeong (徐厚廷) in 1733

In 1733 (the 11th year of King Yeongjo's reign), a group made up of Seo Hujeong and his party settled in Ryukyu.[27] The group that drifted with Seo Hujeong can be found below, in Table 2.

<Table 2> Members of Seo Hujeong's Ryukyu Drift Party, 1733[28]

Generation	Name	Age	Relation	Name	Age	Relation	Name	Age
1	Kim Pilsun	56	son	Kim Joongman	15			
2	Seo Hujeong	43	wife	Kang Ilmae	32	daughter	Seo Oksim	12
3	Park Giman	42	wife	Magjin	38			
4	Seo Husun	36	wife	Myungjin	26			
5	Choo Moohag	26	wife	Hyojung	27			

The 11 members of Seo Hujeong's group were comprised of six men and five women. A relatively detailed description of their drift and repatriation from Ryukyu is recorded in Records of the Border Defense Council (備邊司謄錄)[29], which records foreign relations of the late Joseon Dynasty. The group's

---

27 "Records of the Border Defense Council (備邊司謄錄)" the 18th book, 29 August, in the eleventh year of King Yeongjo's reign, 'a separate record about a person who has drifted and returned'.

28 Okinawa Prefecture Historical Sources, pre-modern era 5, Record of Drift Relationships.

29 Jeong Hami (2015), "Identification of the Joseon people and Response of the Ryukyu Kingdom: in the case of Kerama Islands in 1733", *The Korean Journal of Japanology* 104, pp.316-318.

experience is well summarized in the following quote:

> The drifting party was 11 people from Duryongpo, Hansan, Seomyeon, Geoje-eup. On August 2, 1735 (the year of Eulmyo), Kim Pilsun and others who lived in Geoje, returned from Beijing, and were sent to the local government. After they were interrogated, the recorded documents were brought directly to the king. They interrogated them once again to identify the drifting route and the tributes that were given when they were sent back home. As they have been living in foreign lands, it is safe to write off the Tongyeongjeon (統營錢), which he had borrowed from the local government since the amount was not large. When I asked the official to dispose of it, The King allowed it.[30]

First of all, the motive for Seo's drift to Ryukyu was that it was difficult to live in Gyeongsang-Province at that time, due to a bad harvest, so they borrowed 50 nyang with the purpose of paying it off later by doing business. Seo led his family and left Tongyeong on August 20, 1732 (the year of Imja) to do business in Gangjin, Jeolla-Province. Later, when he went out to the sea on November 8, 1733 (the Year of the Pig), waiting for the wind to return to Tongyeong, a storm broke out in the night and they drifted into the high sea on the 21st.

After this group, Ryukyu permanently posted a sentry to watch over Joseon drift-people who were required to stay in a shelter. This was to block the free passage of the Joseon people and block their access to the residents of Ryukyu.

---

30 *Records of the Border Defense Council* (備邊司謄錄) the 18th book, 29 August, in the eleventh year of King Yeongjo's reign, "a separate record about a person who has drifted and returned".

In particular, they made sure that the Joseon people did not know that they used Japanese in Ryukyu, including Japanese era names, and currency. This was because Ryukyu people feared that the Joseon people would divulge the relationship between Ryukyu and Japan to Qing.[31] However, while Seo Hujeong's group stayed in Ryukyu, the treatment was good.

It was the same treatment from start to finish. Many people came and gave us food. The taste of food was not different from that of Joseon and the refreshing taste of alcohol was like soju. Having been with the people here for months, I have come to understand a little bit of dialect. When I asked the name of the country, they said Ryukyu. To explain the scenery of Ryukyu, the hills were high, and the fields were narrow. The farm was large, and the rice paddies were small. Men wore Go, a garment with two crotches that sews legs under separate bottoms, and women wore Sang, a dress in skirt form. Both men and women tied their hair. They were just like men and women in Joseon. Geoncheokdu, a bandana, was hard to distinguish because it was like a horsehair-woven headband. Women pinned a binyeo (a Korean traditional ornamental hairpin) on the head. The crops are harvested in June by sowing seed in December, and in October by sowing in June. The capital was far away compared to the work of the castle site and the military, with a fence around it, and many soldiers were guarding it. Therefore, the records could not come out easily. The hospitality procedure of Ryukyu was sincere, and the national custom was warmhearted.[32]

---

31 *Okinawa Prefecture Historical Sources*, pre-modern era 5, Record of Drift Relationships, "A Diary of Repatriation of Joseons", *Kyorama Island Diary*.
32 *Records of the Border Defense Council* (備邊司謄錄) the 18th book, 29 August, in the

After staying in Naha for four months, Seo's group left the site on March 8, 1734 (the year of Gabin) and arrived at Hujangji on April 20. At that time, the government office provided four silver pieces to each of them in obedience to the emperor's instructions. The local official provided three units of sugarcane, two mosquito nets, and six parasols. Prior to this, on September 25, 1733, Chu Muhak's wife gave birth to a son. On the last day of November of 1733, they arrived on the coast of the 'Yoju' (Ryukyu) province[33] and abandoned the vessel because it was damaged. Many Qing people who were living in Ryukyu came out and took them to a village where they stayed for six days before entering "Yoju-guk" on December 7th. The country provided two sets of men's clothing and three sets of women's clothing and treated them well. On December 24, Seo's wife also gave birth to a son. The Ryukyu people gave her a lot of medicine and sent a doctor to care for her. After staying at "Hujiang" for 13 days, they left on April 10, 1735 (the Year of the Hare) and arrived in Beijing on June 4. After staying in Beijing for 24 days, they left on June 27 and returned home safely. They had come by ship from Yoju to Hujiang, where 'Yoju' means Ryukyu and 'Hujiang' means Namkyung, and by riding oxen from Hujiang to the Yalu River. It was by favor of their king that Seo's group returned to their home country safely. The 50 nyangs from Tongyeongjeon were lost at sea. Even though they returned to the mainland, there was no way to repay it. Therefore, they were allowed to write it off.[34]

Second, the process and procedure for the repatriation of Seo's party in

---

eleventh year of King Yeongjo's reign, "a separate record about a person who has drifted and returned".

33 Usually, Yoju province refers to a district of Jiangxi and Poyang in China. However, it means Ryukyu in here.

34 *Records of the Border Defense Council* (備邊司謄錄) the 18th book, 29 August, in the eleventh year of King Yeongjo's reign.

1735 were as follows.[35] The twelve residents of Gyeongsang-Province, who were repatriated from Qing in 1735, were actually sent back to Joseon two years after landing on Tokashiki Island of Ryukyu in 1733.[36] During the late Joseon Dynasty, the repatriation of Joseon drifters from Ryukyu was usually carried out using tribute ships. This is because the vessels used by drifters were too old and dangerous to tow to Qing, and as such, they were often burned without being repaired, irrespective of them being Chinese or Korean. In 1733, after being inspected, the ship of the Joseon drifters on Ryukyu was deemed so old that Ryukyu eventually ordered its disposal by incineration, under the precedent of dealing with Chinese fishing boats. Therefore, it was necessary to escort them by tribute ship at this time, but since 1734 was a year without a tribute, a separate ship[37] was prepared and escorted.

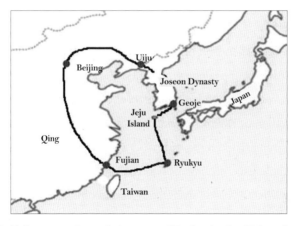

<Figure 2> Drift Sea area and repatriation route of Ryukyu by Seo Hujeong's party in 1734

---

35 *Dongmunhwigo* (同文彙考) Vol. 2, Vol. 66, "Drifter-Joseon People", Year of the Eurmyo.
36 *Kyorama Island Diary*.
37 Kazuyuki Toyomiyama (1996), "The Satsuma Diplomacy of the Ryuku Kingdom in the Mid-term", *New Modern History,* Sinjinbuchuoraisha, pp.216-220.

The sailors (25 people) who were selected to repatriate Seo Hujeong's party left Naha on March 9, 1734 (the year of Gabin) after holding a ritual to pray for a safe voyage at the temple, before leaving Ryukyu the next day, on March 10. It was on April 4 that they went to Tokashiki Island where the Koreans were picked up from their accommodation, before arriving at the Fujian Province of Qing China on April 8. After arriving in Fujian province, they reported to the official of Fujian that they had brought in the Joseon people and handed them over to the government official of Fujian province on May 8. After coming to Beijing, these drifting people stayed at the Hoedonggwan. In Qing China, they were led by an interpreter (Goryeo Tongsa) to the Uiju of Joseon by land. Leathers, clothing, and wagons were also provided during the escort service and the drifters were guided by government officials. In 1735, Qing escorted a Korean-language interpreter to Uiju, because there was no diplomatic mission from Joseon dispatched to Qing that year.[38]

Diplomatic documents on the repatriation of Joseon drifters from Ryukyu were sent to Joseon, either along with diplomatic delegation or to the border by an interpreter from Qing, or Jamun, one of the diplomatic documents, written from the Ceremonies Board in Qing. The Joseon people who had drifted to Ryukyu were repatriated to Joseon via Fujian-Beijing of Qing China. The exchange of diplomatic documents was made between Qing and Joseon after the fall of the Ming Dynasty, since there was no diplomatic relations between Joseon and Ryukyu.[39]

Third, concerning the expenses used to rescue and repatriate the the drifters of Gyeongsang-Province, in 1733, the items paid by Ryukyu during their six-

---

38 Lee Hoon (1999), op. cit., p.123.
39 *Dongmunhwigo* (同文彙考) No. 4. "A consultation on literature to inform the return of the Ryuku-drifter on Jeju Island", the National Institute of Korean History, p.3599.

day stay from November 29 to December 4 are described in minute detail.[40] It is an especially important information about the rescue of the drifting people. In 1733, Ryukyu did not ask for payment for the relief of Seo Hujeong's party.

Ryukyu provided 11 kinds of goods, ranging from a total of 7 Hap 9 Jae, (Ryukyu's unit of measure), of rice to fish and tobacco per drifting person, on a daily basis for the drifters from Gyeongsang-Province who landed in Ryukyu in 1733.[41] Additionally, the Joseon people frequently requested clothing, soju, combs, hair oil, cattle leather, and the string of Gat (Korean traditional hat), and received what they requested.[42] Moreover, Ryukyu provided daily necessities such as vegetables and new lumber, as well as rice for 20 days (based on distribution of three times a day), to be used onboard the ship when sending Joseon drifters to Qing by the Ryukyu ship.[43] Furthermore, the Joseon drifters were unable to leave the ship immediately due to poor weather conditions in 1733. Twenty days of food was not enough since they stayed onboard in standby status so they requested additional supplies. Except for the fact that the Joseon people were living at an isolated shelter in Ryukyu, they were able to stay in family groupings and their treatment was generally good. Ryukyu provided most of the items requested by the Joseon people, even the soju they asked for to relieve their gloomy foreign life, that was consumed by both men and women. In addition to this, Ryukyu also provided rice to the Joseon people for the Lunar New Year's Day.[44]

Meanwhile, the expenses that Ryukyu had to bear accumulated beyond

---

40 *Okinawa Prefecture Historical Sources*, pre-modern era 5, Record of Drift Relationships, "A Diary of Repatriation of Joseons".
41 Ibid
42 Ibid
43 Ibid
44 Ibid

these. There were also extra expenses for the accommodation and heating for the sentry-duty watching the group while they were in Ryukyu. In order to retrun the Koreans, they had to rent a repatriation ship and hire sailors. The information on the expense of sailors currently available is that 375 silver coins were paid for hiring five Jwasa, government officials, and 1 silver coin for hiring 20 water owners, another name for a government official.[45] In addition to this, the five-month supply of food to be used while the crew went to Qing and returned was also at the expense of Ryukyu. However, about 546 silver coins, for the cost of repairs to the Ryukyu ship, was charged to the Pojeongsa of Joseon, and paid.

From Ryukyu's point of view, not only did they pay for Joseon drifters to stay in Ryukyu, but it also cost a considerable amount in extra expenditure to guard and repatriate them. However, the Joseon Dynasty did not give diplomatic documents or return gifts to Ryukyu for the repatriation of the Joseon drifters.[46] This is probably because Ryukyu's repatriation process was changed in 1696, and as such, no special advice (official document) was sent from the King of Ryukyu to Joseon's king, but was written instead by the Ceremonies Board of Qing, and delivered to Joseon.

As mentioned earlier, there was a woman among the group who gave birth to a son, in 1733, while they were in still in Ryukyu. Ryukyu gave special consideration for pregnant women, and as such, all expenses for pre-birth supplies, childbirth, doctors and nannies for postnatal/postpartum care, were covered.[47] The concern for the health of mothers after childbirth is evident by mushrooms that were provided for medicinal purposes and ginseng soup

---

45 Ibid
46 Ha Woobong et al. (1999), *Joseon and Ryukyu*, Arche, p.227-228.
47 Lee Hoon (1994), op. cit., p.144.

supplied for about one month. Ginseng was then, as it is still now, a very valuable medicinal ingredient and they had paid as much as two thousand nyang (tael) for it. On top of all this, people from Ryukyu also hired doctors, and wet-nurses to breastfeed newborns. The salary for three wet-nurses between December 26-29, was 15 thousand nyang.[48]

The Joseon people who drifted in Ryukyu into 1733 were repatriated to Joseon in 1735. They stayed in Ryukyu for as long as two years before returning home, and this raises the question of whether Ryukyu really paid all the costs free of charge during their long stay. Among the *"Okinawa Prefecture Historical Sources,"* there is a memorandum that petitioned for the employment of a man among the Joseon people, as a sailor in Ryukyu.[49] Their per capita wage was one silver coin per day. It is also difficult to know exactly how long the Joseon people were actually employed as sailors, and whether they were able to cover the entire cost of the Ryukyu stay with their wages.[50] Ryukyu made it a rule to pay for Joseon people's cost of living while there, so that it was free for them. However, it can be said that there was a change to the paid-in repatriation because it was intended to reimburse part of the cost for the wage labor of the drifting people.

However, the cost of transferring the Koreans to Beijing was charged to Qing when they arrived at Fujian in Qing China on the Ryukyu ship. However, Qing had to escort them from Beijing to the Joseon border due to the absence of envoys. The escort cost for this trip was also covered by Qing.[51] As such, Ryukyu was responsible for the relief of the Joseon people from the landing

---

48 *Okinawa Prefecture Historical Sources*, pre-modern era 5, Record of Drift Relationships, "A Diary of Repatriation of Joseons".

49 Ibid

50 Lee Hoon (1994), op. cit., p.135.

51 Ha Woobong et al. (1999), op. cit., pp.223-224.

site, as well as for the expenses during their stay in Ryukyu and until they were escorted to the Fujian Province of Qing China. After that, the cost to Uiju via Beijing was covered by Qing.

IV. The Drift of Ryukyu People in Joseon and the Joseon Sea Area

1. Cases of Joseon Drift by Ryukyu People

During the Joseon Dynasty, Ryukyu sent a goodwill delegation to Joseon more than 50 times in the 15th century. In this process, the two countries actively engaged in exchange activities, ranging from political, diplomatic, defense, trade, and repatriation of drifters. However, in the 16th century, foreign relations with Ryukyu declined rapidly. This was because China's trade ships pushed for direct exchanges in Southeast Asia, Japan, and other countries while the Ming Dynasty eased its isolationist policy.[52] Moreover, in 1592 (the 25th year of King Seonjo's reign), Japan invaded Joseon and started the Imjin War, demanding Ryukyu's cooperation. At this time, Ryukyu rejected Japan's offer and rather cooperated with Joseon and Ming. In 1609 (the 1st year of King Gwanghaegun's reign), Japan's Satsuma-domain invaded Ryukyu putting it under Japanese subjugation.[53] From then, Ryukyu was suspended from trading with foreign countries while under the control of Satsuma though they continued to exchange with Joseon through informal procedures such as repatriation of the drifting people. Such information can be found in the case

---

52 Min Duckki (1999), *History of Ryukyu, Joseon and Ryukyu*, Arche, p.17.
53 *The Annals of King Gwanghaegun*, 8 May, the fifth year of King Gwanghaegun's reign.

of the repatriation of the drifting people in the Ryukyu Kingdom, which was recorded by Joseon in the 15th and 19th centuries.

In the Joseon Dynasty, 22 cases of people drifting from Ryukyu to Joseon were recorded as shown in Table 3. Not many of these have been traced from Ryukyu to the sea area of Gyeongsang-Province. However, through the issues of people drifting directly between Gyeongsang-Province and Ryukyu, we can look at sea area issues such as relationship, exchange, and repatriation between Gyeongsang-Province and Ryukyu in Joseon.

<Table 3> Cases of Joseon drift by Ryukyu people during the Joseon Dynasty[54]

Date of Drift	Date of Repatriation	Drifting site	Outport	Number of Drifting People	Reason for Drift	Way of Repatriation	Repatriated by	
							Document	Repatriation Mission
1418. 8.21		Hansan Island, Gyeongsang Province	Ryukyu	70 Fatalities	Ryukyu Delegation, transport of gifts	Communicate, sent to Seoul		
1429. 8.15		Uljin, Gangwon-Province		15 (1 Fatality)		Interpreter accompany, Japan's cooperation, sent to Seoul, 14 people, Sea route		
1452. 5.11		Chuksanpo, Yeonghae	Ryukyu	12		Ryukyu, the repatriation of the envoy		Envoy Doan, an envoy for the prince's birthday
1497. 10.14		Jeju	Tarama	10	Safflower, fabric, rice transportation	The lord of the Tsushima request, transportation of native products		Shinsira, a fake envoy

---

54 <Table 1> was made and complemented by compiling data from Lee Hoon (1994), "The Choson-Ryukyu Relations as seen by Drifter's Repatriation in the Latter Half of Choson Dynasty", *Journal of Historical Studies* 27, pp.123-124; The Korea-Japan Historical Society (2001), *Research on Korean-Japanese Drifters in Joseon Dynasty*, Kookhak, p.21; Shigeru Kobayashi·Takatoshi Matsubara·Yutaka Rokanda editor (1998), "Timeline of drifts from Ryuku to Joseon in Joseon", *Research on the Diplomatic Records of Ryukyu (Rekidai Hoan)* 9, Okinawa Prefecture Education Research Society, pp.86-117.

Date of Drift	Date of Repatriation	Drifting site	Outport	Number of Drifting People	Reason for Drift	Way of Repatriation	Repatriated by	
							Document	Repatriation Mission
1530. 10.3		Ujukdo, Jeju	Nojima	7	Tributes of rice	via Beijing, 1531 a New Year's Eve mission		New Year's envoy, accompany
1589. 7.23		Jindo	Ryukyu	30	Mercantile	via Beijing		A winter solstice envoy, accompany
1590. 1.1			Ryukyu	1		Liaodong attachment, Request extradition		
1612. 9.9			Ryukyu	9		A document of Seungjeongwon (承政院), via Beijing		A winter solstice envoy, accompany
1613. 1.28		Jeju		merchants	Yellow cloth, silk cloth, transportation of glass, etc.	Assault of drifting ships such as a local official of Jeju		
1790. 7.20 (6.13)	1790. 6.27	Jeju	Ryukyu Naha District	12	Tributes of rice (grain and rice, horse, books)	Sea route		
1794. 8.17 (9.11)	1794	Jeju	Ryukyu	11(4)	Public affairs (clothing, document)	Repatriation by land (via Beijing, Fujian)		Seasonal envoys on the return back (accompanied by an envoy)
1794. 9.11 (7.11)		Yeongam	Ryukyu, Yaeyama Island	3 (7 fatalities)	Official documents (an islander of an island), a public vessel	The evacuation of the Gwangjewon (廣濟院), Stay in Gyeonggi-Province, Payment of repatriation costs		A winter solstice envoy, accompany
1797. 6.7 (leap month)		Jeju	Naha District	7	Popular Romance of the Three Kingdoms, Calendar	Sea route		Ryukyu vessel
	1801		Ryukyu	5				
1820. 6.16 (7.1)	1820.7	Jeju	Ryukyu	5	Lumber	Land route (via Fujian)		Erudite calendar officer, on the return back
1821. 5.20 (6.15)	1821.8	Jeju	Ryukyu	5(6)	Household goods Purchase	Land route (via Fujian)		Erudite calendar officer, on the return back
1827. (26) 2.29 (6.15)	1827	Oenarodo	Ryukyu	3	Merchants	Land route (via Fujian)		Erudite calendar officer, on the return back

Date of Drift	Date of Repatriation	Drifting site	Outport	Number of Drifting People	Reason for Drift	Way of Repatriation	Repatriated by	
							Document	Repatriation Mission
1831. 7.1 (25)	1831	Jeju	Ryukyu Naha District	3		Land route (via Fujian)		Seasonal envoys, on the return back
1832. 8.13	1832	Jeju	Ryukyu Naha	4		via Fujian		Seasonal envoys, on the return back
1860. 6.13	1860	Jeju	Ryukyu Naha	6		via Fujian		Seasonal envoys, on the return back
1861. 10.15		Jeju	Ryukyu			via Japan, Tsushima		Satsuma
1871. 9.23		Naju		22		Sea route		Ship by sea (public procurement)

During the Joseon Dynasty, there were three cases of Ryukyu people who drifted into Joseon's sea area, including Gyeongsang-Province (plus Gangwon-do) and most of them were in Jeju Island except for Jeolla-Province, Jindo and Yeongsan. This was because, among other things, Jeju Island is geographically closer to Ryukyu and open to the ocean. The Ryukyu people were carrying out various activities before drifting, such as carrying a tribute of seed, commerce or official duties.

During the Joseon Dynasty, Joseon and Ryukyu repatriated the drifting people from a friendly position as partners of good-neighbor countries. However, the drifters were repatriated indirectly through Beijing from 1530 (the 25th year of King Jungjong's reign) as direct exchanges ceased due to the issue of falsifying history.[55] Joseon and Ryukyu were repatriated on the premise of friendly relations between the two countries. The Kings of both Joseon and Ryukyu started to repatriate, and continued the repatriation using official missions while exchanging documents. The Ryukyu people, who drifted to Jeju

---

55 The Korea-Japan Historical Society (2001), op. cit., pp.21-24.

Island in 1497 (3rd year of Yeonsangun), were repatriated through Tsushima. In 1530, the Ryukyu people were repatriated via Beijing.[56] Later, repatriation of the drifting people to Joseon took place five times until 1589 (the 22nd year of King Seonjo's reign) when 30 merchants of Ryukyu were repatriated from Jindo. The number of cases seems low considering the external relations between Ryukyu and Joseon in the early Joseon Dynasty. This was because ships had to pass through Kyushu and Tsushima in Japan to come to the sea area of Gyeongsang Province of Joseon, from Ryukyu. However, the opportunity itself had been reduced due to the Japanese pirates who took control of the coast of Gyeongsang-Province. Moreover, if a problem occurred, they went back to the middle of sailing or to a nearby area, not to Joseon.

In particular, the repatriation of the drifters between Joseon and Ryukyu from 1530 (the 25th year of King Jungjong's reign) to 1668 (the 16th year of King Injo's reign) was by an indirect method of repatriation via Beijing.[57] The repatriation was based on the premise of good neighbourly relations between the related countries and repatriation was continued by exchanging documents between the countries. Since Ryukyu was subjugated by Japan in 1609, the drifters were repatriated by a detour via Nagasaki under the repatriation system between Joseon and Japan. Later, when the system of repatriation of the drifting people was established by Qing, they were sent back to Ryukyu through Qing, incidentally in accordance with Ryukyu's procedures for repatriation of Chinese people, most of which were along with a diplomatic delegation.

Ryukyu drifters were repatriated free of charge from Joseon.[58] In the case of the repatriation of Ryukyu people through Japan, Joseon paid goods (such

---

56 Yang Suji, op. cit., pp.123-126.
57 Ha Woobong et al. (1999), op. cit., p.62.
58 Ibid, pp.228-233.

as white rice, fish, vegetables, firewood, dried fish, etc.) every five days during their stay in Joseon. On their return home, they paid rice and lumber to help the repatriation.

2. Drift and Repatriation in Gyeongsang-Province of Ryukyu People

Before the Imjin War, there was a total of five times that Ryukyu people who drifted were repatriated. Among them, there were three cases in the area of Gyeongsang-Province during the early Joseon Dynasty.[59] Firstly, in 1418, when the envoys of Ryukyu settled in Hansando, clothing, and food were provided to them.[60]

Secondly, in August 1429 (the 11th year of King Sejong's reign), 15 Ryukyu people, including Pomogara, arrived in Uljin-hyeon, Gangwon-do. Upon receiving the report, the government let the drifters decide whether they wanted to live in Joseon or not. If they wanted to stay, they would live in the coastal sea area of Gyeongsang-Province. If they wanted to return, they would be repatriated to Ryukyu.[61] Their attire, when found, showed that that were from Ryukyu.

A. In the year 1429, a foreign ship was found in Uljin-hyeon. It turned out that there were fifteen people in all, all dressed in blue. They tied up the hair around their necks, wrapped the head in red cotton with colored drawings, and wrapped his lower body in a large blue garment without pants. On

---

59 *The Annals of King Sejong,* 21 August, 1418, in the first year of King Seongjong's reign.
60 Ibid.
61 *The Annals of King Sejong,* 15 August, in the eleventh year of King Seongjong's reign.

closer examination, they found out that they were from Ryukyu.[62]

B. Fifteen people, including Pomogara, members of the Ryukyu Kingdom, drifted to Uljin-hyeon, Gangwon-do. They were captured and reported as pirates, the officials reported the issue and sent them to Seoul. They gave Ryukyu drifters clothes and shoes, guiding them to the inn.[63]

During this time, a funeral was held for one of the Ryukyu drifters named Imagara (理毛加羅), who had died, and whose remains were eventually repatriated in accordance with the wishes of the remaining 14 people. However, as there was no direct voyage between Joseon and Ryukyu, it was necessary to seek cooperation from Japan. When repatriated, Joseon sent Tongsa Kim Wonjin along with a document sent to the name of King Ryukyu. Joseon also sent documents to ask for the cooperation of Hyuga, Osumi, and Satsuma of Japan. This was the direct repatriation method of Joseon and Ryukyu. In response, the Ryukyu people thanked Kim Wonjin in the following year (1430) when he returned home. The Ryukyu king also promised to repatriate any Koreans who drifted in the future to Joseon. As a result, Joseon and Ryukyu's friendly repatriation of drifters started off smoothly.

Third, in 1452 (the second year of King Munjong's reign), when 12 Ryukyu people were repatriated from Chuksanpo, Ryukyu returned four Joseon people who had been found adrift, to express their gratitude, through Wangsa Doan, in 1453. Unlike the deportation of Joseon drifters, the method by which Ryukyu people were returned to their homeland, depended on when

---

62 *Daedongyaseung* (大東野乘), "*DonggagJabgi*" the first, Seonwonborog (璿源寶錄).
63 *The Annals of King Sejong*, op. cit.

repatriation occurred.[64]

The first Ryukyu group mentioned (1418) was sent back directly; the second (1429) was returned with the assistance of Japan; while the third group (1452) was repatriated through the diplomatic delegations of Ming or Qing. Joseon's government was generous to the Ryukyu drifters in 1429 (the 11th year of King Sejong's reign). When the drifters were to be repatriated, they repaired the ship and provided crops. They also sent documents to the powerful local Japanese family in Satsuma, to ask for their cooperation. Kim Wonjin, the Tongsa, was sent with them, to assist in their safe repatriation.

In the case of 1429, the specific examples of how people who were rescued and repatriated to Ryukyu during the early Joseon Dynasty are as follows: When the people of Ryukyu drifted in 1429 in Uljin-hyeon-Gangwon-do, clothes and shoes were given to the drifting people. In one case in September 1612, Ryukyu drifters were taken to the Bibyeonsa, a conference where ministers of civil affairs and military affairs gathered during the Joseon Dynasty, to decide on the national affairs. The drifters were provided with winter clothes, shoes and hats, separately, to prepare for the upcoming cold, considering that they originally lived in a warm climate.[65] Additionally, five people aboard a Ryukyu vessel, drifted into Jeongui-hyeon of Jeju Island, in 1820. Their goods onboard was in good condition, however, they were not allowed to travel home along the sea route to Ryukyu, because it was stipulated, in principle, that they should be repatriated by land. Therefore, Joseon used local horses to transport the items in the collection of this Ryukyu group to Seoul. For items which were unable to be transported, the Joseon government purchased the goods at a generous price.[66]

---

64 Yang Suji, op. cit., p.126.
65 *The Annals of King Gwanghaegun*, 9 September, the fourth year of King Gwanghaegun's reign.
66 *The Annals of King Soonjo*, 1 July, the twentieth year of King Soonjo's reign.

As such, the Ryukyu drifters were taken to Seoul after receiving first relief measures at the drifting site. This process was called Jeonche (傳遞) or Yuckjeon (驛傳).[67] Jeonche was the method by which the local government official in the area they passed through, would transport the drifting people to the boundary point of his jurisdiction on the way to Seoul, and then hand them over to other officials in the neighboring area. Yuckjeon meant that the local government official in the jurisdiction, transferred the drifting people to other local government officials, starting with the lodging where they settled while moving to Seoul. When the drifters arrived in Seoul, a central government official accompanied the local official to question the group about how they came to to drift to Joseon, in a form of inquisition or interrogation. Ryukyu drifters were also questioned about their arrival in Joseon, by a Japanese person from the Dongpyeonggwan (東平館),[68] who would first record their appearance. In other words, they identified the Satgat, worn on the head, clothing, and the language used. Then they asked basic questions such as name, place of residence, the purpose of navigation, the process of drift, shipment, and so forth.[69] Even when Doan, the envoy of King Ryukyu Zhongshan (中山王) arrived, and a banquet was held in Yeo (the Ministry of Culture and Education), it was said that his words were written down in the records of Yeo, to prove that he was from indeed from Ryukyu.

---

67 Kim Kyungok (2012), "The Real Condition of Casting away on Chosun and Repatriation of Ryukyu-People: Focusing on Chosunwangjoshilok (朝鮮王朝實錄)", *Local History and Local Culture* 15-1, Korean Society for Local History and Culture, pp.129-131.

68 Dongpyeonggwan was built during the early Joseon Dynasty to serve Japanese envoys. In the early days, there were two, Dongpyeonggwan and Seopyeonggwan. They were established to appease the Japanese pirates, but when the Japanese pirates were suppressed during the reign of King Sejong, Seopyeonggwan was abolished and only Dongpyeonggwan was maintained. (*The Annals of King Taejong*, 26 February, the ninth year of King Soonjo's reign).

69 *The Annals of King Yeonsangun*, 14 October, the third year of King Soonjo's reign.

More than 60 Koreans have drifted to Ryukyu, but almost all of them dead, only five old people are still alive. Their daughters and sons are all married to the people of the country, and they are all wealthy. Old people know a little bit of the Joseon language.[70]

The sea area and sea routes that the Ryukyu people drifted in during the Joseon Dynasty are similar to that shown in Table 3. The reason why people from Ryukyu drifted to Gyeongsang-Province during the early Joseon Dynasty was because of the dispatch of envoys to Yeompo, Ulsan, after the opening of the port of Sampo, on their way to trade. The drifting from Ryukyu to Joseon was influenced by seasonal winds since it mostly took place in summer. During the pre-modern period, the route between Joseon and Ryukyu was also open to Jeju Island.[71]

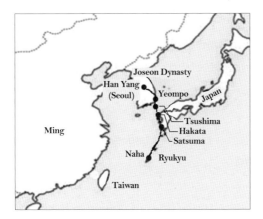

<Figure 3> Drift sea area and repatriation route in Gyeongsang-Province by Ryukyu people in the early Joseon Dynasty

---

70 *The Annals of King Danjong*, 11 May, the first year of King Danjong's reign.
71 Yoon Myeongchul (2012), *Marine History Research Methodology*, Hakyoun, p.217.

The Northeast Asian sea area centering around the Korean Peninsula, changes every year under the influence of seasonal winds. In particular, distress occurred frequently during the winter (November-March) depending on the climate of Siberia and the North Pacific Ocean. Moreover, there were many typhoons in the summer (from June to September) that occurred in the East China Sea through the sea area around the Philippines and Taiwan. The typhoons often arrived on the southern coast of Korea passing through Ryukyu.[72] For this reason, when people drifted into the Jeju sea area, they frequently arrived from Ryukyu.

Meanwhile, in the late Joseon Dynasty, three Ryukyu merchants who had drifted into Oenarodo, Heunghae-hyeon, were escorted to Beijing along a land route.[73] However, the recorded route of Oenarodo - Heunghae-hyeon - Donghae - Gyeongsang-Province was no doubt incorrect, and was more likely Oenarodo - Heunghae-hyeon, Jeolla-Province, instead.[74] As a result, it is believed there was never a case in which Ryukyu people drifted into the sea area of Gyeongsang-Province during the late Joseon Dynasty. This was because Ryukyu were unable to continue their relationship with Joseon, with the Japanese unified government subjugating Ryukyu after the Imjin War.

V. Conclusion

In the Joseon Dynasty, the cases of drifting to Ryukyu from the sea area of Gyeongsang-Province of Joseon, and the cases of drifting to Gyeongsang-

---

72 Kim Jaeseung (1996), op. cit., p.142.
73 *The Annals of King Soonjo*, 16 June, the twenty-sixth year of King Soonjo's reign.
74 Heungyang-hyeon is currently located in Goheung, Jeolla-Province.

Province of Joseon, from Ryukyu are very limited. This is because records of most of the drifts were not kept properly. The drifts that occurred in the East Asian sea area during the pre-modern period were under the principle of free repatriation between countries following the framework of the tributary system. Drifting was a typical maritime accident, however, they also served as opportunities to create new routes in the sea. This is the main reason why maritime history pays attention to drifting.

The unexpected drift and drifting ashore in Joseon and Ryukyu, by subjects of these two countries, served as opportunities to experience and acquire various pieces of cultural information and other knowledge while staying in each other's countries for certain periods of time. The relationship between Joseon and Ryukyu, which are distant, has been affected by political changes in Japan, since the time of foundation of the Joseon Dynasty. Particularly closely related to the activities of Japanese pirates, the issue surrounding the drift of Joseon and Ryukyu people also changed in three stages: Direct repatriation between Gyeongsang Province and Ryukyu, the case of Tsushima or Kyushu's detour through Japan, and repatriation through Ming or Qing China. Among them, the first two used mainly sea routes, while the third used a combination of sea and land routes.

Therefore, the direct repatriation of the drifting people of Gyeongsang Province and Ryukyu was strictly limited to only certain periods in the early Joseon Dynasty. Even though the frequency of drifts between Gyeongsang-Province and Ryukyu was uncommon, these pioneering years became a way of identifying the geographical area, or the physical sea area, leading to the opening of sea routes. During the pre-modern period, people continued to settle over a certain sea route under the influence of natural phenomena such as ocean and tidal currents, and the prevailing winds. This would have been predicated by the constant sacrifice of many ocean-going people who tried to go out to sea.

The cases of repatriation after the drift to Ryukyu by Kim Bieui's party in 1429, and the drift to Ryukyu by Seo Hujeong's party in 1733, were typical examples of Joseon people who drifted into Ryukyu during the Joseon Dynasty. Through these incidents, cultural exchanges between the two countries, and their understanding of the other countries, were deepened. In particular, the two times Ryukyu people drifted into Joseon, during the Joseon Dynasty, between Ryukyu and the coast of Donghae, Gyeongsang-Province can be understood from the same perspective. It is noted that these are rare cases that confirm the sea route to Gyeongsang Province or Ryukyu. Confirming an unusual case draws attention. Additionally, the repatriation route between Gyeongsang Province and Ryukyu differed between the early and late Joseon Dynasty. The reason for this is related to the establishment of the Japanese unified government, which forced repatriation to become indirect, via Ming or Qing, since foreign relations with Ryukyu and Joseon deteriorated. It can assumed, however, that drifting would have continued through the sea routes that were established during the early Joseon Dynasty.

A Study on a British Sailing Ship Harbouring at Yongdanpo in 1797

Lee, Hak-Su

Jeong, Moon-Soo

Ⅰ. Introduction

A foreign ship landed at Yongdangpo (龍塘浦) in Busan (釜山) on September 6, 1797 (October 13, Gregorian calendar) of the 21st year of King Jeongjo's (正祖) reign. The residents of Yongdangpo rowed their boats out of curiosity and flocked around the ship. It had been 200 years since the Japanese Invasion of Korea in 1592 and 140 years since the Manchu Invasion of Korea in 1636. The naval and administrative officials of Busan, surprised by the appearance of foreign ship, boarded and investigated the ship, and then hurriedly reported to the king. The king and the secretaries of the kingdom also discussed countermeasures against foreign sailing. The government instructed them to send the vessels out of the Joseon border by providing necessary supplies following the manual. Only a few high-ranking officials knew about the appearance of the ship and kept it secret from the public.

However, the Yongdangpo incident, the appearance of a British sailing vessel in Yongdangpo, was not an unusual incident. Immediately after the incident, The Catholic Persecution of 1801 occurred. It has been given as a trigger for the Korean Isolation policy that the government blocked the research or influence of new culture or literature from West. In the face of social change, Joseon's privileged class took a defensive stance and tightened security of the boundaries of Gyeongsang-do's (慶尙道) coastal areas. However, despite the crackdown by the government, the Interests of Silhak (實學) scholars of the realistic school of Confucianism, who studied practical matters in the Joseon Dynasty, in the new culture had not diminished, and the number of Christians had rather increased. Coastal residents had drifted to distant seas, sailing outward and the tension between governing forces and those who want to change was heightened.

The Yongdangpo incident has been mentioned partially in several books.[1] However, there was a critical error, which is the main reason to write this article, in order to correct it and to further interpret the meaning of the incident. First of all, this paper identifies the real name of the sailing vessel anchored at Yongdangpo. Next it will not only review Joseon society's attitude toward strangers, but will restore the accuracy of first meeting with the crew members of the sailboat and the residents of Yongdangpo by analyzing the logbook and historical documents of both sides. Finally, it will ascertain the relationship between the Joseon society and the ocean around 1797, and the significance of

---

1 Han, Sang-Bok (한상복, 1988), *Korean Studies in the view of Maritime Studies*, Seoul: Hyesosa, pp.32-36, 45-50; Kim, Jae-Seung (김재승, 1977), *The Maritime Interaction History of Korean and U.K. in Modern Times*, Kimhae: Inje Univ. Press, pp.20-21, 159-191; Park, Chun-Hong (박천홍, 2008), *The Sea of Joseon, where evil spirits appeared,* Seoul: Hyunsilmunhuayeongu, pp.49-85; James E. Hoare (2000), *Captain Broughton, HMS Providence (and her Tender) and his voyage to the Pacific 1794-8, Asian Affairs*, Vol. 31, Issue 3, pp.303-312.

the Yongdangpo incident.

The materials of the Yongdangpo incident helped a lot in the restoration of the accuracy of the incident with the ship's logbook, the voyages[2] published by Captain Broughton, and the remaining accurate and detailed information[3] of the British sailing vessel from the official Joseon society records.

II. HMS *Providence* and *Prince William Henry*

1. HMS *Providence* and Captain William Broughton

On October 13, 1797, the appearance of a British sailing vessel in Yongdangpo was reported to the Royal Court of Joseon. At that time, the generals looked into the vessel in detail, but they did not know which country it was from and where the crew was from. The Yongdangpo incident was studied earlier by Han, Sang-Bok and Kim, Jae-Seung. Referring to Broughton's voyages, in 1988 Han mentioned that HMS *Providence* ran aground near Okinawa and her tender came to Yongdangpo.[4]

Kim refers to both Broughton's voyages and reports, describing the fact that the ship ran aground and that the tender was called HMS *Province* as well.[5] Park, Chun-Hong also referred to the research results of Han and Kim

---

2 William Robert Broughton (1804), *A voyage of discovery of to the north Pacific Ocean*, London: British Library, Historical Print Editions.

3 *Annals of the Joseon Dynasty* (朝鮮王朝實錄), *Seungjungwonilgi* (承政院日記), *Ilsungrok* (日省錄), *Selected Poems and Essays of Chungdasan* (鄭茶山詩文選), *Chung, Dong-Yoo* (정동유), *Jooyoungpyeon* (晝永編).

4 Han, Sang-Bok, op. cit., p.47.

5 Kim, Jae-Seung, p.25, Kim was confusing the types of the two ships, calling them "87-ton Sloop-type sailing ship" and "400-ton Schooner *Providence*." but "87-ton Schooner

and wrote that the tender was renamed *Providence* right after it ran aground.[6] However, both are not consistent with the facts. Because the name of the tender that arrived at Yongdangpo was *Prince William Henry*.

From a gunship first launched in 1637 to a minesweeper scrapped in 1953, twelve ships of the British Navy have been named HMS *Providence*. The Sloop-of-war HMS *Providence*, commanded by Commander Broughton was launched in April 1791 as a full-rigged ship and operated for six years until it was stranded in May 1797. The vessel, built in London's Perry & Co., Blackwell Yard, was used as a trading ship for the West Indies, with a total of 406 tons, three decks, 32.9 meters long, 8.9 meters wide, and 100 crew members.

When the *Bounty* was lost due to a sailor riot, the British Navy needed a ship to take its place. The British Navy purchased the *Providence* built and placed just in time and assigned Commander Bligh to collect breadfruit trees. In January 1793, Bligh arrived in the West Indies with the *Providence*, unloaded breadfruit trees on Jamaica and other British islands, and returned to England in August 1793. The *Providence* was re-rated as a sloop on September 30, 1793.

William Broughton began his career as a midshipman at the age of 15 and commissioned as an officer at the age of 18 in 1789. After his commission, he immediately joined the 74-gun *Superb*. In January 1782, he was promoted to lieutenant in the Royal Navy and served in 68-gun *Burford*. When he fulfilled the period of a contract on 19 July 1784, he did not serve for about four years.[7]

Prince William Henry" and "400-ton Sloop-type sailing ship" is correct.

6 Park, Chun-Hong, op. cit., p.63.

7 Andrew David ed.(2010), *William Robert Broughton's Voyage of discovery of to the north Pacific 1795-1798,* Hakluyt Society, London: Ashgate, pp.lii-liii.

<Figure 1>The *Providence* (detail), from a watercolour by George Tobinc. 1791.
Mitchell Library, State Library of New South Wales (David. ed., p.xxix)

After returning to the Navy in June 1788, Broughton was promoted to lieutenant commander and was appointed captain of the Brig HMS *Chatham* on May 18, 1790, for the first time, to accompany the north-west Pacific expedition led by Commander George Vancouver. On October 3, 1793, Broughton was promoted to commander, and this time, he was appointed captain of the *Providence*. Repairs caused a long delay and the ship was unable to leave the port. He arrived in north-west America in February 1795 and tried to join the Vancouver Expedition. However, he eventually decided to explore the Asian coast of the Pacific independently because he was unable to locate Vancouver.

Broughton explored the Asian Coast between the latitudes of 35 and 52 degrees north, including the Kurile Islands, Japan, Okinawa, and Taiwan for four years (1795-1798). In September 1796, he charted the coast of Honshu and the east coast of Kyushu. Then, he decided to winter at Macau, where the British naval base was located. Broughton purchased the *Prince William*

Henry, a small-sized schooner ship, in Macau on December 29, 1796, judging that he needed a ship to assist the *Providence*.[8] In ocean exploration, it was common for two ships to team up to explore. The auxiliary ship was necessary to prepare for the risk of a possible stranding, to be used as a close-range probe, and to transport essentials such as food, drinking water, and firewood to handle a long exploration. *The Prince William Henry* was 87-ton and 28 meters long, with two sails, about one-fifth of that of the *Providence*. The ship's name came from the name of Prince William Henry (1743-1805) who was the brother of King George III (1760-1820). He served as a military officer and was named the head of the Field Marshal shortly before his death.[9] Broughton, meanwhile, was promoted to captain during his voyage of exploration on January 28, 1797.

That year, on April 11, 1797, Captain Broughton left the port of Macau to resume exploration near Sakhalin Island in the North Pacific, carrying 15 months of drinking water and food on both the *Providence* and the schooner *Prince William Henry*. On the evening of May 17, 1797, the *Providence* was wrecked when it hit a rock near Miyako Island in Okinawa. After struggling to save the ship all day, Broughton and his crewmen eventually gave up the ship and carried the navigational equipment and documents to the schooner. Fortunately, Broughton's personal diary, ship's log, and longitude measuring precision watch, Arnold Chronometer 45, were in the salvage and there were no casualties.[10] The next morning Broughton and his crewmen were able to salvage riggings such as small anchors, ropes, and sails from the wreck, but they had to give up food. Broughton and the rest moved to Hirana village, near

---

8 Ibid, p.215.

9 Colin Matthew and Brian Harrison (2007), "Prince William Henry" in *Oxford Dictionary of National Bibliography*, Oxford: Oxford University Press; Jane Roberts, *Royal Landscape: The Gardens and Parks of Windsor*, New Haven: Yale University Press.

10 Andrew David, op. cit., pp.125-127.

Miyako Island and anchored there. He returned safely to Macau after receiving supplies from residents.

2. The Schooner *Prince William Henry* and Captain William Broughton

After arriving in Macau, Broughton reported to the Royal Navy that the *Providence* was stranded, expressing his intention to continue his exploration of the north Pacific. Broughton's June 15 diary reveals his plans for future exploration as follows.

> The Schooner could not contain more than 5 months provisions. ... We now sail'd a second time in the prosecution of the voyage, not indeed with most flattering hopes of success, as the season was far advanc'd & the vessel in many respects ill-suited to the purpose. But still there was a prospect of acquiring a geographical knowledge of the Tartarean and Corean coasts; nor did I wish to fail in any endeavour that might promote the improvement of science by the discovery of parts of the world as yet but imperfectly known. The officer and the men were equally well dispos'd with myself to do our respective duties and we departed in good health.[11]

Broughton and his 35 crewmen continued north along the east coast of Honshu with the *Prince William Henry*, leaving Macau on 27 June 1797. Passing Okinawa and Japan, they stopped by seaside villages to get drinking

---

11 Ibid, pp.136-137.

water and firewood, and even sought a map of the Japanese island in Muroran, south of Hokkaido. However, residents generally wanted the Broughton companies to leave quickly and demanded to keep secret that they obtained a map from them.[12] Broughton later sailed into the Tartar Strait on the west coast of Sakhalin in early September passing Hokkaido. Finding the shallows at the north end of the Tatar Strait, Broughton thought that Sakhalin was connected to the mainland and turned back to the Gulf.[13] However, this was a strait, not the mainland, and Broughton's conclusion later proved false when the British navy was blocked at the Gulf of Tatar during the Crimean War, and it made them dismayed.

The *Prince William Henry* got out of the Tatar Strait and turned south along the coast of the east sea of Korea near Vladivostok. Passing Musudan, Yeongheungman, and Ulsan, Broughton stayed in Busan for nine days from October 13 to 21 due to a lack of drinking water and firewood.[14] The *Prince William Henry* which sailed from Yongdangpo with drinking water, firewood, and some food, explored the southern coast of Jeju Island. After discovering that there were no islands to the south of Jeju Island, Broughton turned north to explore Joseon's west coast. He discovered Soheuksan Island (now Gageo Island) south of the Heuksan Island in the west sea of Joseon. After this, Broughton, who determined that there were no more islands off the west coast of Joseon, turned to the south. He then anchored in Taipa, Macao, on November 27 sailing via Okinawa and Taiwan. Broughton temporarily discontinued writing the ship's log as he arrived in Macau. He stayed in Macau until January 21, 1798, writing the sea chart.

---

12 Ibid, pp.xlviii-xlix.
13 Ibid, pp.xlix-l.
14 Ibid, pp.184-190.

Anticipating a court-martial for the loss of the *Providence*, Broughton then went to Madras port (now Chennai) in India in March to report to his commander, Peter Rainier of the East Indies base. After he heard that commander Rainier was in Trincomalee, Sri Lanka, he headed there. The crew, who visited Yongdangpo, were paid off in Trincomalee, where there had been a major naval base since 1795. Captain Broughton was court-martialled on May 19. Fortunately, the court held Officer James Giles Vashon, the duty officer at the time, responsible, and Broughton was found not guilty.[15]

After handing over *Prince William Henry* to Commander Rainier on May 24, 1798, Broughton arrived in England on February 6, 1799, via Madras on June 15, 1798. Broughton wrote his book *A Voyage of Discovery to the North Pacific Ocean* and published it in 1804 while serving in the Navy for only half of his salary for two years. The *Prince William Henry*, which was handed over to commander Rainier, was renamed HM Schooner *Providence* with the approval of the commander in Trincomalee and officially listed as a British Navy asset.[16] This is how the *Prince William Henry* was renamed the *Providence*. The authors estimate that this period would have been in late May or early June 1798. The date of registration of the ship is 1796 because the date of registration was applied retroactively to the time when Captain Broughton purchased the ship. For this reason, the authors believe that the British sailing vessel, which landed in Yongdangpo in October 1797, should be corrected to the *Prince William Henry*.[17] HM Schooner *Providence* was briefly assigned

---

15 Ibid, pp.226-227.
16 Ibid, p.li.
17 A study showing a British sailing ship in Yongdangpo was Prince William Henry was first brought up by Jeong, Moon-Soo to the Korean academic community, followed by a paper by Kim, Nack-Hyeon and Hong, Ok-Sook. Jeong, Moon-Soo(2018.3), *Comprehensive Report on the History of British Sailing Ship's Visiting Yongdangpo and*

to the East India Company's naval base before being assigned to the British fleet. The *Providence* was commissioned as a firearm to attack the French fleet during the Battle of Boulogne on October 2, 1804, led by Admiral George Keith Elphinstone. After loading it full of gunpowder, it was likely to have approached French combat ships and was struck before sinking.

Even after the *Prince William Henry* in 1797, Britain continued to send sailing ships to explore the near seas of Joseon and to demand commerce from Joseon. Commander Murray Maxwell, the captain of the Frigate *Alceste*, and Commander Basil Hall, the captain of the Sloop *Lyra*, visited the five islands and off Gusan and Seocheon-gun in Korea's west sea from September 1 to 10 to measure the depth of water and prepare a sea chart.[18] They were able to visit the west sea of Korea to complete the survey mission of Broughton, which was not completed in 1797. Maxwell's crewmen departed from the coast of Gunsan around 10 a.m. on September 10 and arrived in Jeju Island late in the evening for a brief stay before hurriedly leaving Joseon after drawing up a map of the coasts of Jeju Island.

---

the Establishment of Master Plan for Symbolization of the Sailing Ship, Nam-gu, Busan, pp.29; Kim, Nack-Hyeon, Hong, Ok-Sook (2018.4), "Captain Broughton's Exploratory Voyage around the North Pacific (1795-1798) and its Significance", *Cultural Interaction Studies of Sea Port Cities*, No. 18, pp.194-195.

18 Basil Hall (1818), *Account of a voyage of discovery to the west coast of Corea and the great Loo-Choo Islands,* Philadelphia: Abraham Small.

III. Yongdangpo, a contact zone between British and Joseon cultures

1. British in Yongdangpo

The *Prince William Henry*, brought by the Broughton and his crews, was the first foreign ship to dock in Joseon. So what were the crew members of the ship like? At the end of the 18th century, the British navy was a mixture of civilian sailors forcibly drafted in addition to volunteer soldiers, and prisoners who chose to serve as sailors for exemption from prison terms. It is assumed that the crew of the British Navy's crew, including the whalers, were usually men of similar history to the *Bounty* crew. Also, the working conditions were generally poor due to frequent wars at the time. On the other hand, the *Prince William Henry*'s crew members were 35 regulars selected from 115 people, so they were better than average.

In October 1797, the 10 years had passed since *La Boussole* commanded by Captain La Pérouse passed the East Sea and the southern sea of Korea, the *Prince William Henry* stayed for nine days in Yongdangpo until they left. The records are relatively clearly described in the ship's log of Broughton.

As we approach'd the Land we perceiv'd several villages scatter'd along the Shore which appear'd much broken & likely to afford Shelter altho' its external View presented rather an inhospitable prospect. We all saw some Fishing Boats to Seaward (Friday 13 October). … Having spoken a fishing Boat with whom by signs we comprehended the NW opening wou'd admit of Anchorage, We bore up at 1/2 past Noon. … We therefore turn'd up toward the Bay and came to an Anchor in 4 fathoms, Sandy bottom. ... In the morning we had fair and pleasant weather & our Decks soon full of men, Women & Children whose curiosity induc'd them to come off. ... After breakfast we went in search of water & soon found a convenient run of excellent sort. ... After taking some Altitudes for the Watch & Observing distances for the Longitude we took a Walk round the village attended by a numerous party of inhabitants. ... Many villages were scattered round it, and to the North a large Town seemingly surrounded by a Wall with Battlements. Some Junks lay near it in a Bason surrounded partly by a Mole. Another Mole appear'd to the West of a Similar Form near some White Houses of Superior construction Enclosed by a thick Wood. All the Villages seem'd to abound in People and the Harbor equally so by the infinity of Boats sailing about. They were similar in figure tho'inferior in Workmanship to the Chinese Boats. They made use of Skulls & Matted Sails. ... In the afternoon we were visited by some Superior People who were dress'd much better & treated with great deference by the Common Sort. ... After Dinner we endeavour'd to explain who we were and what we came for, but I fear we comprehended each other very in differently. They however seem'd satisfied with their entertainment & took their Leave. ... On our return on board we found the Schooner crowded with People nor cou'd we get rid of them till near Dark and then with great difficulty, using almost violence to get them into their Boats. (Saturday 14 October)[19]

The most urgent task for the crew was to find drinking water and firewood.

---

19 Andrew David, op. cit., pp.184-185.

With the help of the residents, it was easy to find the spring water and convenient because the distance from the ship was close. Jaseongdae (子城臺) was likely surrounded by walls in the distance. They must have known by looking at the battlement that it was a wall where soldiers were stationed. White houses are assumed to be Choryang Waegwan (草梁倭館). The crew members also witness many ships working in and out of Busanpo (釜山浦). On the 14th, the day after the ship's arrival, the first official visitor was Park, Jong-hwa (박종화), the Busan Chumsa (釜山僉使) in Jwasuyeong, Gyeongsang Province. It seems that the naval forces in charge of the first line were the first to investigate the foreign ship.

We had no Boats come near us till after breakfast when two came with Company Superior to any we had yet seen. … They had in each Boat some Soldiers who carried Spontoons or Spears with flags of Blue Satin, the field & their Arms in yellow Characters. … One of principal Men who had been on board before, bro't us a present of Rice, Salt fish & Seaweed. After many enquiries respecting us these Great Men express'd a strong desire that we should sail & having informed them of our wanting Wood & Water they promised to send us some by way of hastening our departure. I also requested they wou'd send us a Bullock as we saw them grazing on the Shore which they did not seem inclined to comply with and as Money appear'd of no value we could not procure any, having no other means to induce them. … In the Afternoon they sent us some water in Jars & Tubs. (Sunday 15 October)[20]

---

20 Ibid, p.186.

On October 15, Broughton and his crews received a visit from Jeong, Sang-woo (정상우), a Dongnaebusa (東萊府使). He was escorted by soldiers with spears. The Dongnaebusa served dried fish, rice, and seaweed as gifts to strangers as a local administrative officer and commander. At that time, Joseon apparently tried to abide by this principle for foreign ships that drifted in because they were paying for the cost of the Busan Waegwan or the stay of the people who had drifted in. Meanwhile, the British tried to buy grazing cows on the coast for money, but the Dongnaebusa refused to allow it, so they could not buy beef.

The British saw that the residents who came to see them were quarantined by the Dongnaebusa. They probably got the impression that it was a measure of concern for unnecessary friction. The Dongnaebusa ordered the Yongdangpo residents to provide water and firewood, and so they provided the British with the necessary supplies in an orderly manner.

> As the violence of the wind permitted, we were employ'd watering and they also sent us off both wood and water (Monday 16 October). In the afternoon we had some deputies from the Great Men to know if we had wood & water enough & when we meant to sail. … After taking some Refreshment & having satisfied their curiosity they took leave (Tuesday 17 October). We were supplied throughout the Day with Water; of wood we had already receiv'd sufficient Quantity. … In the afternoon we were compleat with water and our Friends were very desirous we shou'd Sail. I endeavour'd to make them understand we meant to remain two days more to observe the Sun (Wednesday 18 October). We had some Visitors in the morning to expedite our departure but I assur'd them we cou'd not sail till one day after the Sun appear'd (Thursday

19 October). We were necessarily employed preparing for Sea & our Friends again came to know when we intended leaving them. ... Soon after They Landed (as if they still suspected our intention) they sent off four boats with a Flag & Soldiers in each who anchor'd on each side of us as I would not permit their coming on board. In the Afternoon they left us to ourselves (Friday 20 October). Before day light I left the Vessel to compleat a Sketch of the Harbor. We however returned at 1/2 past 7 Am. ... At breakfast we receiv'd a Visit from one of their Principal Man, who was highly pleas'd at seeing our preparation for Sailing. I presented him with a Telescope and a Pistol, the only two Articles he seem'd desirous of possessing & we parted much pleased with each other. We soon after got under way & Made sail out of the Harbor (Saturday 21 October).[21]

Besides visits of both the Busanchumsa and Dongnaebusa, Broughton and his crewmen were dispatched almost every day by the Jwasuyeong (Headquarters of the Busanchumsa) and Dongnae-Gwana (Administrative Office of the Dongnaebusa) to monitor the ship and urge them to leave quickly. On the other hand, they received both curiosity and practical support from the residents of Yongdangpo. The residents provided them with plenty of water and firewood and provided directions to locations.

During their stay in Yongdangpo, Broughton made a map of Busanpo and examined 38 Korean words and 26 plants. The Korean words are numbers from 1 to 10, words for navigation such as stars, wind, water, fire, etc., names of body parts such as eyes, nose, mouth, and precious items such as gold,

---

21 Ibid, pp.186-188.

silver, cattle, and pigs.[22] Broughton expressed his impressions on the Koreans as follows

> They were well acquainted with fire arms and Great Guns, and yet during our stay we saw no sign of offensive weapons whatever among them. Nor did they seem any way apprehensive of the small power we possess'd. ... We had very much excited their attention & curiosity particularly our Woolen Clothing. As a Commercial People one would suppose they were conversant in Barter but they did not appear anxious to make any changes whatsoever. They have Horses & Black Cattle, Hogs & Poultry. On them I think they set a great value. ... Money indeed they had no idea of money, at least our Coins & Spanish Dollars. Yet they fully understood the Value of Gold and Silver of which they make use in workmanship of Knives &c. Their Grounds were cultivated in Japanese Manner in Ridges between the Hills & to their Rice Grounds by Drains they easily convey Water.[23]

From the British's point of view, it can be seen that the residents of Yongdangpo were rather warm and friendly to the foreigners rather than being hostile to them. In the 17th century the Hamel also recorded that Joseon people treated them with wonder, warmth, and goodwill. Captain Basil Hall, who came to Korea in September 1816, 20 years after the visit of Broughton in Yongdangpo, also left detailed records of Koreans' kindness and the related records of Napoleon.[24]

---

22 Broughton (1804), op. cit, pp.391.
23 Andrew David, op. cit., pp.188.
24 Basil Hall (1818), op. cit.; Basil Hall (trans. by Kim, Suk-Joong 2003), 바실 홀, 김석중

Broughton's book, published in 1804, would have provided a direct driver for warships, rovers, merchant ships, and whaling ships of Western powers to visit the port of Busan. It seems likely that various Western vessels would have referred to Broughton's book when they visited the port of Busan for intermediate supplies, such as drinking water, firewood, food, and as a port of refuge, or rest during their voyage. A typical example would be the case of the whaler *South America*, a U.S. whaling ship, which landed in Yongdangpo in 1852.[25]

2. *Prince William Henry* docked in Yongdangpo

The mountainous area of 170, Yongdang-dong, Nam-gu, Busan, is sea cliffs and sea caves, where the granite coast has been developed by the erosion of waves to give its superb view (Monument No. 29 designated by Busan City). The surrounding mountain area was called Yongdang because it looked like a dragon surrounding a pond. The name of Sinseondae (神仙臺) located in the mountain behind Yongdang originates from the remains of a white horse's fresh footprints on the rock "Mujedeung (무제등)" at the top of the mountain.

According to data from 1888, the population of Dongnaebu (東萊府) was 27,275 at that time. Dadaejin (多大鎭) was under the jurisdiction of Dongnaebu, included in Gyeongsang Jwasuyeong. In the jurisdiction of Dadaejin, there were 16 dongs, including Sahamyeon (沙下面), Namchonmyeon (南村面), and Yongdangpo, which was one of the dongs belonging to Namchon-myeon. There were 43 households in Yongdangpo,

<hr />

옮김 (2003), *A 10-Day Joseon Voyage,* Seoul: Samguagoom, pp.18-100.

25 Kim, Jae-Seung, op. cit., p.26,

with 122 residents. The jurisdictional population of Dadaejin accounted for about 20% of the total population of Dongnaebu.[26] As there is a gap of about 100 years from the time of the Yongdangpo incident, this data only provides us with a rough estimate. Most of the residents of Yongdangpo were fishermen.

Yongdangpo is the easiest port of approach to Busan. For this reason, although there were no naval forces deployed in Yongdangpo during the mid-Joseon Period, Busan was transformed into the largest naval base in Korea after the Japanese Invasion of Korea in 1592. A seven-tier system was established in Jwasuyeong, Gyeongsang Province, and all the troops under Jwasuyeong were virtually concentrated on the coast of Busan.[27]

The naval forces in Jwasuyeong, Dongnaebu officers, and Yongdangpo residents did not feel threatened by the British sailing ship because they believed they were well-protected. In addition, *Prince William Henry* was a small sailing ship. The records also state that the length of the British sailing ship was 18 fa (把) (one fa is about 1.5 meters per length; 27.54 meters) and seven fa (10.71 meters) wide. The ship of Joseon Tongsinsa, Korean missions to Japan, which was dispatched from 1607 to 1811, was 34.5 meters long, 9.3 meters wide, and 137 tons in total.[28] Of course, the ship was the largest ship to be built using the best technology at the time, as it was a ship for a mission. In the 16th century, the length of the *Turtle Ship* (龜船) was 30 meters and its width was 9-10 meters, and the *Panokseon* (板屋船) was larger than the

26 Kim, Hyun-Goo (김현구, 1989), *Explanation of Dadaejin Public Documents, Historical Documents of Dongrae* 1, Seoul: Yeogang, p.24.

27 Kim, Kang Sik (김강식, 1997), "Local Administration and Official Residence of the Dongnae Region in the 17th-18th Century", *Portcity Busan* 11, p.45.

28 Cultural Heritage Administration of Korea (2017.6.22.), "Joseon Tongsinsa ship in the historical records reproduce in it's real size," *Policy News of Cultural Heritage Administration of Korea.*

Turtle Ship. The ships from Hujochang in Miryang or sailing from the Gimhae warehouse to Mapo in Seoul were also large enough to sail with 1,000 or 2,000 straw bags of rice.

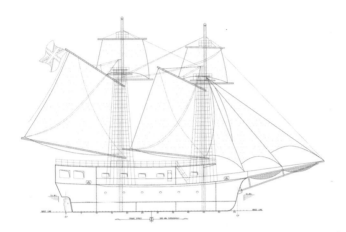

<Figure 2> The design of *Prince William Henry*, restored by MNC Engineering, based on the records provided by the authors

When the British sailing ship appeared, the handling of both Gyeongsang Jwasuyeong and Dongnaebu was shrewd and rapid. Gyeongsang Province governor Lee, Hyeong-Won (李亨元) and naval commander Yoon, Deuk-Gyu (尹得逵) hurriedly sent a report to the king after receiving the report of the foreign ship from a subordinate department.

Lee, Hyeong-Won, a governor of Gyeongsang Province, said, "A ship from a foreign country has drifted in off the coast of Yongdangpo in Dongnae. All 50 people on the ship braided their hair, and some people wore a white Jeonlip (soldier's felt hat), on their heads, and some tied it on their backs, which looked like the same as ours. They were wearing black woolen clothes, which looked like our Dong Dal Yi (military uniform), and they wore a pair of pants underneath.

They all have high noses and blue eyes. When I asked them the name of the country and the reason for drifting, they did not understand Chinese, Japanese, or Mongolian words. I gave them a brush to write something, but I couldn't figure out what they wrote because it looked like a cloud or a mountain. The length of the ship is 18 fa long, and 7 fa wide, and they say not a single droplet can penetrate it because it's made solid and precise by placing cryptomeria wooden boards on the left and right sides and under each other fixed with copper and iron pieces."

"I ran to Yongdangpo and saw one of the men who had drifted in, and his nose was high and his eyes were blue, seemingly Westerners," said naval commander Yoon, Deuk-Gyu. "When I saw the items on the ship, all of them were Western goods, including glass bottles, telescopes, and silver coins. I can't understand the language or the sound of the words, and only the four letters of Nanghasagi came out, which is the Japanese word for Janggido (長碕島), which probably means this ship drifted from Janggido and arrived here. He is blowing wind with his mouth, pointing his hand around Daemado(對馬島), apparently waiting for a favorable wind," they reported, and I ordered to let them go when the wind blew as they wanted.[29]

The report by the governor of Gyeongsang Province and the commander of the Naval Forces seem brief, but if you look at *Ilseongrok* (日省錄), the officials of Busan responded with a close and agile manner until they raised

---

29 *The Annals of the Joseon Dynasty*, the 21st year of King Jeongjo's reign-September 6.

the report to the king.

Lee, Hyeong-won, the governor of Gyeongsang Province, received a report on September 6 (lunar calendar) that a foreign ship was spotted in Yongdangpo by Lee, Deuk-Joon (李得遵), a Jwasusa in Gyeongsang Province. "Tell the Dumopo (now Gijang 機張) Manho(military officer) Park, Jin-Hwang (朴震晃) to guard the ship and Jeong, Sang-Woo (鄭尙愚) of Dongnaebu to protect it together. We don't know where this ship came from and we don't understand what they say, so we have to call in a lot of translators and instruct them to do it in various ways, and send down an official document to give them plenty of food and side dishes, and to keep them out of the country", he said.[30]

On September 10, Yoon, Deuk-Gyu, the commander of the Naval Forces, reported that he had sent an interpreter to investigate the foreign ship. "Dongnaebusa Jeong, Sang-Woo said that a foreign ship, not a Japanese ship, appeared in Yongdangpo. I ordered Dumopo Manho Park, Jin-Hwang to spy on them and Park, Chi-Gum (朴致儉), an interpreter in charge of civil affairs at the Waegwan (倭館), to visit and investigate the ship. On August 27, 'Park, Jin-Hwang was unable to investigate, so I ran to Yongdangpo instead, and they were like Westerners, and their belongings were a mirror, glass bottles, and telescope. Please send an interpreter in Jwasuyeong urgently', said the Busanchumsa making an urgent request. So I sent Cho, Joong-Taek (趙重澤,) who is fluent in Chinese, urgently to the ship by horse, and sent Lee, Deuk-Joon an official letter to appoint Jwasuyeong Woohu (military officer) Kim, Seok-Bin (金錫彬)

---

30 *Ilseongrok*, the 21st year of King Jeongjo's reign-September 6.

to an investigator. I ordered him to investigate the ship in detail and find out the situation with Dongnaebusa Jeong, Sang-Woo."[31]

There were two lines about how the reports reached the king from Busan. One is Gyeongsang-gamsa (governor) and the other is the commander of the Naval Forces. Both got reports from the Gyeongsang-jwasusa and Dongnaebusa, but the Gyeongsang-gamsa could order or direct only for the two who made a report. The commander of the Naval Forces, on the other hand, could give instructions to the Jwasuyeong-Woohu, Busanchumsa, and Dumopo Manho, interpreters, and his men, including the Dongnaebusa.

Regarding the Yongdangpo incident, *Ilseongrok* describes it in more detail than in the *Annals of the Joseon Dynasty*.

Westerners of the foreign ship looked about 60 centimeters taller than Joseon people. They looked different because of a high nose and a straight forehead. The sailing ship was almost the same size as Joseon's freighter, which can handle two to three thousand straw bags. The entire ship is surrounded by copper boards, and the inside of the ship was pure copper. The breeding grounds for dogs, pigs, and ducks were also strangely clean. There were eight or nine large and small masts on the ship, and there were a lot of cabins made of boards on the front and back of the ship. There were three large cannons like our cannon on the back of the ship. The tools on the ship were four iron anchors, five anchor ropes, two large sticks used for sails, two sails of white cotton, one helm, ten oars, ten ropes, three pots, and many other water bottles, bowls, rice, and beans stored in the bottom of the ship. Side dishes were

---

31 *Ilseongrok*, the 21st year of King Jeongjo's reign-September 10.

duck meat, pork, salt, and pastes.[32]

Investigators estimated that the size of the ship was the same as that of a large-sized freighter. Unlike Joseon's ships, they found copper around the ship to keep water from leaking, and to keep livestock in the ship for fresh food ingredients. They also record that the animal cage was strangely clean. Records of the British sailing vessel are also shown in *Juyeongpyeon* and *Selected Poems and essays Chungdasan*. The point is as follows.

"There was a small boat to fetch water, but after it did, it must be put back on the ship. The coat and pants were both too tight, barely enough for the limbs to fit in, and it was hard to bend knees." "The Busanchumsa, Dongnaebusa, and other officers were all on board to investigate the ship. When they got on the boat, the foreigners encouraged them to sit on a box in rank. Since it was hard to communicate with each other, they asked the foreigners to see their stuff with body language. The foreigners showed them rice and beans, which were like ours. A silver coin without a hole was like the money used in their country. The foreigners showed them a book, but they couldn't understand it because it was a foreign language. The shape of the book was similar to ours. There was a gun, which was only 21 to 24 centimeters long, but it was exquisite. The ball hit the back of the gun, and when foreigners pulled the trigger and dropped it, it hit the stone and caught fire."

"When they (the Busanchumsa, Dongnaebusa, and other officers) tried to search for what was kept inside, the foreigners shouted angrily

---

32 *Ilseongrok*, the 21st year of King Jeongjo's reign-September 6.

all together, and they flinched and dared not get close. When the foreigners saw a cow going on the hill, they put their hands on their foreheads and asked them (Korean officers) to give beef, but Korean officers declined. The next day, when the wind blew, the foreigners opened their arms and whistled, which seemed to mean that the foreigners could sail in the face of the wind. When the foreigners hurriedly pulled the anchor and fired three large cannons at the back of the ship, the ship was pushed by that force, and it went as far as our Korean officers could see at that moment."[33]

The Joseon officials' investigation skills into the foreign ship were highly regarded, and the descriptions in the reports were detailed and meticulous. Based on these Korean records, the authors believe that the *Prince William Henry* will be able to restore the original version.

Meanwhile, based on a report, there is a different point of view between the local administration and the navy about the *Prince William Henry*. On the day king Jeongjo received the report of Yongdangpo, he ordered, "since the ship is intact, let them leave as soon as they want, without waiting for a directive, just as the rule in Honam (湖南)[34] last year." As there were cases in Honam where the drifting foreign ship was sent away immediately, he meant to let them leave if they wanted instead of detaining them.[35] However, the Yongdangpo incident

---

33 Chung, Yak-Yong (1982), *Selected Poems and essays Chungdasan,* vol. 9, Seoul: National Cultural Promotion Association, pp.167-168; Chung, Dong-Yoo (2016), *Juyeongpyeon*, Seoul: Humanist, pp.134-135.

34 In November 1796, a foreign ship, which had drifted to Nakwol-do, Yeonggwang-gun, Jeolla-do (전라도 영광군 낙월도), was ordered to leave immediately without waiting for a reply from the government, and to be strictly punished for delaying the administration of the government. *Seungjungwonilgi*, the 20th year of King Jeongjo's reign-November 30.

35 *Ilseongrok*, the 21st year of King Jeongjo's reign-September 6.

did not end like this, but a report from Yoon Deuk-Gyu made a disturbance again on September 12, 21st year of King Jeongjo's reign.

Park, Jong-Hwa (박종화) Busanchumsa, hurriedly told me after he received a report from Gaeunpo (now Ulju-gu 울주) Manho Oh, Heung-Dae (오흥대) … He said that "The wind blew and the foreign ship raised the sail and was ready to depart. We escorted the ship to Oryukdo (五六島) and it sailed quickly over the southern sea." The report from Jeong, Sang-Woo, Dongnaebusa, arrived. "We were waiting for the order from the Government's message to ask them after giving the foreigners firewood, water, food, and side dishes. On September 2, when the southeast wind blew, the foreign ship set sail without interrogating. Since there was a rule to allow them to return as they wanted, we escorted them to the coasts of Oryukdo." Jwasusa Lee, Deuk-Jun's report was the same.[36]

Yoon, Deuk-Gyu was angry that the foreign ship was sent away without a rigorous investigation. According to his account, there was a pattern in how they investigated at that time. 'Together with the interpreter, it was a set rule to draw the hull after a foreign ship had drifted, enter it as an official document, record each of the species in detail, and report to the king when it was all set.' However, they didn't follow the rule and made an excuse that it was difficult to investigate everything. They have been very negligent because we have not looked into them carefully. We should have not let them leave so easily, considering the political situation and preventing troubles in the future.

---

36 *Ilseongrok*, the 21st year of King Jeongjo's reign-September 12.

Park, Jong-Hwa, the Busanchumsa, and Gaeunpo Manho Oh, Heu-ng-Dae, the guardian, should be dispatched first, and then the official in charge of the crime should bring a charge against their negligence. In the case of Lee, Deuk-Jun and Jeong, Sang-Woo, they sent the foreign ship before the investigation, but there was no such rule. If even an interpreter could not communicate, they should have reported with a good reason and waited for further orders. However, they were careless with the rule, and they should take the blame for mistakes and neglect of their responsibilities. Let the official in charge of the crime make a close inquiry into their guilt."[37]

Yoon, Deuk-Gyu was afraid that the responsibility would come to him, so he raised a report to the king that the Gaeunpo Manho, Bu-sanchumsa, Jwasusa, and Dongnaebusa should all be punished. King Jeongjo, who received Yoon, Deuk-Gyu's report, rather scolds him severely. "I'm sure the king ordered last time not to wait for my further instructions, but to let them leave when the wind blows again, as in the case of Honam last year. As a leader if he didn't know there was such an order, what would it be like and what would it be like if he knew and intentionally committed the crime? ... Let this report go back down."[38]

As can be seen here, it was institutionalized to repair and provide food and drinking water to the ship if it was damaged. There was a rule to repatriate the ship after the repair. King Jeongjo and the government decided that if there were no need for repairs, there would be no need to hold the ship. About 20 days after the *Prince William Henry*'s departure, King Jeongjo and his men

---

37 Ibid.
38 Ibid.

discussed the Yongdangpo incident as follows.

"Someone told us that, regarding the foreign ship in Dongnae (Yongdangpo), they seemed to be an Aranta (Dutch) person, but where is
Aranta?" said the King, "Earlier, there was also a ship of Aranta in the
reign of Hyojong (孝宗), and I remembered that Aranta is located in the
southwestern part of China. It has only just been a member of the Chinese
province. According to the history of the Ming Dynasty, it is called Haran
(Dutch), so-called Taiwan these days," said Lee, Seo-Gi (李書九), the
head of Border Defense Council. Wooeuijung, the second vice-premier,
Lee, Byung-Mo (李秉模) responded agreeably, "I'm so satisfied with his
response. We really need to employ someone who reads like him."[39]

Although Joseon's government does not discuss the true meaning of the
incident and its countermeasures over the Yongdangpo incident, it can be
seen that it has some knowledge of the world situation of the time. Taiwan
became a colony of the Dutch East India Company in 1624, and its residents
were being severely exploited. Unbearable residents unsuccessfully revolted
against the Netherlands in 1625, but more than 8,000 were killed by soldiers
from the Dutch East India Company. At that time, Dutch ships were mainly
trading with Japan, with Taiwan as their port of call, and Joseon was generally
aware of these facts. In April 1661, Zhèng Chénggōng (鄭成功) attacked
the Dutch army of Taiwan's Jeokgamseong (赤嵌城) with 25,000 troops in
350 warships, and then attacked Daemanseong (now 安平). The Dutch army
surrendered in 1662, and after the execution of Zhèng Chénggōng, the Qing

---

39 *The Annals of the Joseon Dynasty*, the 21st year of King Jeongjo's reign-October 14.

army set out to Taiwan and occupied Taiwan in 1683. It is highly likely that Joseon intellectuals understood that the Netherlands was ruled by Qing. Lee, Seo-Gu mentioned the fact that Aranta ship came to Jeju Island in 1653, during the reign of Hyojong. It seems likely that it was Hamel and his crewmen, who drifted to Jeju Island

IV. Conclusion

The Yongdangpo incident was a symbolic event in the late 18th century that showed characteristics of the international situation at the end of the Joseon Dynasty, in which Western powers gradually expanded their influence to the East. The maritime exploration of Western powers, including the British Navy, was eventually in preparation for the acquisition of colonies or lucrative trade in East Asia. Captain Broughton's approach to Yongdangpo was also part of the ocean exploration for this purpose. On the other hand, Joseon's intellectuals did not fully grasp the intentions of the Western powers, including the British, and showed that they lacked preparation for them. Despite this historical background, the Yongdangpo incident symbolizes characteristics of Busan as a sea port city.

This paper is a study on the British sailing ship that stayed in Yongdangpo for nine days in October 1797 (the 21st year of King Jeongjo's reign). The authors suggest that this paper has the following meaning. First, the ship that visited Yongdangpo in Busan at the end of the 18th century has been previously considered to be the *Providence*, but the authors have showed why it should be changed to the *Prince William Henry*. Second, Korean records of this foreign ship, which approached Yongdangpo, estimated that it was almost the only data on the British Schooner, *Prince William Henry* in the late 18th century. In addition, analysis of these records suggests that the *Prince William Henry*, which drifted to Yongdangpo, could be restored. Third, when contact between different cultures occurred in Yongdangpo, Busan, the two different cultures showed efforts to communicate instead of taking a hostile attitude, especially Yongdangpo residents felt the homogeneity of foreign sailors beyond other cultures, by providing goods needed for navigation to British sailors in need. Through the studies as above, we could confirm that Busan already had characteristics of a sea port city, such as the historicity of exchange of goods, people, ideas, culture, openness or internationalism, and cultural interactions, at the end of the 18th century.

Meanwhile, the Yongdangpo incident provides us with another challenge: the starting point for the Korea-British interaction of culture and economy. Until recently, historians have described history from a European or Western perspective, and have excluded the non-European and non-western perspective over the past few centuries, even denying the history of non-European countries. The history we are trying to see is the interaction between countries interacting with each other, the transfer between countries that have become closer, and the cultural interbreeding and combining phenomena caused by the expansion of Europe. In order to get a correct grasp of history from that perspective, it is necessary to localize and relativize the categories and values of history, mode of existence, and thought in Europe, i.e. Euro-centralism while depriving Europe of the standards it has laid out for other continents and the rest of the world. Therefore, the authors insist that the Yongdangpo incident of the *Prince William Henry* should be noted and remembered because it is regarded as the starting point for Korea-U.K. exchanges, rather than the advanced British heroic imperialist maritime history. It is not the independent history of Korea and Britain that means more to us, but the history of the accumulation of exchanges between Korea and Britain. At this point, the maritime characteristics and openness of the sea port city of Busan are being highlighted again.

The National and Transnational Characteristics of Korean Merchant Seafarers - Focusing on the period of the shipping industry from 1960-1990

Choi, Eun-Soon

An, Mi-Jeong

Introduction

Since liberation from Japanese colonization, the Korean shipping industry has laid the foundation for the modern era, and the role of merchant seafarers has been at the center of modernization. However, despite the fact that the modernization of Korea began with maritime development, it is true that the role and contribution of Korean merchant seafarers has not been properly evaluated by academia or the general public for a long time. The study of seafarers in Korea began in the 2000s and is mainly related to the employment and status of seafarers as ship manpower management. This seems to be because whenever problems occurred for seafarers, studies to solve legal and social problems followed. Although these studies have contributed greatly to improving the rights and welfare of seafarers, they have not managed to improve the general public perception of them. To improve distorted social perception, it is necessary to expand the methodology and themes of the existing research, and to pay attention to the lives of seafarers and their history, as well as their important role in, and contribution to, society.

Our research aims to focus on the sailing experiences, lives and worldview of merchant seafarers who have promoted Korean modernization and industrialization from the perspective of 'Bada Humanities.' The main research subject is merchant officers, who were active in the "Capitalism Growth Period",[1] in which the Korean shipping industry rapidly grew over about 30 years from 1960s (more precisely from the mid-sixties to the early nineties). During that period, merchant officers had different seafaring careers and experiences in terms of origin, age, sailing period and type of ship. However, we assume that their working conditions, environment and world of experience were due to the fact that this period coincided with Korea's national reconstruction and industrial development.

We limited the research scope to this period of thirty years because during this period the shipping industry experienced several twists and turns of the economy, and the supply and demand of crew personnel and the industrial environment changed greatly with the advancement of technology. This period was a time when the shipping industry grew rapidly due to the fostering of export-led industries in the 1960s, and Korean merchant officers began working on foreign ships, contributing to foreign currency income. Conversely, after the 1990s, when the growth of the shipping industry began to slow down,

---

1 Son, Tae-Hyun(2011) divides Korean shipping after liberation from Japanese colonization into three periods as follows : the first is the Period of Shock of Advanced Capitalism (after liberation ~ the establishment of Korea Shipping Corporation, January 1, 1950). The second is Capitalism Formation Period (January 1, 1950 ~ around 1965) The third is 'Capitalism Growth Period' (after around 1965). *Korean Shipping History*, With Story, p. 248,293.

the turnover rate of Korean seafarers on land increased due to the growth of the domestic industry and the improvement of income levels. As foreign seafarers began to fill the jobs of Korean seafarers, the previous on-board labor environment and other structural changes began to take place. In other words, before and after the 1990s, it can be said that the difference between the sailing experience and the working environment of seafarers was remarkable.

This study examines the aspects and characteristics of Korean seafarers, especially 'merchant officers,' onboard labor and crew culture for about 30 years, from the 1960s to 1990s, and how the sailing profession influences the lives and worldviews of Korean merchant officers.

Regarding the research method, it seems that the existing seafarer research has mainly relied on quantitative research methods. However, in addition to these quantitative studies, it is necessary to conduct qualitative studies that allow seafarers to directly express their voices and perspectives. In this context, our study has attempted to clarify the onboard lives of seafarers and the reality of labor, through interviews with merchant officers in their fifties and sixties who were active during this growth period of capitalism. There were three major themes to our interview: the motives of becoming a merchant officer, the experience of intercultural contact, and the professional consciousness and worldview gained through seafaring. The history of the interviewees can be seen in Table 1.

<Table 1> List of interviewees (as of 2017)

Name	Year of birth (age)	Boarding period	Job title	Current occupation	Hometown	Residency
Lee (1)	1948 (69)	1973-1978	2nd engineer - 1st engineer	C.E.O. of ship parts trading company	Incheon	Rotterdam, Netherland
Park	1953 (64)	1977-1981	3rd officer - cap.	Professor	Gochang	Busan,Korea
Kim	1953 (64)	1978-1996	3rd officer - cap.	Professor	Incheon→Seoul	Busan,Korea
Kil.	1957 (60)	1981-1994	3rd engineer - chief engineer	Professor	Jangheung → Seoul	Busan,Korea
Cho	1961 (56)	1984-1989	3rd officer - 1st officer	C.E.O. of seafarer recruiting company	Busan	Naypyidaw, Myanmar
Lee (2)	1966 (51)	1985-present	3rd officer - cap.	Captain	Naju	Sydney, Australia

I. The peculiarity of the development of the Korean shipping industry

1. Overseas work of seafarers and national contribution

The salient characteristics of the development process of Korea Shipping are summarized as follows. First, the development of shipping is in line with the modernization and economic development of Korea. Second, despite the lack of large capital of shipping, training of maritime manpower was given priority. Third, Korea, which was a 'backward' country, sent out 'high-end' merchant seafarers overseas.

As Tae-Hyun Son argues,[2] Korea's maritimeization (or development of

---

2 Son, Tae-Hyun, op.cit, pp.251-252.

the Korean shipping industry) was "forced maritimeization" in that Korea, which became a virtual "island" due to the Korean War and division between North and South Korea, had little choice but to seek a way to maritimeization because of the disconnect with the continent. Since the division made the southern part of the Korean peninsula maritime, South Korea was able to escape from the long continent-oriented thinking

Korea's maritimeization began under the Cold War system in 1962, with five years of economic development for national reconstruction. In this sense, the development of the Korean shipping industry, that is, Korea's maritimeization is also Korea's modernization.

It can be said that the emergence of a professional group called 'Korean merchant officers' are due to the teleological validity that cannot be separated from national reconstruction and national economic development. If we call them the 'first generation' of Korean merchant officers, who were active under national reconstruction and the World Cold War, Korean nationalism lies at the center of their world point of view. This is a Korean peculiarity.

In addition, one of the priority tasks that would drive modernization and maritimiezation of Korea right after liberation from Japan, was the construction of shipping as a cornerstone of national development, and at the same time, training of shipping talent to drive the accumulation of capital in shipping. At that time, pioneers of shipping laid the groundwork for the training of Korean merchant officers.

According to Jin-Hyun Kim[3], the development path of the shipping industry, being contrary to advanced countries, is the peculiarity of Korean shipping. In this respect, the education of merchant officers plays an important

---

3 Kim, Jin-Hyun (1998), The Way of Maritimeization, "Road to advancement", Ocean 21st Century, Nanam, pp.19-21.

role as a contributor to the accumulation of capital in the shipping sector, beyond simply providing technical force. As seen in the title of a newspaper article <1,000 seamen soothe 30 million hungers>, seafarers' overseas expansion was linked to the development of Korean Shipping, not only by earning foreign currency, but by acquiring management know-how about the shipping industry. In the 1970s, navigator Seok-Hwan Kang said, "The seafarers at that time did their job like anchors to keep them safe by being lodged in the bottom of the sea. However, they had the 'anchor spirit' that the Korean economy stood up by fulfilling the duties of seafarers."[4]

Another peculiarity of Korea's shipping was that, Korea, as a less developed country at the time, sent high-quality seafarers to overseas employment. This was due to the cultivation of excellent human resources through higher education. The practice of the world shipping industry in the 1960s was that seafarers from underdeveloped countries were employed mainly on small, old ships at low wages. On the other hand, Korean seafarers were often employed on large, capital-intensive, state-of-the-art ships with relatively high wages, and the international evaluation of the qualifications of Korean seafarers was high. In other words, Korean maritime crews broke the prejudice that overseas-employed seafarers who came from underdeveloped countries were simple workers (lower-level seafarers), and they were paid equal or similar wages to higher-level seafarers of advanced countries. This was an unprecedented case. The evaluation that "the sincerity of Korean overseas seafarers raised trust in the whole of the Korean people and helped secure foreign investments in the development of Korean shipping at the

---

4 Munhwa Ilbo 2005.10.25. "1,000 seamen soothe '30 million hungers" No. 4269, http://www.munhwa.com/news/view.html?no=2005102601030702225001 (Retrieved : 2017.12.01).

time"[5] widely promoted the image and status of the nation as a single-person company in world shipping. It means that they were subjects of economic diplomacy.

Korea Maritime University (opened in 1945)[6] was a representative higher education institution that was in charge of training the majority of merchant officers at that time. We would like to call the graduates of this university the first generation of the merchant officers, who are the main pillars of Korean modernization. From Tae-Hyun Son's classification of shipping periods, these are the generations that experienced a period of rapid growth in the 1970s, starting with capitalist growth (after about 1965). The interviewees for our study are mostly in their fifties/sixties, and except for Mr. Lee (2), who was a graduate of maritime high school, they were maritime seafarers from Korea Maritime University.

The first-generation of maritime manpower who were educated in the political and economic situation of Korea under the division and the Cold War regime can be seen as having a different spirit than those of today's young seafarers. At least, the interviewees we met often expressed a sense of mission for national development and pride, as pioneers in the Korean shipping industry. In addition, among the highly educated merchant officers, there are many people who formed a class leading the shipping industry by growing up as capitalists or maritime experts in the shipping sector in Korean society. The classmates listed by Mr. Lee (1) varied as follows shipping company (vice) presidents, executives, ship owners, professors, pilots, inspectors, supervisors, consultants, professional merchants, ship equipment manufacturers, etc.

---

5 Ibid.

6 The name of Korea Maritime University (KMU) changed to Korea Maritime and Ocean University (KMOU) in 2013.

Among them, there are many people who are active in foreign countries such as the United States, Singapore, Thailand, Australia, etc. He emphasized that all of the students who joined Korea Maritime University at the same time have lived exemplary lives with pride of being graduates of the university.

2. Conflicting images of seafarers : *Jack Tar* and *Madoros*

In western society, the name *'Jack Tar'* was often given to mean a common sailor or member of a ship's crew. The name became widely used during the British Empire in the late 19th century, when many Jack Tars had particularly unsavory reputations as being violent and drunk when in port. Nowadays, *Jack-tar* is a slang-term used mostly for merchant seamen of ranks below officers. Compared to Jack Tar's image, it is difficult to find images of Madoros[7] in European literature or other sources.

In the case of Korea, the image of a seafarer is summarized in two opposing ways. There is the image of Jack Tar, which corresponds to a 'Baetnom' (뱃놈 in Korean language, *ship guy* in a literal sense)', who speaks harsh and vulgar words, and that of Madoros, who glorifies the merchant officer and a leading economic player in Korea. The negative image of 'ship guy', like that of Jack Tar, is due to the notion that 'anyone can work onboard a ship'. In other words, they have the image of a person who decided to get on board regardless of their educational background, career, or age, with a feeling of escape or despair

---

7 Jeon, Young-Woo (2014), 「Role and value of seafarers: the necessity of fostering national seafarers」, Korean Institute of Maritime and Fisheries Technology Report, p.77. The word *madoros* comes from the Dutch word *matroos*, meaning 'sailor'. Originally, in the process of transliterating Dutch *matros* several times in Japan, it was settled as *madoros*, and this Japanese style notation is mainly used in Korea.

from land.

In the lyrics of songs that were popular in the 1960s, Madoros is equated with positive notions and images of patriotism, masculinity, loyalty and romantic guys. Songs about Madoros began with 'The Song of Madoros,' sung by Seok-Yeon Kang in 1933, followed in 1939, by 'Madoros Park' by Nyeon-Seol Paek. Since then, there have been many popular songs with *'Madoros'* in the title, where the positive image is revealed - 'Danny Madoros,' 'My brother is a handsome Madoros,' 'First Love Madoros,' 'American Madoros,' to name a few.

As Myoung-Gyu Park summarizes,[8] the image of Madoros is as follows: the clothes that symbolize the cutting edge of the trend of an era, a seaman in black-rimmed glasses making a trip with a pipe, a young cadet with sophisticated manners, a guy in work clothes smeared with oil, who has the guts and confidence. These images had flavored an era.[9] In this way, while Madoros was the image of envy and positivity in popular songs, it seems that in film, the more negative seaman-images of Jack Tar were more imprinted on the public. 'Madoros Park' often appeared in movies as a representative image of Jack Tar. This image, symbolized by the movie, *Madoros Park* (1964) seemed to have been stamped on the memory of the public under the influence of the movie in the sixties. However, it seems that Madoros' negative image began to turn into a positive image as the public directly experienced excellent merchant officers produced by higher education institutions. There was a social perception that merchant officers were elites who received university education at a time when it was difficult for anyone to attend university. We can say that

---

8 Park, Myoung-Gyu, "Maritime Marketing's Historical Review of Madoros' Popular Songs: Focusing on Shipbuilding and Shipping", *Hanbada*, 8, pp.6-8.

9 Ibid., p.22.

merchant officers wearing white uniforms and captain's hats were images of cool, middle-class men with manners and moderation. As such, the positive image change of Madoros seems to be related to the situation of the Korean economy at the time. In the 1960s, Korea lacked an industrial base and jobs. In Busan, wages were so high that there was a saying, "If you become a seafarer, you save your family."[10] Madoros must have had the image of a wonderful man in command of his life, while being responsible for the livelihood of his family.

According to data analysis of Korean pop song albums released from the 1920s-1980s, the songs with the lyrics of 'Madoros' were the most popular. It illustrates that merchant officers, imaged as Madoros, were enviable professions at the time. In particular, the expression 'Madoros' appears 437 times in popular songs, during this time frame, with half of these concentrated in the 1960s.[11] This shows the boom of the shipping industry in the sixties and the popularity of Korean seafarers who ventured overseas. There was a certain degree of social perception that merchant officers were contributing to the national economy and industry.

In fact, Korea's first seafarers' transmission was mainly through overseas employment. The foreign currency they earned greatly contributed to the Korean economy. Of course, working on a foreign ship bound for international destinations despite the hard work and danger, was due to the individual's financial need for a better life for himself and his family. For example, compared to workers on land in the sixties and seventies, the salary for

---

10 Media Pen (2016.5.31.), "Shipbuilding and shipping industry crying over shipping laws... let's not forget the miracle of Madoros" http://www.mediapen.com/news/article_print/154200 (Retrieved: 2017.12.01.).

11 Kyunghyang Biz (2016.12.16.), "Madoros, the profession most mentioned in popular Korean songs until the 1980s" http:biz.khan.co.kr/print.html (Retrieved: 2017.12.01.).

merchant ship crew almost trebled in amount.

In this way, the character 'Madoros' reflects the atmosphere of the times, when people envied to become merchant seafarers 'to eat and live'. It was relevant to the social paradigm at that time, whereby people preferred shipbuilding and shipping jobs.

II. Korean merchant officers' onboard labor and crew culture

1. Who became a merchant seafarer?

The majority of those who wanted to become seafarers, whether in Europe or Korea, chose to do so, due to economic needs. If there was any difference, the process of becoming seafarers would have been different.

Korean merchant seafarers were elites who were professionally educated/ trained, through university. Mainly, after the graduation, they enter the occupational group that corresponds to senior level seafarers such as captain, first officer, second officer, third officer, engine chief, second engineer, etc. At that time, to become senior level seafarers, they had to enter a specialized higher education institution. For this, they also had to pass the entrance examination with grades at a high level. According to Mo-Ryong Gu,[12] in the case of Korea, during the process of rural areas losing their economic importance due to export-led growth policies, farmers and poor urban dwellers often became seafarers for economic reasons.

The professional attractiveness of becoming a seafarer was because of

---

12 Gu, Mo-Ryong (2013), *Marine landscape*, pp.207-209.

the high wages. Most seafarers we interviewed were often children of poor families, who chose the seafarer profession to raise their family, or as a means to escape poverty.

Mr. Lee (1), one of the interviewees, was born in a rural area, and entered Korea Maritime University to escape poverty, overcoming opposition from his parents. After hearing stories from nearby acquaintances, his parents said, "They say that Korea Maritime University is a very good university... Madoros look very nice." Mr. Cho, another of the interviewees, also entered Korea Maritime University because he thought that if he was exempted from the military, he could make money quickly and relieve his parents of their money troubles. Mr. Lee (2) also quit high school in Gwangju without discussing this with his parents, and after hearing people say, "You have a good job and make good money," he entered Busan Maritime High School. In the case of Mr. Kil, he said that he had decided to enter KMU, because he could quickly enter society if he was exempted from military service. The exemption from military service is also related to economic reasons.

However, it would be too simplistic views to say that they chose to be seafarer simply for economic reasons. In addition to financial benefits, other reasons were heard through the interviewees. In particular, Mr. Kim did not think that being a seafarer was a good career. However, even after leaving university in the '70s, there were few employment opportunities, and it was seafarers who could legally depart Korea, when it was impossible to go abroad. So, he said, "I entered KMU with the idea that 100% employment was possible after graduation." Thinking about his options, he continued, "I thought - shouldn't I have to look around the world and die? I will never see a foreign land until I die. This made me really sad." In this way, through the interview, it was found that economic reasons, exemption from military service and experience in foreign culture were some of the many motives for becoming a seafarer.

On the other hand, if we ask the question, "Who became a merchant officer?" the answer would be 'unconstrained individuals.' Through the interviews, we were able to discover that it was the interviewees themselves who chose their seafarer careers. The interviewees studied very well in high school, and they entered KMU after getting information from their seniors or teachers about going to university and finding employment. In particular, Mr. Kil went to KMU due to the recommendation of a high school teacher, without knowing that students in this university will be trained on board. Considering the situation at the time when people were busy eating and living, most parents did not care whether their children studied well. His parents, also, did not interfere with their son's school, work or career. It was the same in the case of other interviewees.

Through the interviews, we found that the merchant officers at the time were 'independent subjects' so that they could make decisions about their careers themselves, and that the temperament of independence was demonstrated in their later studies, and work.

2. Onboard hierarchy and community culture

The ship is a physical space for maritime labor, but it is also a cultural space where seafarers live together. As David Kirby & Meluza-Liza Hinkanen puts it, being onboard a ship is entering an unpredictable and dangerous environment, which requires special skills and knowledge.[13] Therefore, we

---

13 David Kirby & Meluza-Liza Hinkanen, translated by Jeong, Moon-Soo et al. (2017), *Baltic and North Sea*, Seoul : Sunin, p.292.

can say the seafarer culture that is different from that of being on land. In being different from what is found on land, a ship has a closed structure that travels the oceans, constantly moving and being exposed to the dangers of nature at any moment, which necessitates strict discipline onboard. In other words, as Marcus Rediker[14] summarizes, the labor and life of a seafarer, who lives a lifetime with the sea, is basically to overcome the dual situation of the opposition between nature and humans, and between humans and humans. It seems natural then, that seafarers' unique language, habits, rules and values are created due to the nature of the ship's closed environment, mobility and double opposition. This is why seafarers are regarded as unusual types that are difficult for people on land to understand.

In the age of sailing ships in the past, sailors had difficulties in labor that had to cope with the infinite power of nature. Nowadays, however, due to developments in technology and science, the number of personnel on board has decreased. Therefore, it has become even more vitally important to maintain the hierarchical work-order environment, in which a minimum number of personnel is required to demonstrate maximum capabilities.

"How can a sense of community and culture be formed between members of the ship?" Contrary to the common belief that hierarchical order will be a factor of conflict on board, the basic premise of community culture onboard is a strict hierarchy, in order for safe navigation. For example, in the case of university training ships, there is a saying that "even the president cannot sit in the captain's chair."

The uniforms and epaulets worn by the captain and officers indicate their rank and symbolize their authority and responsibility. According to

---

14 Marcus Rediker, translated by Park, Yeon (2001), *Between the Devil and the Dark Blue Sea*, Kachi, Seoul.

international treaties or agreements, the required number of crew members, such as the captain, officers (1st, 2nd, 3rd), chief engineer, engineers (2nd, 3rd), etc. is determined according to the size of the ship. Comparatively, merchant officer ranks correspond to military officers. Similarly, a Bosun, No. 1 Oiler, Chief Cook, etc. correspond to the rank of sergeants, while other crew members are equivalent to regular soldiers. The titles used by seafarers onboard are also strict. Despite the culture of seniority in Korean companies, officers do not honor elder junior seafarers and always call them by their title. In most cases, it is known that work orders are made like the relationship between officers and soldiers in the military.

On the other hand, a ship's work space is arranged in the order of bridge, engine room and deck, according to the hierarchy. The residential and living spaces are separated according to hierarchy, also, and the officers and soldiers eat separately. In addition, the size and location of cabins differ depending on the rank of the crew. For example, the captain occupies the largest cabin, located farthest from the bridge. The position of other cabins is determined by following ranks.

However, there seems to be a limit to maintaining the hierarchical order onboard through a system or physical space. "What else is needed in onboard work?" "How can trust and bonds be formed between the captain and the crew, the executive seafarer and the junior seafarer?" We would like to answer these questions with *seamanship*, as the basic quality of officers.

According David Kirby & Meluza-Liza Hinkanen[15], seafaring is a profession in which seamen must acquire unique skills in a wide range of fields and work with their own efforts. Safety is important in narrow ships. Ensuring

---

15 David Kirby & Meluza-Liza Hinkanen, op.cit., pp.338-339.

this safety is the most important job for the expertise of each position. In Northern Europe, seamanship, which was required of merchant seafarers in the early 20th century, became the basis for collective evaluation of individuals in onboard positions. Even the officers and the captain were critically evaluated by the crew, and the captain often consulted with experienced and reliable skilled sailors who were in charge of the deck. A good seamanship can resolve two confrontations during the voyage: one between humans and nature and the other between humans and humans. In extreme crises, the seafarer's superior skill and mental power, which is seamanship, become the qualities utilized to overcome adversity. If officers and sailors respect each other's expertise, they can reduce possible conflicts.

In this way, a ship is an "organization," and the crew culture is essentially based on organizational culture. According to Smircich, "Organizational culture provides members with a sense of unity and increases system stability, which affects the satisfaction and productivity of members."[16] Class division is an element of identity. Hierarchies indicate where an individual belongs in a community.

Working onboard is a combination of each crew member undertaking their own role, and working in collaboration. Each person must fulfill his own position while cultivating a sense of community by collaborating with colleagues. As such, seafarers are integrated into their onboard roles, crew culture and the wider professional maritime community. Within the time frame in question, Korean merchant seafarers came from different socio-economic backgrounds, but the group consciousness of the "destiny community" was

---

16 Quoted in Shin, Hae-Mi et al. (2017), "The Effect of Characteristics of Ship Organizational Culture on Job Satisfaction and Turnover", *Korean Journal of Port Economics*, No. 33-3, Korean Port Economic Association, p.122.

clear. Mr. Lee (1) still thinks of his 'mates' who studied, ate and lived together with him every day until graduation, as members of his family.

"He confessed that we all lived together. Like comrades who share the same destiny, the harder and harder it was for us, the more we united. We steadily overcame many difficulties and endured well, by growing our dream for the ocean." Just as the word *Madoros* has the meaning of "a fellowship with a meal," it implies that the crew members of ships are groups sharing a common destiny.

III. A fluid life and a borderless worldview

1. Isolation and mobility

Whether in years of the past or today, the seafarers' sense of isolation that they are 'far from land' has not changed. This is no doubt due to the inescapable maritime work-environment of life at sea. The very nature of working onboard an ocean-going vessel, is being exposed to dangers at sea, and unlike life on land, crew members need to solve problems themselves, while being away from their families, for long periods of time. In other words, working onboard can be summarized as: the solitude of solving problems (with ship isolation), distance from family and distance from society. Often, a difficult job can be referred to as part of the '3D industry' (i.e. dirty, difficult, dangerous), but the seafaring profession is said to be a 4D industry with the addition of a D for *distance from family*. A survey conducted for this research found that the number one reason for ending employment as a seafarer is the isolation from family [couple, children, relatives] (51.5%).[17]

The length of time for ocean voyages for the first generation of Korean merchant seafarers was long, from several months to as much as over a year. Voyage length varied from ship to ship during the booming years of shipping, when seafarers were scarce, but their voyage schedules were tight and their routes were often global. It was a time when long and distant voyages made isolation and separation from family especially difficult, when the seafarers often described their ship as 'a prison without bars.'[18] They suffered from self-alienation and even felt alienated from their own families. They would have had two different points of view as they were positioned at the boundary between their own onboard culture and land culture, or transnational culture and Korean culture. Seafarers who are constantly moving, experience the culture of another with curiosity and interest in a strange place, but when they return to their hometown, they cannot share the experience with their family and friends.

According to David Kirby and Meluza-Liza Hinkanen, the sense of disparity of the seafarers returning from the voyage, "it is as if the hometown remains the same, but it seems that he is the only one who has changed. Because of a new sense of distance from the different experiences of himself and his family, another voyage could almost make him think of it as comfort (which can relieve this sense of distance)."[19] If so, what is the specific

---

17 Sisa Journal (1998. 05. 14.), "The tide of unemployed people due to crew recruitment... 4D industry old words" http:www.sisapress.com/journal/articlePrint/86511 (Retrieved: 2017. 12. 01.).

18 Ha, Yoo-Sik, "The Contrast of Madoros Fighting the Sea", *Busan History and Culture Exhibition*, http://busan.grandculture.net/Common/Print?local=busan (Retrieved: 2017.12.01.).

19 David Kirby & Meluza-Liza Hinkanen, op.cit., p.335.

difference between the experience of a seafarer and his family? We intend to partially interpret this difference with the time difference between at sea and on land.

When a ship goes out to sea, it sails 24 hours a day. In other words, the sailing watch must be held for day and night. The sailing watch consists of three shifts of four hours each, and three officers working twice a day for four hours.[20] In this way, there are no separate days and nights in the time rhythm of the watch duty, and because the officers and engineers work in shifts according to the watch duty, the daily routine is repeated 24 hours a day, 365 days a year. It can be said that there is no concept of regular working hours on a ship, such as office hours, closing time, weekends, etc. Seafarers have a working rhythm that is not easily compatible with family anniversaries, or holidays. Although it is pleasurable for seafarers to see family and relatives again when they return home, the rhythm of daily life on land seems to be unfamiliar and make them feel alienated. Perhaps they view the sea as a place to find their identity, sense of purpose and security.

Another feature of crew culture is mobility. Seafarers cross national boundaries and encounter various cultures around the world. Because they move constantly as part of their careers, it is difficult to be settled in their hometowns. Where is the seafarer culture formed? It is integrated into two spaces: ships and ports. In the strict hierarchical order onboard and constant shift-work hours, seafarers form their own language, discipline and relationships. Therefore, they come to the port of call, where they stay for short periods of time and are able to find relief from the isolation and alienation felt onboard, by enjoying time with other crew members in finding entertainment

---

20 Na, Song-Jin (2006), *The Stories of 77 Ships Written by Madoros*, Samho Advertising Planning, pp.368-369.

and drinking in common areas in the port. Here, the family is not the object of resolving these feelings

In this way, the isolation and movement of seafarers are two sides of the same coin. As long as they move, isolation always follows, and they continue to move to relief their isolation again. However, they cannot be settled because this is the life of seafarers.

As Gu, Mo-Ryong says, "a seafarer is a cosmopolitan".[21] He forms a new identity as he travels back and forth between his hometown and the world. Two spaces in different directions, the aspiration for the hometown and the world, are mixed in the consciousness of the seafarer. That's why when he comes to land he wants to go to the sea and when he is at sea, he wants to go to land. In this sense, his life is fluid, but paradoxical.

2. Cross-border life and thinking

Port in French has the etymology of Latin *portus* which relates to 'passage'.[22] As Nicole Lapierre[23] discusses, a door separates two spaces, but at the same time, connects them again. Mobility through a door is revealed as the dynamics of opposing things - moving from closed to open, from inside to outside, and from discontinuity to continuity.

In this way, considering that the word *port* relates to 'passage', the function of a port is also similar to that of door. If so, a port is both an open door to the

---

21 Gu, Mo-Ryong, op.cit., p.263.
22 *Littré Dictionnaire de la langue française*(1963), tome 6, Gallimard/Hachette, Paris, pp. 121-122.
23 Nicole Lapierre, translated by Lee, Se-Jin (2007), *Pensons Ailleurs*, Purensup, p.43.

outside world and a door that is an entrance at the border. Those who leave and enter ports most frequently are the seafarers. It can be assumed that seafarers then, whose very careers are remarked by embarking on voyages and engaging in transnational living and employment are characterized by open-mindedness, transnationality and 'borderless thinking'. They are different from those who are accustomed to continental thinking.

In the case of Korea, it is possible to see a cross-border education method in the training of merchant officers. The lifestyle of Korea Maritime University's Maritime Science student dormitory, called the 'boarding dormitory' is the same as that at sea. At this dormitory, students wear uniforms and live under strict rules. This is part of a practical education that allows students to easily adapt to the life onboard after graduation, by experiencing the habit of working and living 24 hours a day on a merchant ship. Such education can be said to be a non-boundary education method that has the students thinking of life at sea, even while on land, without separating the land and the sea.

While in the dormitory, students use the same jargon used onboard. For example, there is an organization called the 'military department', which operates like an autonomous student organization, where the titles of the student-members are the same as those of the executive officers on the naval ship. Thus, it is organized by titles such as 'officer on duty', 'deputy officer', 'honorary officer', 'facility officer', 'staff member', etc. In addition to this, in relation to the rules of life at sea, *going out* is referred as '*landing*', *prohibition from going out* as '*landing prohibited*', *late boarding* as '*embarkation delay*' and *general cleaning* as '*deck cleaning*'. There are other terms used such as *absence, internal training*, and *personnel check*, etc. The primary reason for the overall management and control of student life, is the preparation for on-ship training in the 3rd year, but ultimately, it could be argued, the greater advantage to be gained is the acquisition of a borderless worldview that does not differentiate the land and the sea.

In a slightly different dimension, the non-boundary characteristics of seafarers also appear in the professional world. Korean merchant officers tend to change their employment between land and sea based jobs, depending on the highs and lows of the shipping industry. Occupational and social mobility are more easily changeable, compared to other industries. In other words, it is not particularly difficult to find maritime-related jobs on land, with seafaring experience, after the cessation of life at sea. This is because there are special maritime fields that require seafaring experience and related qualifications, and employment linkage is easily made through the personal network of the same generation or alumni. For example, based on long-term embarkation experience, it is possible to advance into an offshore plant position, a shipping supply business, a shipbuilding equipment business, a ship repair business, an oil supply business, or even a ship brokerage company etc. There are few professional boundaries for merchant officers. They can work anywhere, at sea or on land.

The subjects we interviewed had a clear view of the country and a sense of duty, due to the political and economic situation in Korea, at that time, but they also had a transnational experience earlier than anyone else, and had an open worldview. During the period of rapid growth in the shipping industry, merchant officers were a globalized professional group first of all, when it was difficult for diplomats to go abroad. They were able to see, hear, and understand different cultures and ways of thinking, directly or indirectly, traveling to and from the ports of many countries around the world. Upon returning to their hometown, they would have proudly presented their families, relatives, and acquaintances with novel items from abroad. In addition, the knowledge learned and experience of being in other cultures, were good topics for conversation. Like this, it could be assumed that, with the amount of travel undertaken to numerous countries, seafarers developed an appreciation for cultural relativism, whereby an acceptance of cultural practices, different from their own was acquired.

From the viewpoint of cultural relativism, Mr. Park remembered the characteristics and culture of foreign seafarers he met on multinational ships. He recalls the first Japanese seafarer as being a friendly person who laughed well and maintained good relationships, and the Greek captain as someone who spoke a lot, very quickly. Mr. Kim also explained about the gypsies he met when he was docked in Gdansk, Poland, saying "They don't care about what people think of them and don't hesitate to do things that people hate." It can be said that these two navigators understood Korean culture and other cultures, because of their cross-border experiences.

Moreover, in the anecdotes of Mr. Park, we found that a British captain also had a cultural relativist view of Koreans and Korean culture. The following is what the British captain told Mr. Park when he was onboard as second officer for four months: "I have worked with Indians, Filipinos, and Eastern Europeans, but I am working with a Korean for the first time. I went to the bridge to see you working and I can trust you now. You do paperwork especially well. I'll believe you now, so do what you've been doing." It is regarded as the first work evaluation of a Korean seafarer by the British and an expression of understanding and acceptance of Korean culture. It can be said that these two people, from different countries and cultures, while experiencing their nuances firsthand, underwent a process of cultural interaction with curiosity and openness that led to understanding. Working in a multinational environment, whether on a voyage or in contact with various people in a port, means not just meeting individuals, but experiencing their culture. Because seafarers are exposed to transnational work environments, inherent to their careers at sea, they are open to the cultures of others and not trapped by the borders of a country.

IV. Conclusion

This research has tried to illustrate the onboard work and living conditions experienced by first-generation Korean merchant officers who were active in the growth period of capitalism in Korea. In addition, the characteristics of crew culture and the worldview they shared together, has been highlighted.

After Korea's liberation, maritimeization was another name for modernization. The emergence of a professional group called Korean merchant officers was closely related to Korea's national reconstruction and national economic development. They were not just salaried workers, but the leaders in the modernization of Korea. They guided national economic development and directly experienced the world economy and culture beyond borders. In this sense, the roles and contributions of the merchant officers who promoted Korea's maritimeization and modernization cannot be overlooked.

The first-generation merchant officers who were active in the period of division and the Cold War, had a firm patriotism and a sense of professional mission. At the same time, they were 'global citizen or global being' who developed cultural relativism and an open worldview across borders. Furthermore, their contributions and roles were made in a more difficult era, and it is clear that the 'independent being' who chose to become seafarers developed close bonds to overcome the dangers and solitude of their profession. It could be said that if the first-generation merchant officers had not overcome their ordeals, it would have been difficult to form the professional group called 'merchant officers' in Korea.

Due to the intrinsic nature of maritime labor, the problem of onboard isolation and mobility remains today. However, those seafarers who have been active from the 1990s till the present, who are tentatively named 'second-generation' merchant officers, have different experiences and values from their predecessors. Moreover, innovation in maritime education is required in the era of the 4th Industrial Revolution, which predicts a future with unmanned ships. If follow-up studies on the work and life of Korean merchant seafarers can be continued, it will be meaningful from a historical and educational perspective.

Chapter

3

The Projection of Nation-State Sovereignty on the Oceanic Space

A Study on Russia's Deer Island (絶影島) Leased Territory in the Late 19th Century

Kim, Seung

I. Introduction

Russia's Deer Island lease was one of the important measures to understand the internal and external political situation of Northeast Asia in the late 19th century. However, Russia's Deer Island issue has so far only been studied at a recapitulative level. As a result, even the exact location and size of the leased territory that Russia had demanded remain unknown in most academic circles.

Therefore, this article focuses on three points. First of all, the reason why Russia was able to justify the lease of Deer Island, was due to Japan's installation of coal storage on Deer Island in 1885. Thus, this paper will begin by examining the situation of Deer Island after the opening of the port and Japan's installation of coal storage on Deer Island.

Secondly, it would like to take a closer look at timeline of Russia's lease process, the response of pro-Russian officials in the Joseon government, and the opposition of the Independence Club against it. Russia's Deer Island lease began in August of 1897 and came to a finish with Russia's acceptance of the

"General Foreign Settlement at Deer Island," a decision of the first and second foreign envoys meeting held in Seoul in February of 1898. After this, it will demonstrate the fact that the "General Foreign Settlement at Deer Island" was a policy in which Britain was trying to assure the open ports of the Korean Peninsula after the Sino-Japanese War. In addition, it would like to consider that the fundamental cause of Russia's abandonment of Deer Island was deeply related to Russia's occupation of Lüshun (旅順) in December of 1897.

Third, this article examines Japan's response to Russia's Deer Island lease. Japan was willing to accept the lease if the size was equal to the initial lease Russia first agreed upon. However, after confirming the vast scale of Russia's demanded territory, Japan took the lead in stopping Russia's lease in cooperation with Britain. In the process, Japan drew in the contents of the Treaty of Commerce and Navigation between Korea and Great Britain, signed by Joseon and Britain in April of 1884, claiming the logic of "Deer Island equals the areas within 4km of concessions," which had never been raised before. Japan's response strategy had moved toward allowing the Japanese to individually occupy the land of Deer Island through the Japanese government's national subsidy.

Japan developed the strategy to stop Russia's Deer Island lease as the justification and reasoning Japanese' land ownership. Here, Japan's motivation was hidden under the idea that the Deer Island lease would not end up as a problem between the Joseon government and Russia, but rather a matter between the Russian and Japanese governments. Japan's strategy through the medium of land ownership became an important strategy for Japan to target General Foreign Settlement at each newly opened port to be established on the Korean Peninsula, including Mokpo. This article would like to confirm that the very starting point of this strategy can be observed through Russia's Deer Island lease.

Ⅱ. The Situation of Deer Island after the Open Port and Japan's Installation of Coal Storage

During the Joseon Dynasty, there were ranches, sacrificial rites, fisheries, and prohibited forests in Deer Island. Additionally, it was a place of sacred rituals held to pray for safe travel for missions from Joseon and rain in times of drought. In particular, Deer Island was used as a source of wood, firewood, and charcoal needed by Choryang Waekwan because it was close to the main land. However, it was only after the open port that people entered Deer Island more frequently, and the cultivation of resources began in earnest.

When an outbreak of cholera began in May of 1879 at the port of Busan, Japan requested the establishment of a disinfection center and an infectious hospital on Deer Island. The Joseon government authorized the installation of a quarantine camp. Later, in the case of cholera at the port of Busan, the Joseon government permitted the Japanese to set up a temporary quarantine camp and a market for the Japanese. Meanwhile, as the number of Japanese in the Japanese Concession in Busan increased, the collection of firewood from Deer Island also increased. As the number of Japanese people entering Deer Island increased, the Joseon government set up Deer Island Camp in April of 1881 by moving the ranches to other places and to monitor the entry and exit of foreign ships.[1]

After the Deer Island-jin was installed, the island underwent many changes. With the relocation of ordinary people along with the naval forces dispatched to Deer Island, where only a few caretakers lived on the ranches, Deer Island had transformed into a major area inhabited by Joseon people near the port of Busan. Moreover, the land of the ranches facing the Japanese Concession

---

1 *Seungjungwonilgi* (承政院日記), 1881.2.26; 1881. 4.1.

in Busan began to be cultivated in earnest. Meanwhile, in December of 1885, after four years of the installation of the Deer Island-jin, coal storage was established on the site of the Japanese navy. Considering that Britain occupied Geomundo Island in March of that year to prevent Russia from moving south,[2] Japan's securement of coal storage was ideally timed for their overall regional strategy.

The size of the coal storage Japan set up on Deer Island was about 1.6ha, and it was under the that they would pay 20 silver (won) for the storage every year to the Joseon government. This gave precedent for additional coal storage of Japan in December of 1890 on Wolmido Island of Incheon. The scale was the same as Deer Island. However, in the case of Wolmido, Japan promised to pay 80 won to the Joseon government every year. The difference in the amount of money between Deer Island and Wolmido Island was due to the difference in land prices. Japan fulfilled the payment conditions for both Islands until 1909.

The coal storages of Japan in both islands were based on formal negotiations between Joseon and Japan. Therefore, it seemed likely that there was no major problem. The problem, however, was even though Japanese people were banned from owning land on Deer Island, it actually happened. Especially after the Sino-Japanese War, Japanese land ownership increased on Deer Island. The Joseon government had notified the Japanese whenever the opportunity was available that they cannot own land, because Deer Island is not a concession. Though this was only a superficial theory. Japanese land ownership, in reality, increased over time. In this situation, Russia's Deer Island lease was proposed in 1897, then Japan further encouraged the

---

2 Choi, Deok-gyu (2016), *A Study on the Change of Modern Korea and East Asia*, Seoul: Gyeoninmoonhwasa.

purchase of land on Deer Island to stop Russia from obtaining the lease. On top of that, as the land of Jeolyeongdo Island was being sold at a bargain price by the Joseon louts, the land encroachment of Deer Island had been rapidly progressed since 1897.

III. Russia's Demands of Deer Island Lease and its Process

In January of 1892, Japan prepared its own protocol regarding the establishment of the Bokbyeongsan cemetery in Busan before it formally signed an agreement with the Joseon government in August of that year. Therefore, Japan built up a cemetery over Bokbyeongsan for the Japanese navy and army in the size of 11.6ha. When Japan built up the Bokbyeongsan cemetery, Russia also wanted to lease the Sapyeongsan, currently known as Bosusan [寶水山] neighboring Bokbyeongsan, from the Joseon government in May of that year.

The basis for Russia's insistence on the Sabyeongsan lease was in the "Treaty of Commerce and Navigation between Korea and Rusia" signed in May of 1884. According to the treaty, "If a Russian warship examines the waterways and the geomantic topography of the situation in the coastal waters of Joseon, the Joseon government should deservedly help." However, Russia did not even actually lease the entirety of the area surrounding Sabyeongsan.[3]

It was in the summer of 1895, after the Sino-Japanese War, that Russia began to engage directly in the Korean Peninsula. Е.И.Алексеев, a commander of the Russian Pacific Fleet, had an audience with King Gojong in July of 1895, and surveyed the coast of the Korean Peninsula between July

3 Busanbu (釜山府 1936), *History of Busanbu* (釜山府史原稿), 6, pp.438-439.

and August of that year. On July 24, the Russian warship Отважый entered the port of Busan. The Russian fleet's survey of the Korean Peninsula strained the diplomatic relationship with Japan. The Japanese minister in Seoul at the time immediately ordered the Japanese consul in Busan to investigate and report on the land status of Deer Island. Japan also did not have a clear understanding of its people's land ownership at that point.

Meanwhile, Russian minister, K.I. Weber, in Seoul, demanded the pro-Russian foreign minister of Joseon to loan the site of coal storage in Deer Island. The reason why Russia demanded the Deer Island lease was Russia, which had focused on advancing to Manchuria, had changed its direction to the center of the Korean Peninsula, as it faced resistance from Qing.[4] Weber (K.I. Weber) wanted the area to the west of the coal storage of Japan in Deer Island. However, a government official in Busan, who was ordered by the central government, reported to the central government that public opinion in-the-field was not favorable because the site Russia wanted, was a tactically advantageous position in the port of Busan. The Japanese minister also asked the Joseon government to reject Russia's demand, hinting that they were willing to return the coal storage on Deer Island.

However, the pro-Russian foreign minister of Joseon was intimidated that both Japan and Russia could insist upon the withdrawal of coal storage in Deer Island. Surprised by this, the Japanese minister gave up persuading the foreign minister of Joseon and sought to stop Russia's lease with the help of British Consul J.N. Jordan, Busan Customs Chief G.H. Hunt, and the Korean Chief Financial Officer, J.M. Brown, who were in charge of Joseon's finances.[5] In a

---

4 Hyun, Gwang-Ho (2007), *The Korean Empire, Russia, and Japan*, Sunin, pp.27-28.
5 *Records of Japanese Legation of Great Han Empire* (駐韓日本公使館記錄) vol. 12, *Russian Leased Land for Coal House in Deer Island* (絶影島露國石炭庫用地, 1897. 8. 26) "Secret

word, Japan tried to block Russia's demand through a collaborative effort with Britain. This joint effort was possible because of the cooperative relationship between Britain and Japan to keep Russia in check after the Sino-Japanese War. In fact, Britain was always worried that Russia would occupy the port of Busan and turn it into a naval base for the Far East Fleet.

Russia sent a foreign minister to Busan on August 26, 1897, shortly after they demanded the Joseon government address the Deer Island lease. A Russian official, who arrived in Busan on August 29, aboard a Russian warship, launched an investigation into Deer Island and demanded the size of about 3ha to the west of coal storage of Japan. It was twice the size of the coal storage of Japan. However, the area requested by a Russian official was selected by J.M. Brown, who was in charge of Joseon's finances in 1895, when he came to Deer Island and selected a reserve site for each country's concession. In addition, the Japanese already owned a portion of the land in the area.

The Japanese minister claimed to the foreign minister of the Joseon Dynasty that the size of land for the coal storage was appropriate, except for the quantity of land owned by the Japanese. The Japanese government's claim was unpleasant to Joseon's foreign minister. However, he eventually accepted the idea because ordinary officials from the Ministry of Foreign Affairs of the Joseon government wanted to accept it. However, the Russian official in Busan strongly countered that he could not accept the decision of the Ministry of Foreign Affairs. The Russian official acted this way because he knew that under Joseon's law, Japanese people could not own land on Deer Island. In fact, until then, Japanese people who owned land on Deer Island were not

Document No 60" (機密第60號), "Leased Land in Deer Island" (絶影島借地 1897. 9. 24).

recognized by the Joseon government. In addition, there were no certificates of land ownership handed over from the Joseon people.[6]

Under these circumstances, the Japanese consul in Busan ordered Japanese people who purchased land from Deer Island to receive at least a bill of sale. Meanwhile, the Japanese consul reminded his superiors in Japan that it was urgent to come up with countermeasures. When a Russian official came to Busan in August of 1897, he had an official document issued by the Joseon government. The document indicated the granting of land equivalent to that of the Japanese coal storage area, yet failed to specify a location. Therefore, the Russian official toured Deer Island and chose the western region, about a kilometer from the coal storage.

However, even the land that Russia had requested was located within the territory that J.M. Brown had assumed and measured as concessions of each country in 1895. As shown in the area of the dotted line in Map below, it was a diamond-shaped area of land measuring 910m in the north and 350m in the south, facing Youngmisan, currently Gwangbok-dong Lotte department store. The Japanese Concession measured 310m on the west and the east, and is located on the east side of the map. The area was half the size of the site for the General Foreign Settlement Area that the Korean Chief Financial Officer J.M. Brown planned.

---

6 *Records of Japanese Legation of Great Han Empire*, vol. 12, *The Case of Russian Government's Leased Land in Deer Island for Coal House* (露國政府 當港絕影島 石炭貯藏所 借地件) (1897. 8. 31.).

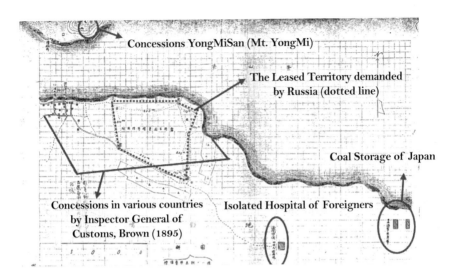

Concessions YongMiSan (Mt. YongMi)

The Leased Territory demanded by Russia (dotted line)

Coal Storage of Japan

Concessions in various countries by Inspector General of Customs, Brown (1895)

Isolated Hospital of Foreigners

<Map> The location of the Leased Territory demanded by Russia on August of 1897[7]

However, the area demanded by the Russian official was completely different from the place expected by the Japanese consul in Busan. The Japanese consulate expected that Russia would demand the western region of the coal storage of Japan with a little flat, water valley, and a little field around the shore. However, the area chosen by the Russian official was "a completely unexpected place with no water source and only a flat terrain." Moreover, Japan confirmed that the area requested by Russian officials was large and suspected that Russia had other intentions for the use of the land than just coal storage.[8]

Later, the Russian official had a land survey conducted and repeatedly demanded a senior official of the Korean Ministry of Foreign Affairs to grant

---

7 *Records of Japanese Legation of Great Han Empire* (1897. 9.6), Annex, "Secret Document No 31".

8 *Records of Japanese Legation of Great Han Empire*, vol. 12, *The Case of Russian Government's Leased Land in Deer Island for Coal House* (露國政府 當港絶影島 石炭貯藏所 借地件) (1897. 8. 31.).

the land on September 22. However, the Korean government countered that they could not accept Russia's demand because it was a region designated for future General Foreign Settlement. The position of the Joseon government changed within a month. In September of 1897, the Joseon government proposed a General Foreign settlement plan the same as that of the British, American, and German ministers, which was devised in 1895.

In fact, after the Sino-Japanese War, the measure was taken against the new British settlement on the Korean Peninsula. The UK's plan came from its strategy of achieving economic benefits by realizing the balance of power and strength of world powers on the Korean Peninsula. The way Britain gained economic benefits was to push ahead with J.M. Brown, a British national who was in charge of the Joseon government's finances, by taking control of customs. The United States, Germany, and France also supported the British position.

However, Japan and Russia, which sought superior positions on the Korean Peninsula after the Sino-Japanese War, did not like the plan. Mokpo and Jinnampo were opened in the form of a General Foreign Settlement on October 16, 1897,[9] as the interests of the Korean government and the Western powers were matched. In other words, the Joseon government's proposal for General Foreign Settlement at Deer Island in September of 1897 was linked to the open port of Mokpo and Jinnampo, which were under consideration at the time.

Meanwhile, Russia sent a warship into the port of Busan on January 21, 1898. Two Russian military officers and 20 sailors who were aboard the ship landed on Deer Island, planted dozens of pine trees, and set a guard on the site of their planned coal storage area. The Japanese consul in Busan met with a Russian captain and informed him that the place where the Russian navy

---

9 Son, Jeong-Mok (2001), Studies on the *Urban Transformation in the Period of Opening Time of Ports*, Seoul: Ilgisa, pp.274-284.

planted the trees was Japanese owned land. The Russian captain said he was willing to compensate for the land. In this process, on January 30, the Russian captain received a reply from the Joseon government from a Korean official. The contents of the reply were by no means favorable to Russia.

IV. The First and Second Foreign Envoys Meeting and Plan for General Foreign Settlement at Deer Island

With Russia's Deer Island lease still unresolved, the foreign minister of Joseon notified J.M. Brown, Korean Chief Financial Officer, of a meeting to set up a General Foreign Settlement at Deer Island on February 11, 1898. On February 14, the first foreign envoys meeting was held with ministers of Joseon, as well as the United States, Britain, Germany, and Japan. At the meeting, the Korean Foreign Minister announced a policy to establish a General Foreign Settlement at Deer Island. However, due to the absence of Russian and French ministers at the first meeting, the plan for General Foreign Settlement at Deer Island had not been finalized.[10]

Russia informed in advance that they would not attend the first foreign envoys meeting unless the issue of coal storage leased to Russia in Deer Island was on the agenda. Russia chose to be absent when their requests were not addressed. After the first meeting failed to finalize the plan, the foreign minister asked the Japanese minister to hold another meeting. During the process, the foreign minister of Joseon was replaced. Russia put pressure on the Joseon government. The newly appointed foreign minister informed the Russian

---

10 Documents Collections of Customs (總關去函) (file 17832) book. 5. Drafts of Great Powers' Concessions at Deer Island (起案 釜山港絕影島豫定各國租界一事 1898. 2. 11).

minister in February of 1898 that he would approve the site for the coal storage in Deer Island. He also informed the Japanese minister that it would withdraw the General Foreign Settlement at Deer Island.[11]

Surprised by the Joseon government's decision, the Japanese minister held the second foreign envoys meeting on February 28. Russia was absent from the meeting and diplomatic ministers from the United States, Britain, France, Germany, and Japan were present. The ministers and consuls of each country who attended the meeting decided to finalize the plan for General Foreign Settlement at Deer Island and to expand the size of the site to 90ha in accordance with the cases of Mokpo and Jinnampo. In the end, the second meeting applied the opening method and scale of Mokpo and Jinnampo, which were signed in October of 1897. Russia also accepted the decision of the second meeting. It was for two reasons that Russia accepted the decision.

The first was the rapidly changing situation in Northeast Asia. The second was the extreme opposition from the Joseon people to the lease. Firstly, the rapidly changing situation in Northeast Asia meant Germany's occupation of the Chinese Gulf of Jiaozhou on November 14 and Russia's occupation of Lüshun on December 19, 1897. Since the Sino-Japanese War, Russia had been at odds with its cabinet members over its foreign policy direction toward Manchuria and the Korean Peninsula. The basic axis of conflict was the polarity between S.Y. Witte and M.N. Muraviev, the Minister of Foreign Affairs. Witte and Muraviev clashed in their views on political, economic, and military diplomacy. For example, there was the location of an ice-free port that Russia should secure in Northeast Asia, the expansion of naval forces in East Asia, the analysis of the British and Japanese responses these policies would

---

11 *Records of Japanese Legation of Great Han Empire*, vol. 12, "Planing of Great Powers" Settlement of Deer Island (絶影島各國居留地 設定件 1898. 3. 18).

bring about, and the establishment of a Korean and Russian Bank.[12]

When Germany occupied the Chinese Gulf of Jiaozhou, Russia held a Cabinet meeting on November 26, and engaged in a heated debate. The meeting concluded that the Lüshun would not be occupied. A few days later, however, Muraviev reported to Emperor Nikolai II that Britain would take the lead if Russia did not take over Lüshun. Inspired by this, the emperor finally reversed the decision of the Cabinet meeting and granted permission to occupy Lüshun. Thus, Russia occupied Lüshun on December 19 and signed a treaty with Qing on March 27, 1898, to lease the facilities of both Dalian and Lüshun ports and surrounding military territory for 25 years.

Britain and Japan immediately protested against Russia's occupation of Lüshun. On December 30, Britain put eight ships of the Eastern Fleets into Jemulpo and sent two of them in Lüshun. It then leased land of China's Weihai on April 19, 1898.[13] Against this backdrop, Russia had set out to finalize negotiations with Japan. Finally, on April 25, 1898, the Nishi-Rosen Convention was signed in Tokyo between R.R. Rosen, the Russian minister in Japan, and Nishi Tokujiro, the Japanese foreign minister. The contents of the treaty were favorable to Japan.

As such, Russia had tried not to provoke Britain and Japan as much as possible since the occupation of Lüshun. Therefore, Russia could no longer challenge the issue of the Deer Island lease as it was originally conceived. The second reason Russia accepted the results of the second meeting was the fierce opposition of the Joseon people. This was closely related to the Korea policy

---

12 Choi, Deok-gyu (2008), op. cit., see the first and second chapters.
13 Song, Geum-Young (2005), *Russia's entry into Northeast Asia and its policy on the Korean Peninsula(1860-1905)*, Kughakjaryowon(國學資料院), pp.279-282; Son, Jeong-Mok (2001), op. cit., p.278.

of Russian minister Alexei de Speyer, who was newly appointed to the post in September of 1898. Unlike his predecessor, K.I. Weber, Speyer pushed ahead with Russia's policies unconditionally and with great urgency. As a result, he faced fierce opposition from the independence club. King Gojong also suspected Russia after returning to the palace from the Russian legation. As a result, Joseon and Japan could maintain an amicable relationship at the end of 1897, unlike the period of Korea's royal refuge at the Russian legation.[14]

Eventually, Russia accepted the decision of the second foreign envoys meeting in February of 1898, on account of its policy not to further escalate tensions in Northeast Asia following its occupation of Lüshun. Russia's abandonment of the Deer Island lease was only a temporary setback by the Ministry of Foreign Affairs. Russia has not scrapped its basic policy of securing an ice-free port on the Korean Peninsula. As Russia stabilized its control of Lüshun and strengthened its naval power in the Pacific Ocean, securing Russia's ice-free port on the Korean Peninsula became an urgent priority. The result was the lease of Masanpo, in June of 1900.

Japan, which blocked Russia's Deer Island lease earlier through the second meeting, immediately took measures to buy a large amount of land on Deer Island. The method was supported by the Japanese Ministry of Army. Japanese individuals ostensibly owned the land with money provided by the Japanese government, thus the land was actually managed by the Japanese Consulate in Busan. The plan was to strengthen the Japanese government's influence on the land around the open port by offering it to the Japanese Army when the issue of Russia's Deer Island lease was fully resolved. By August of 1898, the land owned by the Japanese was at least 7.6ha in Deer Island.[15]

---

14 Hyun, Gwang-Ho, op. cit., pp.129-133.
15 *Records of Japanese Legation of Great Han Empire*, vol. 13, "Russian Coal House in the Deer

The 'General Foreign Settlement at Deer Island' plan adopted at the second meeting was finally approved by the Joseon government on May 27, 1898.[16] This put an end to Russia's Deer Island lease issue. What is noteworthy here is that when the Joseon government finalized the plan of General Foreign Settlement at Deer Island in May of 1898, another important agenda was decided first. It was to open three ports - Sungjin (城津), Gunsan (群山), and Masan - and set up a market (開市場) in Pyeongyang.[17]

However, the three ports that the Joseon government promised to open were to opened under General Foreign Settlement like Incheon. In October of 1897, the Joseon government opened ports in Mokpo and Jinnampo, followed by Seongjin, Gunsan, and Masan in May of 1898, because of fears over Germany and Russia's occupation of Jiaozhou and Lüshun as a form of Leased Territory. In other words, King Gojong first opened a port that world powers hoped would be a General Foreign Settlement on the Korean Peninsula to prevent certain countries from monopolizing the port. In short, the Joseon government kept the powers in check by operating General Foreign Settlement at the open ports.[18]

Later, in August of 1898, the Joseon government ordered a Busan official not to sell houses and lands owned by Koreans to foreigners within the area planned for the General Foreign Settlement at Deer Island.[19] Moreover, they

---

Island Acquiring from Japanese real estate" (絶影島 露國石炭庫敷地中日人所有土地賣買件, 1898. 5. 28; *Records of Japanese Legation of Great Han Empire*, vol. 13, "Prohibition of Dealings Real Estate in Deer Island "(絶影島土地賣買禁止件, 1898. 8. 29).

16 *Official Documents sent to the Administrations* (各部指令存案) (File 17750) book 1, no. foreign 37 (外三十七號, 1998. 5.27).

17 *The Annals of the Joseon Dynasty* (朝鮮王朝實錄) King Gojong reign 35(1898. 5. 26).

18 Moriyama shigeru (森山茂德 1987), *Studies on the Korean-Japanese Interaction History* (近代日韓關係史研究), Tokyo: Tokyo Univ. Press.

19 *Records on the Dongnae Port* (東萊港報牒) (file 7867-2) book 5, "Degree No. 31" (訓令第三十一號, 1898. 8. 12).

were ordered not to issue documents proving the ownership of land purchased by the Japanese. Upon hearing the news, the Japanese consul sought to secure the right of Japanese land ownership, as the British could own land within four kilometers of a concession, based on the Treaty of Commerce and Navigation between Korea and Great Britain in April of 1884.[20] Two strategies were hidden beneath/underneath Japan's logic of "Deer Island equals the areas within 4km of concessions," which had never been raised before.

First, if the logic of "Deer Island equals the areas within 4km of concessions" is carried out, the controversial issue of Japanese land ownership in Deer Island could be solved at once. Secondly, based on the logic, the Japanese could supersede the expected General Foreign Settlement area in Deer Island. Japan's strategy was to create a situation in which countries seeking to use the General Foreign Settlement area must first deal with the Japanese who own land. That meant that countries seeking to use the General Foreign Settlement area had to deal with the Japanese government, not that of Joseon. This is because many of the Japanese owned the land with the monetary support of the Japanese government.

It is worth noting that the issue of Russia's Deer Island lease had prompted Japan to establish a strategy to block the expansion of the western powers on the Korean Peninsula through the medium of land ownership by its citizens.

V. Conclusion

Deer Island, which was used as a ranch and a national ritual site during

---

20 *Records on the Dongnae Port* (東萊港報牒) (file 7867-2) book 3, "Report No. 26" (報告第二十六號, 1898 8. 31).

the Joseon Dynasty, was built to isolate patients when cholera broke out in the port of Busan after its opening. It was also used as a site for the dismantling of whales, and as the population of Japanese in Japanese concession in Busan increased, it was used as a source of firewood. As the number of uses of Deer Island increased, the Joseon government dismantled the ranch and installed Deer Island-jin in April of 1881, considering the importance of national defense. The Ranch, which was landlocked, was reclaimed by migrants and privatized. Originally, the site of the ranch was nationally owned land. However, with the illegal purchases of the land by Japanese individuals, the Japanese government realized their goal of usurping the land from the Korean government. All Japanese land encroachment was illegal because foreigners were prohibited from owning land in Deer Island.

Meanwhile, in 1885, when Britain occupied Geomundo Island, Japan installed coal storage with a size of 1.6ha in December. The installation of coal storage of Japan in Deer Island has since become an excuse for Russia to call for the Deer Island lease. Russia had rapidly strengthened its influence on the Korean Peninsula since King Gojong's refuge at the Russian legation in February of 1896. Russia's demand to lease Deer Island, which began in August of 1897, was caused by this situation. Japan was willing to accept Russia's demand if the area was about the size of its coal storage. However, the leased territory demanded by Russia was twice the size of the coal storage. Japan tried to stop the Russian lease with the help of Britain.

In order to address the issue of Russia's lease, the Joseon government held two rounds of meetings with foreign envoys. At the first foreign envoys meeting held on February 14, 1898, the General Foreign Settlement plan of Deer Island was discussed. However, the plan was not finalized because Russia was absent. As the foreign minister of Joseon was replaced by a pro-Russian figure, it moved toward accepting Russia's demands. However, Japan held the second meeting on Feb. 28 to finalize the plan and to expand the scale of General Foreign Settlement to 90ha. Russia accepted this decision. Russia's acceptance of the decision was related to Russia's occupation of Lüshun in December of 1897. This sparked a strong backlash from Britain and Japan. In the face of heightened tensions in Northeast Asia, Russia did not want to provoke Britain and Japan anymore, even with the issue of the Deer Island lease.

The Joseon government officially adopted the General Foreign Settlement at Deer Island plan, which was also adopted at the second foreign envoys meeting in May of 1898. This also thwarted Russia's lease attempt at a single stroke. Meanwhile, Japan began to claim the logic of "Deer Island equals the areas within 4km of concessions," which had never been raised before August of 1898. Japan's logic was part of its strategy to strengthen its influence over the General Foreign Settlement of newly established ports on the Korean Peninsula by using land ownership as a medium.

Namely, after the Sino-Japanese War, Japan found itself no longer able to set up its own concession by the checks of Western powers. In response, Japan pushed for a strategy of large-scale land ownership by Japanese citizens, who received national subsidies from the Japanese government, in the newly open ports. Japan's strategy was to create a phase in which the Western powers had to negotiate first with the Japanese who owned land when they wanted to use General Foreign Settlements. Due to this strategy, negotiation with the Japanese and the Western powers actually meant negotiations with the Japanese government. It is worth noting that Japan's strategy of leveraging land ownership began with the process of dealing with the problem of Russia's lease on Deer Island.

A Sea Agreed upon as a 'Sea' : Territorial Dispute and Settlement of the Caspian Sea

Woo, Yang-Ho

I. Introduction

The Caspian Sea, located in Central Asia, is strange for us. From the map, the sea lies deep in the western outskirts of Russia, even on the Eurasian continent. Unlike the Caspian Sea, the adjacent "Black Sea" is connected to seas such as the "Aegean Sea" and the "Mediterranean Sea," so the Caspian Sea has the characteristics of a completely isolated inland Sea.

Although the Caspian Sea was surrounded by many countries for a long time, it stayed out of the public eye. Then, in the 20th century, various resources such as energy, minerals, and fisheries were discovered in this area, and as economic value rose, competition for exploitation and preoccupation began. The debate over "Is the Caspian Sea a Sea, or not?" also began at this time.

Was the Caspian Sea originally a "sea?" Or is it a sea defined or agreed upon as a 'sea?' So far, the international situation surrounding the Caspian Sea is closer to the latter. Still, many consider the Caspian Sea a "great lake."

There is also an ostensible reason for being geographically closed and low in salinity. However, the reason why the Caspian Sea, which already means "sea," has faced claims that it is not internationally recognized as a "sea" is clear. It is due to the issue of 'sovereignty' among its coastal countries. The five countries along the coast of the Caspian Sea - Russia, Iran, Kazakhstan, Azerbaijan, and Turkmenistan - were in conflict and dissension over their sovereignty from 1991 to 2018.

Today, the Caspian Sea also has many other problems as well as the claims from the five coastal countries. Due to the complicated interests of the many coastal countries, the Caspian Sea has been called "the Mediterranean Sea between the Middle East and Central Asia." Since the Caspian Sea is completely isolated, there is a lack of water flowing out from rivers. Water quality and water resource problems have long been emerging, and the environmental conditions of living things have deteriorated as well. There are also many problems with environmental pollution caused by oil and gas development, and the development and construction of infrastructure across the borders. As various types of international conflicts over the Caspian Sea increase, we need more specific information, international legal status, and academic research on them.

This article examines the regional opening of the Caspian Sea and the causes and progress to date of territorial issues. It will also study in detail the positions of coastal countries, especially those related to territorial issues, and analyze in-depth the recent changes in the situation.

II. The Overview and Major Status of the Caspian Sea

1. Locational Introduction to the Location and its Geography

The Caspian Sea in Central Asia covers about 370,000 square kilometers of sea, about twice the size of the entire Korean Peninsula. The southern and northern ends are about 1,200 kilometers apart and the coastline is about 7,000 kilometers long, it is the largest inland sea in the world. The maximum depth is about 1,025 meters and the average depth is about 184 meters, allowing large ships to travel without difficulty. On a map basis below, the water depth in the north is relatively shallow, while the farther south you go, the deeper the water becomes.[1]

Figure 1. Geography of the Caspian Sea in Central Asia

---

[1] Wikimedia (2019), https://commons.wikimedia.org/wiki/Category:Maps_of_the_ Caspian_Sea#/media/File:Caspianseamap.png.

The Caspian Sea is geographically surrounded by five countries: Russia, Kazakhstan, Azerbaijan, Turkmenistan, and Iran. The Caspian Sea, the world's largest "inland body of water" and "inland sea," is so wide that it is divided into north, central, and southern regions along the border. It is divided into the northern part, which borders Russia and Kazakhstan, the central part facing Azerbaijan and Turkmenistan, and the southern part by Iran. In other words, the coasts of a total of five countries, including southwest Russia, Azerbaijan, Turkmenistan, Kazakhstan, and northern Iran, surround the Caspian Sea.

It is named the Caspian Sea in the respective languages of Azerbaijan, Armenia, Kazakh, and Georgia, besides English, Russian, and Turkish. Major ports in the Caspian Sea include Russia's Makhachkala, Astrakhan, Azerbaijan's Baku, Kazakhstan's Atyrau and Aktau, and Turkmenbasy of Turkmenistan.[2]

2. Discovery of Resources and Rise of Competition in Coastal Countries

The Caspian Sea, located in the center of the southwestern Eurasian continent, is also on the geographical border between Europe and Asia. Because it has always been at the crossroads of civilization between the East and the West, it has historically been an essential area for hegemonic competition on the Eurasian continent. Until the modern age, however, the Caspian Sea remained relatively stable geopolitically until the end of the 20th century.

During the Cold War, the Soviet Union and Iran jointly managed the entire

---

2 Gisreportsonline (2019), https://www.gisreportsonline.com.

Caspian Sea in two halves above and below through the Russo-Persian Treaty of Friendship in 1921 and the Treaty of Commerce and Navigation in 1940. The boundary was a line that crossed today's Azerbaijan region of Astara and Turkmenistan's Gasan-Kuli. This left the Soviet Union with about 85 percent in the northern and central Caspian Sea, and Iran with about 15 percent in the southern part.

The Caspian Sea has undergone major changes in the international order and diplomatic relations since the early 1990s when the Soviet Union collapsed. With the dissolution of the Soviet Union in 1991, a series of newly independent states were set up in the Caspian Sea. Central Asia's Kazakhstan, Azerbaijan, and Turkmenistan, which gained independence from the Soviet Union, have advocated for sharing sovereignty of the coast of the Caspian Sea. The United States and Europe have also crept into the Caspian Sea, where there was a temporary vacuum in sovereignty. This brought in complex contemporary geopolitical interests between the countries.

Meanwhile, the decisive event that brought the Caspian Sea into the world's spotlight was "the discovery of resources." Various resources, including energy resources such as oil, natural gas, and minerals, have been found along the coast of the Caspian Sea, and commercial production has begun, drawing keen attention from coastal countries and global corporations.

Kazakhstan, Azerbaijan, and Turkmenistan were newly independent countries from the Soviet Union in the early 1990s. The discovery of resources in the Caspian Sea was like sweet rain in a drought for them. As an independent nation, they had the task of building their own national economy. Although they gained independence from the Soviet Union, they could not escape the shadow of Russia both economically and industrially.

The energy resources of the Caspian Sea were relatively urgent and important in these countries. Except for Russia and Iran, the new coastal states of the Caspian Sea have been called the "second Middle East," thanks to the discovery of the energy resources and have had great opportunities for economic and industrial development. The issue of sea border and territorial conflicts among the coastal states of the Caspian Sea was important since it was directly linked to whole national development.[3]

The current oil reserves at the bottom and coast of the Caspian Sea are about 50 billion barrels, about 5 percent of the world's reserves. Potential future oil reserves are estimated to reach 260 billion barrels. This would be the world's second largest after the world's number one in the Middle East. In other words, the Persian Gulf would be the only place in the world known to have more oil than the Caspian Sea. The amount of natural gas reserves in the Caspian Sea is estimated to be around 8.4 trillion cubic meters.

About 70 percent of the oil field representing the Caspian Sea's resources has been drilled off the coast of Kazakhstan, Azerbaijan, and Turkmenistan. All of these coasts are in the northern Caspian Sea, where the water is relatively shallow, the continental shelf is well developed, and conditions for oil exploration and energy development are easy. Moreover, since the Caspian Sea is completely surrounded by four sides, it is easy to transport oil and natural gas by land.[4]

---

3 Croissant, M. P. and Aras, B. (Eds) (1999), *Oil and Geo-Politics in the Caspian Sea Region*. Greenwood Publishing Group, pp.1-57.
4 Zeinolabedin, Y., Yahyapoor, M. S. and Shirzad, Z. (2011), "The Geopolitics of Energy in the Caspian Basin", *International Journal of Environmental Research*, Vol.5, No.2, pp.501-508.

III. The Beginning and Progress of the Caspian Sea Territorial Dispute

1. The Beginning of Conflict: Is the Caspian Sea a Sea? Or is it a lake?

The definition of the Caspian Sea is no different from the question of its legal status and its ripple effects have a decisive effect on coastal countries when setting sovereignty. There are mixed views of the Caspian Sea as a "small inland ocean" and the "world's largest lake." It is hard to conclude that the Caspian Sea is a complete sea or a complete lake since neither are historically nor scientifically complete.

The controversy is bound to escalate once it is passed on to national relations or diplomacy. The reason for making different claims over the same area is simple. Practically, jurisdiction varies depending on what the Caspian Sea is defined as, and the amount of resources and economic benefits each coastal country can occupy also varies greatly.[5]

The difference in view of "how should the Caspian Sea be defined?" is the starting point of the territorial dispute by related countries. There have been three types of specifically discussed arguments here:

First, the position that views the Caspian Sea as a "sea" applies the current United Nations Convention on the Law of the Sea (UNCLOS), which was enacted in 1982. UNCLOS, which applies in common to international waters, has been ratified by 166 countries around the world and recognizes rights to '12 nautical miles of territorial waters' and '200 nautical miles of exclusive

---

5 Ghafouri, M. (2008), "The Caspian Sea: Rivalry and Cooperation", *Middle East Policy*, Vol.15, No.2, pp.81-96.

economic zones.' A nation can also claim "exclusive jurisdiction over the continental shelf" on its own shores and have a right to claim international community to navigate international waters. In other words, if it is defined as a sea, part of the Caspian Sea is included as individual territory of the neighboring countries. So, each country has exclusive rights to undersea resources and fishery resources along the coastal border of their land.[6]

Secondly, there is the position that views the Caspian Sea as a "Lake" where neighboring countries can consult and set boundaries freely by applying the "Legislation on Transboundary Lakes," which is internationally customary in the field of environmental protection. In other words, if the Caspian Sea is defined as a lake, the UNCLOS does not apply at all because it is not a sea.

However, the large lake would be managed equally by the relevant coastal countries. For example, if a lake has five coastal countries, it divides the entire body of water by exactly one-fifth. All buried resources should be jointly developed by all coastal countries and precisely share their interests equally.[7]

Third, apart from the dispute of whether the Caspian Sea is a sea or a lake, there has also been a "new alternative, a third arbitration proposal" aimed at ending territorial disputes permanently. It is the position that since the Caspian Sea has both the main features of a 'sea' and a 'lake,' a special third standard for this area should be applied separately.

In other words, it should be defined as "a lake as a special sea" or "a sea as a special lake" and create and apply a separate "convention" agreed upon by coastal countries. This is a possible "way of agreement" because the

---

6 Kapyshev, A. (2012), "Legal Status of the Caspian Sea: History and Present", *European Journal of Business and Economics*, Vol.6, pp.25-28.

7 Bajrektarevic, A. H. and Posega, P. (2016), "The Caspian Basin: Geopolitical Dilemmas and Geoeconomic Opportunities", Geopolitics, *History and International Relations*, Vol.8, No.1, pp.237-264.

Caspian Sea is in a completely isolated environment and the borders of coastal countries are clearly defined. As we will discuss in detail later, this alternative resulted in the settlement of territorial disputes between the coastal countries in 2018.[8]

2. The Contradictive Perspective and Position of Coastal Countries

The five coastal countries with borders on the Caspian Sea had three different positions. Some countries, including Russia and Turkmenistan, had a reversal of their original positions and policies. The different perspectives and positions of each coastal country are summed up as follows.

First of all, Russia saw the Caspian Sea as a lake in the early days like Iran but changed, to view it as a sea to claim sovereignty. After the collapse of the Soviet Union, Russia, along with Kazakhstan, was occupying the northern part of the Caspian Sea, where there are large deposits of oil. Russia also began to pay attention to its own coast of the Caspian Sea after a new oil reservoir was discovered along the coast of nearby Kazakhstan and the continental shelf. In the mid-1990s, Russia learned that there were resources on the seabed. It changed its position from Iran's position at that time and announced that the Caspian Sea was a Sea. Russia, in particular, expressed its territorial claims to the seabed and sea levels differently to others. They insisted that the seabed should be divided according to the principle of equidistance, where a 'median

---

8 Kofanov, D., Shirikov, A. and Herrera, Y. M. (2018), "Sovereignty and Regionalism in Eurasia", In *Handbook on the Geographies of Regions and Territories*, Edward Elgar Publishing, pp.10-88.

line' equidistant from the shoreline of each coastal country is used as the boundary. This is also an international legal principle in the United Nations' maritime law that often compartmentalizes "exclusive economic zones (EEZ)." They also argue that sea and sea levels should be left as joint jurisdiction zones of the five coastal countries to ensure each other's freedom. Kazakhstan and Azerbaijan have endorsed this changed claim from the start.

Secondly, Iran was in the opposite position to Russia. Iran had the shortest coastline of the Caspian Sea and so had a narrow area of jurisdiction. They hoped to maintain their interests as they did in the former Soviet Union, which divided the Caspian Sea equally. Iran was also aware of its deep, relatively small resources along the southern coast of the Caspian Sea. Iran feared that its territorial waters would be limited to areas where development and exploration would be difficult if it became a "sea." Therefore, as in the past, it never recognized the Caspian Sea as a sea and has maintained its argument that the five countries should share exactly 20 percent of the total benefits from resource development equally.

Third, Azerbaijan's position, which emerged as a newly independent coastal country, is basically similar to that of Russian's position. Namely, that the Caspian Sea is an obvious "sea" it has been in the past, as well as now, and that it has 12 nautical miles of territorial waters, airspace, and 200 nautical miles of exclusive economic zone under UNCLOS. Azerbaijan in particular since its independence, has insisted that the Caspian Sea is "sea" most consistently and strongly. It was the most advantageous to them to share sovereignty according to the length of the coastline of the coastal countries.

Fourth, Kazakhstan has the longest coastline, 2,320 kilometers long. They stuck to its sea sovereignty as "international waters" that can secure about 30 percent of the territory. Kazakhstan is a traditional ally of Russia, preferring to negotiate sovereignty with neighboring countries in a peaceful manner. The reason according to adherence of Kazakhstan seems to be that it prioritized relations with neighboring countries and practical national interests.[9]

Fifth, Turkmenistan saw the Caspian Sea as a "lake" and then later reversed its position to a "sea." In 1991, Turkmenistan agreed with Iran's position that the Caspian Sea was a "lake", but since the 2000s, it has accepted Kazakhstan and Azerbaijan's position of it being a "sea." Turkmenistan's coastline is about 650 kilometers long from east to west, about 15 percent less than the total of the total Caspian coastline. Thus, it agreed with Iran's claim at first, then gradually tilted toward accepting the territorial claims of Azerbaijan and Kazakhstan.[10]

Here's a brief summary of the positions of each country until recently: Russia, Kazakhstan, and Azerbaijan claimed the Caspian Sea as a 'sea.' Therefore, they insisted that the sovereignty of the Caspian Sea be divided according to the length of the coastal border. On the contrary, Iran and Turkmenistan insisted that the Caspian Sea be a 'lake', not a 'sea.' It should therefore be divided equally regardless of the border. Of the five coastal countries in the Caspian Sea, three countries and two countries differed at first, but as time went by, four coastal countries, excluding Iran, agreed to lay claims to it as a 'sea.'

Conflicts in the Caspian Sea continued until 2003 but entered a phase of full-scale negotiations in 2004. Russia, Azerbaijan, and Kazakhstan are located in the northern part of the Caspian Sea, which has many undersea resources and so had

---

9 Mottaghi, A. and GharehBeygi, M. (2013), "Geopolitical Facets of Russia's Foreign Policy with Emphasis on the Caspian Sea", *IAU International Journal of Social Sciences*, Vol.3, No.3, pp.53-59.

10 Contessi, N. (2015), "Traditional Security in Eurasia: The Caspian Caught between Militarisation and Diplomacy", *The RUSI Journal*, Vol.160, No.2, pp.50-57.

the fiercest conflict. They took the lead in the trilateral negotiations in 2003.[11]

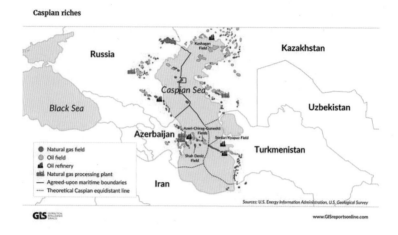

Figure 2. The distribution of resources in the Caspian Sea and the negotiation section between the countries of the coast

On May 14, 2003, Russia, Azerbaijan, and Kazakhstan signed a tripartite treaty on subsea compartments in the northern Caspian Sea on the basis of bilateral agreements, clarifying the oil and natural gas development zones along each coast. At this time, the debate over the identity or nature of the Caspian Sea, for which all coastal countries were concerned, was put aside for a moment for the practical effect of narrowing the differences in their positions and to progress in consultations. Iran and Turkmenistan in the central and southern parts of the Caspian Sea watched the process and were not directly involved, so substantial progress was made.

It was still not a fundamental solution, but in the northern part of the

---

11 Hafeznia, M. R., Pirdashti, H. and Ahmadipour, Z. (2016), "An Expert-Based Decision Making Tool for Enhancing the Consensus on Caspian Sea Legal Rregime", *Journal of Eurasian studies*, Vol.7, No.2, pp.181-194.

Caspian Sea, where existing resource development facilities were concentrated, the agreement between the three countries was meaningful. Moreover, the agreement enabled Russia to complete the redrawing of boundaries with both the left and right sides of the Caspian Sea for the first time among the Caspian coastal countries.[12]

IV. Resolving territorial disputes and Potential Conflicts

1. Resolving Territorial Disputes: a Sea Agreed upon as a 'Sea'

Controversy and conflict have grown over the years, with no exact standard in international law on whether the Caspian Sea is a "lake" or a "sea." The situation of territorial disputes and conflicts over the Caspian Sea, especially among the coastal countries, lasted for nearly 30 years from 1991 to 2018. By August 2018, however, the five coastal countries reached a tentative agreement on the Caspian Sea to be "a sea of special status," neither a sea nor a lake. This agreement was not achieved instantaneously.

As discussed earlier, the results of the negotiations have accumulated over the years and are based on existing bilateral and trilateral agreements. As a result, after many twists and turns over the long years, the Caspian Sea has become "A Sea Agreed upon as a Sea" following the agreement by the coastal countries in 2018. The Caspian Convention seems to have three main points.[13]

---

12 Kim, Y. and Blank, S. (2016), "The New Great Game of Caspian Energy in 2013-14: Turk Stream, Russia and Turkey", *Journal of Balkan and Near Eastern Studies*, Vol.18, No.1, pp.37-55.

13 Lashaki, A. B. and Goudarzi, M. R. (2019), "Evolution of the Post-Soviet Caspian Sea Legal Regime", *In The Dynamics of Iranian Borders*, Springer, Cham, pp.49-68.

Firstly, that the Caspian Sea should be defined as a "sea of special status" and mutually recognizes both "international waters" and "exclusive economic zones." Up to 15 nautical miles (approximately 27.78 km) of the sea from the land coastline of the five coastal countries were designated as international waters and airspace in the same sense as territory. They agreed to recognize each other's "exclusive fishing rights as economic zones" up to 25 nautical miles (approximately 46.30 km) from the coastline. Like other sea cases in the world, the mid-Caspian waters have been set for common use by its coastal countries. This seems to be the middle ground achieved from Iran's concession of its position that the Caspian Sea is a 'lake,' and the position of others that it is a 'sea.'

Secondly, that ownership of resources on the seabed shall be finalized according to the agreement between the parties under international law, and judgement on final and permanent ownership shall be withheld for now. It has been agreed that the issue of undersea territorial imputation for further resource development needs to be resolved again in the future through a further agreement among coastal countries. This seems to reflect the Iranian position. Regarding its short coastline on the south side of the Caspian Sea, they have relatively little resources on the seabed and its deep water makes the development of resources difficult.

Third, the agreement was made to ensure that outside military forces would never be allowed to enter the Caspian Sea, only those of the five coastal countries. Under the agreement, including the future activities of warships and aircraft belonging to external countries, no new "harbor" or "facilities" can be created for military purposes by outside assistance. Activities such as external national ships' navigation, fishing, scientific research, resource development, and installation of industrial infrastructure are possible only if they are subject to sub-rules under the agreement. There seems to be a relatively strong military force at present, and the claims of Russia and Iran, which are competing with outside powers, have been included.

2. Meaning and Evaluation of the Caspian Sea Treaty

Under the Caspian Sea Treaty in August 2018, a number of existing large problems have recently entered a phase of solution. The most representative is Russia's decision in 2019 to allow the installation of pipelines to Europe from Kazakhstan and Turkmenistan, located on the east coast of the Caspian Sea. The energy pipeline, which must pass through western Russian waters and coastal territories to reach Europe, has not been properly realized for nearly two decades due to opposition from Russia. The Caspian Sea Treaty has made it possible for diverse means to transport vast amounts of resources buried in the Caspian Sea to outside high-consuming areas. It is also stated in the treaty that the countries where pipelines cross only need to agree on construction. Considering the problem that Iran and Turkmenistan have not signed onto the UNCLOS and now, in the Caspian Sea, the two countries have also been given special rights to the seabed. Additionally, there is also a clue that the problems of the past, for which the coastal countries have not cooperated, can be solved one by one.

The "Caspian Sea Treaty" was not easily progressed until it reached the final conclusion. It has important implications not only for the sovereignty of the Caspian Sea but also for the development of diplomatic relations throughout the coastal countries. For example, the preliminary work on the treaty took at least 10 years, with diplomatic authorities and officials from the five coastal countries holding more than 60 rounds. In the process, clear facts about each other's situation and position have been exchanged. Moreover, interest and understanding seems to have deepened between the countries. This is a meaningful point where negotiations and agreements can set a good precedent for resolving international maritime territorial disputes.

On an international perspective and normative level, the Caspian Sea Treaty can be taken in a sense as the 'first constitution' for the countries. This is because all the interested countries participated in the treaty and recognized each other's position with official documents. Therefore, the treaty is expected to guarantee security and political stability among the coastal countries over the long run. One positive assessment of achieving the treaty is that now the intense territorial disputes that had dragged on for at least two decades has ended.

3. Potential Conflicts and Possibilities of Disputes

The Caspian Sea Treaty does not seem to have completely resolved the long-standing conflict over the Caspian Sea. Specific discussions on this may be made as follows:

First, the Caspian Convention has some restrictions and proviso clauses. The convention states that "it does not immediately resolve existing maritime territorial disputes between Azerbaijan and Turkmenistan, or existing maritime territorial disputes between Azerbaijan and Iran." However, future measures to resolve existing territorial disputes in coastal countries are at the level of stating that they will be based on this agreement. In particular, Turkmenistan and Azerbaijan, which have similar periods of independence and national power, have yet to resolve the territorial disputes and are in a continuous state of military tension.

Second, with no detailed agreement on the status of the Caspian Sea, including ownership of undersea resources, the "grounds for quarrel of political conflict" seem to remain. Problems are bound to happen all the time on the unclear 'border lines of the sea.' The agreement of "common use and management of waters other than territory" also seems problematic. The leaders of the coastal countries signed the treaty together in 2018, stressing that the treaty was not the final end. They stated that continued cooperation and communication in the future would be necessary. Especially in the case of Iran, the treaty is, "only an agreement on the nature and legal status of the Caspian Sea, and any further excessive interpretation should be avoided." Iran is the country that has suffered the most from the treaty. They have only gained their sovereignty for the part with the deepest water and shortest coastline. Iran is on the verge of isolation due to old diplomatic friction with the U.S. and economic sanctions because of nuclear weapons. Their concessions were inevitable at a time when cooperation between Russia and neighboring countries was more urgent.

Third, the possibility of armed conflict or a security crisis has not been permanently resolved. As the past debate over "sea" or "lake" ends with "sea" for now, Russia and other countries are now trying to have the military authority of the sea. In the Caspian Sea, the Russian navy, has for the past three decades been a state of great force with its inherited Soviet Union-era military power. However, the treaty explicitly includes a clause banning all foreign troops, non-signatories, from being stationed in the Caspian Sea. There is a possibility that the rest of the world will not agree with that clause. The arms race for control of the Caspian Sea is an invisible danger for the future.

Fourth, the treaty will not be the perfect solution both internationally and diplomatically. On the coast of the Caspian Sea, there is a mixture of countries that are on good terms with the U.S. and countries that are not. This corresponds to Russia as well. On top of that, the interests of global corporations and investors in Britain, France, and China are also intertwined. Therefore, there is always a high possibility that they will conduct proxy wars. Although the treaty has given peace and stability exteriorly, it is persuasive enough to point out that it may be entering a more complicated international situation.

V. Conclusion

Today the dispute related to the division of marine territory or the sovereignty over the sea is one of the most difficult issues to decide by international convention. This is why there are many maritime territorial disputes around the world, but very few resolved cases. The issue of the Caspian Sea's identity regulations and territorial division was also a complicated equation from the beginning. All the stakeholders along the Caspian Sea had their own positions on borders and sovereignty, and those positions also have their own grounds.

However, the Caspian Sea Treaty in 2018 was created due to a combination of the finite nature of energy resource stores, the specificity and international pressure of development deadline, the pursuit of existing connectivity and practicality of coastal countries, environmental protection and security issues.

Many experts, including the authors of this study, will agree that the treaty has settled the territorial disputes among the five Caspian coastal countries.

The geopolitical importance of the Caspian Sea in Eurasia has also been reaffirmed. The Caspian Sea is expected to mark a new turning point in development. Since the region is stabilized, the participation in collaborative projects by Western advanced countries and global corporations is increasing. Coastal countries are promoting the benefits of minimizing the "risk" of future investment or cooperation to global corporations or external countries.

However, considering the current situation and geopolitical and geologic trends in the Caspian Sea that will unfold soon, "optimism" and "pessimism" are still intersecting among experts. In this regard, the international situation in the Caspian Sea, a key location linking Central Asia, Europe, and the Middle East, has important economic and diplomatic implications for all countries in Europe and Asia.

The Maritime Boundary Dispute between Slovenia and Croatia

Gojkošek, Matjaž
Jeong, Moon-Soo
Chung, Chin-Sung

I. Introduction

"Borders exclude and include, they are functional and symbolic at once, they help us to construct national, regional, local and European identities, they generate conflicts between people at various levels of interaction - and sometimes they even generate conflicts within people."[1] The topic of border disputes is a complex one, involving a variety of different aspects, which makes them notoriously difficult to resolve. International law still does not contain a clear, prioritized set of norms. Disputes often flare up after they become linked with important economic or social interests. Such areas may also be subject of historically based claims, cultural factors or demands for

---

[1] Dorte Jagetic Andersen (2011), *Life in the Shadows of Geopolitics: Everyday Practices and Public Discourse at the Croatian-Slovenian border*, Centre for International Border Research working paper series, WP23/2011, Felfast, p.15.

self-determination by their inhabitants.[2]

From the 1950s, the delimitation of maritime zones is one of the main topics of international law. The period could be characterized by the tendencies of coastal countries to enforce sovereignty over increasingly larger sea areas. Maritime territorial disputes, to a great extent, threaten peace and stability all over the world. In Europe, the problem of demarcation has become even more pressing after the collapse of multinational states, such as Yugoslavia, where maritime boundaries were yet to be determined.[3]

From the need to determine the boundary and Slovenian junction to the High Seas, the maritime border dispute between Croatia and Slovenia came to light soon after the dissolution of Yugoslavia in 1991. After years of failed attempts to peacefully resolve the dispute and reach an agreeable solution on their own, the two Republics submitted their dispute to Permanent Court of Arbitration (PCA) on November 4th, 2009. Despite few unresolved issues along the land boundary, the fiercest and most important issues of dispute were all directly, or indirectly, connected with the Bay of Piran (or Savudrija/Piran) and Slovenia's 'Junction to the High Seas.' Almost eight years later, on June 29th, 2017, the PCA issued the Final Award and determined the course of the maritime and land boundary between Slovenia and Croatia, and Slovenia's 'Junction to the High Sea.'[4]

---

2 The Carter Center (2010), *Approaches to Solving territorial conflicts: sources, situations, scenarios and suggestions*, Mimeo: Carter Center, VI.

3 Mitja Grbec (2002), "Razmejitev morskih pasov v mednarodnem pravu: določitev meje na morju med Republiko Slovenijo in Republiko Hrvaško", *Pravnik*, Vol. 57, No. 4-5, p.255.

4 The Hague (2017a), Press release, 29 June 2017: "Tribunal Determines Land and Maritime Boundaries in Final Award (long version)," The Hague: Permanent Court of Arbitration.

II. Attempts at dispute resolution before entering the PCA process

Following the World War II, the area from north of Trieste to the Mirna River in the south, was part of the Free Territory of Trieste. In 1954, the Territory was dissolved. The area was provisionally divided between Yugoslavia and Italy. The division was made final by the Treaty of Osimo in 1975.[5] In accordance with a basic international law, succession or the disintegration of countries has no influence on the validity of treaties and the provisions that determine state border or territorial regimes. The border with Italy thus could not be changed.[6] The federal government of Yugoslavia had successfully covered the internal conflicts between Slovenia and Croatia.

When Slovenia and Croatia both proclaimed their independence on June 25th, 1991, they simultaneously declared their mutual recognition, and that there were no outstanding territorial claims between them. Roughly one year after independence, countries jointly formed commission to demarcate their 670 km long shared land boundary, which brought to life several disputed points.[7]

The Brioni Declaration stipulated on July 7th, 1991, that the countries were committed to respecting the status quo of the existing border situation of June 25th, 1991. Despite the fact that maritime border between countries had never been officially determined, when it came to the question of control over the

---

5 Matjaž Gojkošek · Jeong, Moon-So · Chung, Chin-Sung (2017), "The Dissolution of Yugoslavia and the Emergence of a New Ethnic Minorities," *Cultural Interaction Studies of Sea Port Cities*, no.17, pp.280-283.

6 Grbec, op. cit., p.261.

7 Gerald Blake. Duško Topalović, and Clive Schofield (1996). *The maritime boundaries of the Adriatic Sea*, Durham: International Boundaries Research Unit, p.19.

Piran Bay, a proclamation of the regional park and their protection, as well as investment planning, and regulation works on the Dragonja River, a leading role belonged to the municipality of Piran.[8] Respect of the territorial status quo, and particularly the principle *uti possidetis juris*, was also the course of events recommended by the Arbitration Commission of the International Conference on the Former Yugoslavia, in 1992.[9]

The history of efforts to peacefully resolve the border dispute between States first started in 1992, with the formation of the first working groups to deal with the border issues. The following year, the two countries established a Mixed Diplomatic Commission for Establishment and Demarcation of Slovenia-Croatia Border and Final Treaty on State Border. The Diplomatic Commission managed to resolve 15 out of 19 remaining land boundary issues, however, it was unable to find an exactable solution in the area of Dragonja River (the course of which has direct impact on the course of maritime border in Piran Bay) or an acceptable solution for the maritime delimitation.[10] In 1995, both Slovenia and Croatia recognized the legitimacy of their claims regarding unresolved land border issues to respecting the status quo on the day of their independence, however failed to recognized legitimacy of each other's maritime delimitation claims. In 1998, after a last unsuccessful meeting, the Diplomatic Commission completed its work, and the border dispute moved to the political arenas of both States.

---

8 Darja Mihelič (2007), *Ribič, kje zdaj tvoja barka plava? : Piransko ribolovno območje skozi čas*, Koper: Založba Annales, p.148.

9 Vasilka Sancin (2010), "lovenia-Croatia Border Dispute: From »Drnovšek-Račan« to »PahorKosor« Agreement. European Perspectives," *Journal on European Perspectives of the Western Balkans*, vol. 2 no. 2, p.94.

10 Simona Drenik (2009), "Arbitražni sporazum: potek pogajanj in dosežene rešitve," *Pravna praksa*, 28.45, p.2.

The dispute appeared to have reached an acceptable solution in 2001, when the Prime Ministers of Slovenia and Croatia, managed to define the entire land and maritime border, and signed an agreement known as Drnovšek-Račan agreement. In the agreement, both parties agreed that Slovenia would receive about 80 percent of the Bay of Piran and a substantial portion of waters outside the bay (about 150km²) and that the disputed terrestrial area south of the Dragonja River was to become part of Croatia.[11] Both parties also agreed that a special two nautical mile long corridor in 'a certain shape of a chimney' would be formed and would have status of the High Seas, and that both 'the chimney' and 'water tower' would not be subject to sovereignty of either state. This solution would, at the same time, ensure open access to international waters for Slovenia and a territorial maritime border with Italy for Croatia.[12] Following its unanimous endorsement from the day before, Slovenian and Croatian governments initialed the Drnovšek-Račan agreement on the July 20th, 2001.

---

11 Peter Mackelworth, Draško Holcer, Jelena Jovanović and Caterina Fortuna (2010), "Marine conservation and accession: the future for the Croatian Adriatic," *Environmental management* vol. 47 no. 4, p.644.

12 Mitja Durnik and Marjeta Zupan (2007), "Borderline dispute between Slovenia and Croatia in the post Yugoslav era: solutions, obstacles and possible therapy," *CEU Political Science Journal*, vol. 2 no. 1, p.83.

<Figure 1> The maritime borders in the Bay of Piran, according to the Drnovšek-Račan agreement, would grant the disputed area to Slovenia and provide a corridor to international waters. (Source: Wikipedia)

Nevertheless, little more than one year later, in September 2002, the Croatian Prime Minster in letter addressed to Prime Minister of Slovenia, explained that Croatia could no longer pursue the conclusion of the agreement, and that its prior initialing had no legal effect.[13] In 2005, after a number of incidents along the 'border', the countries signed the Brioni Declaration to help avoid incidents. The purpose of the declaration was not about solving the border issues, but to ensure respect for the status quo as at June 25th, 1991, and to prevent further incidents. In July 2007, Slovenia proposed for the border dispute to be resolved through conciliation proceedings before the Court of Conciliation and Arbitration of the Organization for Security and Cooperation in Europe (OSCE), which was rejected by Croatia. The following month, Croatia proposed that countries should resolved the maritime part of the dispute through the International Tribunal on the Law of the Sea (ITLOS),

---

13 Sancin, op. cit., p.97.

located in Hamburg. However, this proposal was rejected by Slovenia, since Slovenia insisted on a comprehensive solution of all disputed areas.[14]

In August 2007, the Prime Ministers of both countries reached an informal agreement, the so-called Bled Agreement, which envisaged the submission of the dispute to an international judicial body. The countries appointed a Slovenian-Croatian team of legal experts, with the task of drafting a special agreement for submission of the dispute to arbitration in the International Court of Justice (ICJ). Since the team was unable to make any substantial progress, Slovenia officially concluded the negotiations in March 2009.

A major turning point occurred just before Slovenian parliamentary elections in September, 2008, when Slovenia decided to block the accession negotiations of Croatia with the European Union. The reason for this decision came from the belief that some Croatian actions in this pre-accession process constituted prejudices to the detriment of Slovenia, with regard to the final resolution of the border dispute. In order to lift their opposition, Slovenia wanted assurances from Croatia that it will eliminate all prejudices. In January 2009, the EU Commissioner for Enlargement, Mr. Olli Rehn, opened a new round of negotiations. After several proposals and amendments, he was unable to prepare an acceptable proposal for both parties. In June 2009, Croatia decided to withdraw from further talks. In the following month, however, both Prime Ministers agreed on further negotiations on the basis of three principles: Firstly, the withdrawal of Croatian prejudices in the pre-accession process; secondly, Slovenian consent to Croatia's continuation of the pre-accession process where the obstacles were prejudices to the resolution of the border dispute; and, thirdly, the need to reach an agreement on the resolution

---

14 Drenik, op. cit., p.2.

of the border dispute. In September 2009, the Croatian Prime Minster sent a written statement to the Council of European Union, in which she declared that no document, map, nor any other unilateral act adopted after June 25th, 1991 would have any legal effect on the final settlement of the border dispute. Slovenia withdrew its opposition and the two Prime Ministers agreed on the previously rejected second proposal from Commissioner Rehn. On November 4th, 2009, the Prime Ministers of Slovenia and Croatia signed the Arbitration Agreement, which was afterwards ratified by both States.[15]

III. Arbitration process and confrontation of arguments

The arbitration process between Slovenia and Croatia was launched on January 17th, 2012, in Brussels. The European Commission established a list of candidates from which both parties, a by common agreement, appointed three members including the President of the Arbitral Tribunal. In addition, each party appointed a further member to the Arbitral Tribunal,[16] as would be shown later, in order to protect their country's interests. On April 13th, 2012, the Arbitral Tribunal held its first procedural meeting with the representatives of both governments, and decided on the procedural framework for arbitration. In February 2013, parties submitted their first and written pleadings (Memorials), followed by second ones in November 2013, concerning the dispute between the two countries. The final arguments of both parties were presented in two week-long hearings, where appointed representatives from

---

15 Sancin, op. cit., pp.98-100.
16 European Commission (2012), Press release: "Launch of the arbitration process between Slovenia and Croatia," Retrieved May 2016 at: http://europa.eu/rapid/press-release_ IP12-25_en.htm?locale=hr

both states pleaded their cases on the disputed areas. The hearings, which were not open to the public, were conducted in two rounds and concluded on June 13th, 2014.[17] The task of the Arbitral Tribunal was to determine "the course of the maritime and land boundary between the Republic of Slovenia and the Republic of Croatia."[18]

Croatia argued that the course of the land and maritime boundary must be determined first, and solely by application of international law. The stressed that only after this had been determined could the Arbitral Tribunal consider Slovenia's contact to the High Sea, and the regime for the use of the relevant maritime areas (The Hague, 2014). However, almost five years prior the hearing Drenik explained that the Article 3 (4) of Arbitral agreement clearly states that "The Arbitral Tribunal has the power to interpret the present Agreement", which means that the court is not bound by the order of points a) the course of the maritime and land boundary between the Republic of Slovenia and the Republic of Croatia, b) Slovenia's junction to the High Sea and, c) the regime for the use of the relevant maritime areas in Article 3 (1), and could start with point b) and determine Slovenian junction to High Seas before determining land and maritime boundaries.[19] This was also confirmed during the negotiations, by the European Commission. 'Slovenia's junction to High Sea' and 'the regime for the use of the relevant maritime areas' were to

---

17 The Hague (2014), Press release, 17 June 2014: "Conclusion of Hearing in the Arbitration between the Republic of Croatia and the Republic of Slovenia," The Hague: Permanent Court of Arbitration.

18 Arbitration Agreement (2009), "Arbitration Agreement between the Government of the Republic of Slovenia and the Government of the Republic of Croatia," 4 November 2009, Stockholm. Retrieved Oct. 2019 at: https://jusmundi.com/fr/document/other/en-arbitration-between-the-republic-of-croatia-and-the-republic-of-slovenia-arbitration-agreement-wednesday-4th-november-2009#other_document_6731

19 Drenik, op. cit., p.4.

be determined by the application of 'international law, equity and the principle of good neighborly relations.' According to Croatia's view, 'equity and the principle of good neighborly relations' were only to supplement 'international law' and should not be contrary to it.

Slovenia stressed that its vital interest is its direct geographical contact, to the High Sea (junction), which should be determined in accordance with Article 4 (b) of the Arbitration Agreement.[20] On numerous occasions since 1993, Slovenia clearly expressed that junction to the High Sea was its vital primary interest on numerous occasions since 1993, and was also an absolutely essential condition for Slovenia to sign and ratify the Arbitration Agreement. From the Slovenian point of view, Croatia's vital interest was its accession to the European Union, which was accomplished after the adoption of the Arbitration Agreement. Therefore, this argument is unique by virtue of the task of the Tribunal and application of the law.

Croatia, on the other hand, contended that despite the fierce pressure of a Slovenian EU accession veto, they insisted that its maritime boundary was to be determined only by application of existing international law. As well as firmly maintaining the view throughout the negations and the hearings, that the term 'junction' did not amount to territorial contact with the High Sea, Croatia also claimed that their vital interest in the negotiations were not limited to EU membership, but were mainly focused toon the preservation of its territorial integrity, and that they had never agreed to the notion that its territorial sea right could be determined in any other way than by the strict application of

---

20 Article 4 (b) of arbitration agreement states : "international law, equity and the principle of good neighbourly relations in order to achieve a fair and just result by taking into account all relevant circumstances for the determinations referred to in Article 3 (1) (b) and (c)" (Arbitration Agreement, 2009).

Article 15[21] of the 1982 United Nations Law of the Sea Convention (UNCLOS). As well as they stated that the maritime boundary was thus to be determined from the mouth of the Dragonja River where the land boundary terminus was located, by application of an equidistant line through the Bay of Savudrija/ Piran (which were territorial waters, not internal waters) and beyond, up to the Osimo Treaty territorial sea boundary line with Italy. According to Croatia, the waters of the Bay have to be delimited between countries without regard regardless of their status.

Slovenia, however, claimed the entire territory of the Bay of Piran to be its internal waters, since it is considered an area of historical significance and was under Slovenian jurisdiction in the former Yugoslavia. The bay also maintained the status as internal waters after both countries proclaimed their independence. Therefore, based on the application of *uti possidetis juris* the whole bay belonged to Slovenia. "To the extent Croatia has occasionally patrolled a narrow strip along its coast, this could be dealt with by the regime." Slovenia stressed that in accordance to the second sentence of Article 15, the "coastal concavity and the cut-off effect of the Istrian peninsula and Cape Savudrija, security, navigation, and Slovenia's enjoyment of territorial sea and continental shelf right as a republic of the former Yugoslavia" must be

---

21 Article 15, the United Nations Convention on the Law of the Sea: "Where the coasts of two States are opposite or adjacent to each other, neither of the two States is entitled, failing agreement between them to the contrary, to extend its territorial sea beyond the median line every point of which is equidistant from the nearest points on the baselines from which the breadth of the territorial seas of each of the two States is measured. The above provision does not apply, however, where it is necessary by reason of historic title or other special circumstances to delimit the territorial seas of the two States in a way which is at variance therewith" UNCLOS (1982), United Nations Convention on the Law of the Sea (UNCLOS). https://www.un.org/depts/los/convention_agreements/texts/unclos/unclos_e.pdf

taken into account as unique circumstances.[22] Slovenia argued that 'maritime delimitation', 'junction' and 'regime' referred to in Article 3 (1) (a), (b) and (c) in the Agreement, were distinct issues of the task, and that the Tribunal was obliged to comply with this to its full extent.

Alternatively, Croatia claimed that 'junction' and 'regime' could not affect the course of the boundary. According to Croatian view, 'junction' was limited exclusively to matters of maritime access and communications, if any existed at all. Slovenia's interpretation of 'junction', however, was that the junction as a line joining Slovenia's territorial sea to the High Sea, does not separate Slovenia from the High Seas by Croatia's territorial sea or by potential an exclusive economic zone in the future. Croatia claimed that as a coastal state it has legitimate interests regarding navigation, security and defense concerns. As well, they pointed out, they also continue to have all the right of maritime entitlements, in the area southwards of Point 5 (45° 12.3') of the 1975 Osimo Treaty line, which was excluded from any determinations by the Tribunal.[23] As argued by Vidas, the only way for Slovenia to be territorially connected to the High Sea, is, if Croatia should relinquish its territorial sea area situated north of point 5.[24] This would basically require Croatia to transform part of its territorial sea into High Seas. Slovenia emphasized that the 'regime' they proposed was consistent with the UNCLOS, and "it would involve confirmation that the maritime regime to the south of Slovenia's junction would remain High Seas, a regime which is consistent with Slovenia's claim to a continental shelf", starting at Slovenia's 'junction' down to 45°10' parallel of latitude. Slovenia

---

22 The Hague (2014).

23 Ibid.

24 Davor Vidas (2009), "The UN Convention on the Law of the Sea, the European Union and the Rule of Law: What is going on in the Adriatic Sea?" *The International Journal of Marine and Coastal Law*, 24.1, pp.36-37.

also claimed 12 nautical miles of territorial sea, and that their historic fishing area right off the coast of Istria, now in Croatia's territorial seas, were to be preserved.[25]

IV. Wiretap scandal

On July 10th, 2015, after more than three years from the first procedural meeting with both countries, the Arbitral Tribunal informed both parties, that they could expect a final decision in December 2015.[26] When it already looked likely that the dispute would finally be resolved, a wiretap scandal placed the entire procedure into question. On July 22th, 2015, Croatian the newspaper *Večernji list* (2015) published illegally obtained audio tapes (acting on information first leaked in a Serbian tabloid) of traced telephone conversations between Jernej Sekolec, Slovene judge of the Arbitral Tribunal, and Simona Drenik, the representative of Slovenia's Foreign Ministry before the court. According to *Večernji list*, contacts took place during two telephone conversations on November 15th, 2014 and January 11th, 2015. The conversations included discussion on how to best present materials supporting Slovenian claims and influence the other members of the Arbitration Tribunal to rule in Slovenia's favor. In addition, Sekolec disclosed deliberations of the Tribunal to Drenik, including that Slovenia would get what it wanted when it came to the demarcation of the maritime border, including that Slovenia would be awared at least two thirds of the Gulf of Piran. It was also mentioned that

---

25 The Hague (2014), p.4.
26 The Hague (2015a), Press release, 10 July 2015: "Arbitral Tribunal Schedules Issuance of Award," The Hague: Permanent Court of Arbitration.

the demarcation of the land border was still undetermined, however, and that Slovenia might have to be more lenient in this regard.[27]

Following these revelations, Sekolec and Drenik both resigned after the Slovenian Prime Minister demanded that they take responsibility for the scandal and announced that the Slovenian Government had not been aware of their communications.[28] Slovenia acted fast, and on July 28th appointed French national Judge Ronny Abraham, President of the International Court of Justice, as a replacement for arbitrator Sekolec, however Judge Abraham resigned on August 3rd.[29]

In the meantime, on July 27th after the meeting with political parties represented in the Croatian Parliament, the Prime Minister of Croatia announced that Croatia was irrevocably withdrawing from the arbitration.[30] On July 30th, 2015, Budislav Vukas appointed arbitrator by Croatia, officially resigned, and the following day Croatia formally announced to the Tribunal that due to the scandal it could not further continue the process and was

---

27 *Večernji list* (2015), "EKSKLUZIVNO Donosimo audiosnimku razgovora arbitra i slovenske predstavnice!" Poslušajte! Zagreb: Večernji list. Retrieved May 2019 at: http://www.vecernji.hr/hrvatska/ekskluzivno-donosimo-razgovor-arbitra-i-slovenskestrane-poslusajte-snimke-1015908

28 RTV Slovenia (2015a), "Slovenija išče novega arbitra. Imenovati ga mora v 15 dneh," Ljubljana: Radiotelevizija Slovenija (RTV Slovenia). Retrieved May 2019 at: http://www.rtvslo.si/slovenija/slovenija-isce-novega-arbitra-imenovati-ga-mora-v-15dneh/370240

29 The Hague (2015b), Press release, 5 August 2015: "Republic of Croatia notifies its intention to terminate the Arbitration Agreement – Judge Ronny Abraham resigns from the Arbitral Tribunal," The Hague: Permanent Court of Arbitration.

30 RTV Slovenia (2015b), "Hrvaška odstopa od arbitraže, Haag pa želi pojasnila," Ljubljana: Radiotelevizija Slovenija (RTV Slovenia). Retrieved May 2019 at: http://www.rtvslo.si/svet/hrvaska-odstopa-od-arbitraze-haag-pa-zeli-pojasnilaslovenije/370496

therefore terminating the Arbitration.[31] On August 13th, 2015, Slovenia, in formal statements to the Tribunal, objected to Croatia's termination of the agreement, and expressed that the Tribunal had the power and the duty to continue the proceedings. Slovenia also argued that Croatia could not terminate the Arbitration Agreement, since it had already achieved its vital interest and joined the EU through the operation of Article 9 of the Arbitration Agreement. Slovenia had refrained from appointing another member of the Arbitral Tribunal in order to preserve the integrity, independence and impartiality of the Tribunal, and the ongoing proceedings. They requested that the President of the Arbitration Tribunal replace Judge Abraham, and appoint a new member of the Arbitration Tribunal.

Croatia, however, ignored the invitation to appoint a replacement arbitrator.[32] On September 25th, 2015, the Tribunal announced that it was reconstituted by the appointment of H.E. Mr. Rolf Einer Fife, a Norwegian national, and Professor Nicolas Michel, a Swiss national.[33] In a letter from the European Commission sent to Slovenian and Croatian Prime Ministers, President Jean Claude Juncker and First Vice-President Frans Timmermans expressed support for the continuation of the work of the arbitral tribunal and their satisfaction at the appointment of two new arbitrators. While Slovenia welcomed the position of the European Commission, Croatia replied that they had withdrawn from arbitration and did not intend to comment further

---

31 The Hague (2015b).

32 The Hague (2015c), Press release, 19 August 2015: "Slovenia demands continuation of arbitration proceedings – Arbitral Tribunal clarifies further procedural steps," The Hague: Permanent Court of Arbitration.

33 The Hague (2015d), Press release, 25 September 2015: "Tribunal reconstituted by appointment of Norwegian and Swiss arbitrators, H.E. Mr. Rolf Fifeand and Professor Nicolas Michel," The Hague: Permanent Court of Arbitration.

on moves of the Tribunal, nor participate in its work. They further stated that Croatia did not feel obliged to adopt, or to respond to any decision of the Tribunal.[34] Croatia's formal position was that it was entitled to terminate the Arbitration Agreement, since Slovenia "engaged in one or more material breaches of the Arbitration Agreement within the meaning of the Vienna Convention on the Law of Treaties, such that the impartiality and integrity of the arbitral proceedings has been irrevocably damaged, giving rise to a manifest violation of the rights of Croatia."[35]

In December 2015, the Tribunal set dates for further submission regarding questions arising from the aforementioned wiretap scandal and its intention to hold a hearing on these matters.[36] Croatia, however, did not file any written submission, nor attend the scheduled hearing on March 17th, 2016. Slovenia, on the other hand, filed a written submission and addressed the Arbitral Tribunal at the hearing. Slovenia stressed that the Tribunal should complete its mandate and render an award, since the Arbitration Agreement was based on a *quid pro quo*, and while Croatia's accession to the EU had been achieved, the Tribunal's determination of Slovenia's junction to the High Seas was still outstanding. "Slovenia elaborated that there was no impediment preventing the Tribunal from fulfilling its duty, and that the Tribunal possessed the tools to remedy the effects of any wrongdoing that may have occurred, in order

---

34 RTV Slovenia (2015c), "Cerar pozdravlja podporo nadaljevanju arbitraže iz Bruslja; Milanović: "Hrvaška je izstopila,"" Ljubljana: Radiotelevizija Slovenija (RTV Slovenia). Retrieved May 2019 at: http://www.rtvslo.si/evropska-unija/cerar-pozdravlja-podporonadaljevanju-arbitraze-iz-bruslja-milanovic-hrvaska-je-izstopila/375291

35 The Hague (2016b), Press release, 30 June 2016: "Tribunal Issues Partial Award: Arbitration between Croatia and Slovenia to Continue," The Hague: Permanent Court of Arbitration.

36 The Hague (2015e), Press release, 2 December 2015: "Tribunal sets dates for further submissions," The Hague: Permanent Court of Arbitration.

to attain the object and purpose of the Arbitration Agreement. In particular, Slovenia suggested that the resignation of those involved in the events, the appointment of new arbitrators, and the critical inspection of the official record of the arbitration by the Tribunal constituted adequate means of redressing the purported breach of the Arbitration Agreement. If any additional reparation was sought, the only appropriate remedy for such non-material damages under international law would be a declaration of the wrongfulness of Slovenia's conduct by the Tribunal."[37] Despite the absence of Croatia, the Tribunal decided that it is able and required to continue the proceedings, however the Tribunal expressed regret that Croatia did not explain its concerns more fully.[38]

All further considerations by the Tribunal regarding the territorial and maritime border dispute remained suspended until June 30th, 2016, when the Tribunal issued a unanimous Partial Award concerning the legal implications of the matters set out by Croatia as their response to the wiretap scandal.[39] "In its Partial Award, the Tribunal holds that Slovenia, by engaging in *ex parte* contacts with the arbitrator originally appointed by it, acted in violation of provisions of the Arbitration Agreement. However, these violations were not of such a nature as to entitle Croatia to terminate the Arbitration Agreement, nor do they affect the Tribunal's ability, in its current composition, to render a final award independently and impartially."[40]

---

37 The Hague (2016a), Press release, 18 March 2016: "Conclusion of Hearing in the Arbitration between the Republic of Croatia and the Republic of Slovenia," The Hague: Permanent Court of Arbitration.
38 The Hague (2016b).
39 The Hague (2016a); The Hague (2016b).
40 The Hague (2016b).

V. Tribunal's Final Award

The Tribunal unanimously issued the Final Award on June 29th, 2017, and determined the course of the maritime and land boundary between Slovenia and Croatia, Slovenia's 'Junction to the High Sea' and the regime for the use of the relevant maritime areas. Hereinafter we focus on the maritime determination of the boundary, while taking into the account only land issues related to the maritime determination.

1. The Bay of Piran (or Savudrija/Piran)

"The historic reason for the border dispute lies in changes of borders of the Municipality of Piran. Its cadaster borders were the result of miscellaneous use of land by various local communities."[41]

The Tribunal concludes that the Bay of Piran had the status of Yugoslav internal waters prior to the dissolution of Yugoslavia and remained so after 1991. Therefore, the delimitation must be made on the basis of *uti possidetis juris*. Since there had been no formal division of the bay prior to the dissolution of Yugoslavia, the Tribunal considered that the deliiminatation must be made on the ground of the *effectivités* at the date of independence, especially with regard to the fisheries regulation and police patrols in the Bay of Piran. The Tribunal observes that during the whole period from 1962 to 1991 Slovenia alone organized the management of the fishing reserve in the area. They also noted that Slovenia was more active in their efforts to address

---

41 Primož Pipan (2008), "Border dispute between Croatia and Slovenia along the lower reaches of the Dragonja River," *Acta geographica Slovenica,* vol. 48, no. 2, p.334.

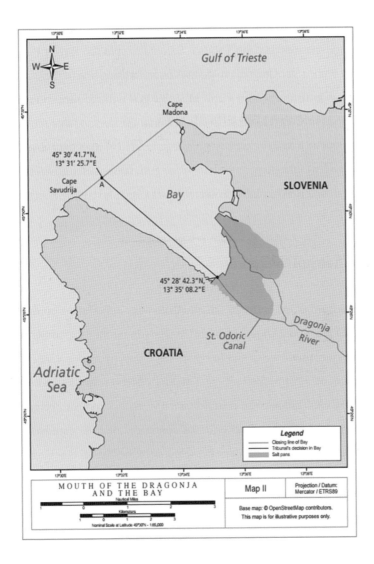

<Figure 2> Mouth of the Dragonja and the Piran Bay. Source: The Hague (2017a. p.9)

the risk of pollution in the area. Regarding the police patrols, the Tribunal recognized that the local police of the Slovenian city, Koper, patrolled the area with two vessels, and that Slovenian police were more active in the Bay than their Croatian counterparts in response to accidents.

Based on these points, the Tribunal decided to split the Bay of Piran, from the mouth of the river Dragonja to point A on the closing line of the Bay (Figure 2), which is a distance from Cape Madona that is three times the distance from point A, to Cape Savudrija.[42] The Tribunal decided and that the maritime border should be a straight line that connects the land border at the mouth of the Dragonja River to the point at the end of the gulf, which is three times closer to Croatia then to the Slovenian side, thereby awarding Slovenia 75% of the gulf.

2. The Territorial Sea

The territorial sea between the countries was delimitated in accordance with Article 15 of the United Nations Convention on the Law of the Sea, and the settled jurisprudence of the International Court of Justice concerning the delimitation of territorial seas. The Tribunal observes that International law calls for the application of an equidistance line, unless another line is required by special circumstances. The Tribunal concludes that the equidistance line must be modified in a way to consider features of the coastal configuration as a special circumstance for delimitation.

The Tribunal observes that it is necessary to accommodate two principles: The first principle is the natural prolongation of the land territory into the sea, and the second is in the words of ICJ, that "the effects of incidental special feature from which unjustifiable difference of treatment could result."[43]

---

42 The Hague (2017a), pp.6-9; The Hague (2017b), Press release, 29 June 2017: "Tribunal Determines Land and Maritime Boundaries in Final Award (short version)," The Hague: Permanent Court of Arbitration. p.3.
43 The Hague (2017a), p.10.

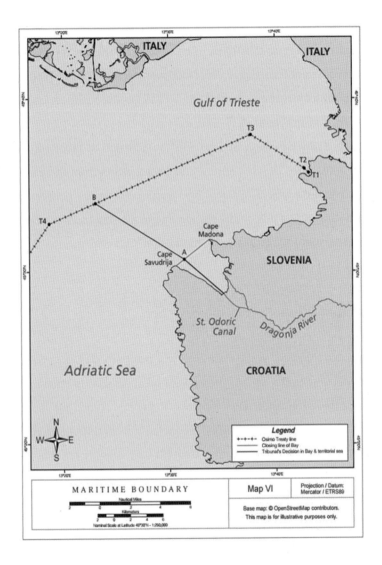

<Figure 3> Maritime Boundary. Source: The Hague (2017a. p.12)

The Tribunal considers that features of the coastal configuration produce an adverse effect if the strict equidistance line is used, and do constitute a special circumstance. The coastline of Croatia turns sharply southward around Cape

Savudrija, so the Croatian basepoints which control the equidistance line are located on a very small stretch of coast where the general (north-facing) direction is different from the general (southwest-facing) direction of the much greater part of the Croatian coastline, which deflects the equidistance line very significantly towards the north.[44]

Therefore, the equidistance line must be adjusted in favor of Slovenia in order to attenuate the 'boxing in' effect that results from the geographic configuration of the area. The determined maritime boundary between the two Republics starts at Point A on the closing line of the Bay of Piran and ends at Point B of the Osimo Treaty line, as indicated on Figure 3.[45]

3. Slovenia's 'Junction to the High Sea'

Slovenia's 'junction to the High Sea' was determined in accordance with international law, equity and the principle of good neighborly relations as laid down by Arbitration Agreement. The two Republics argued the meaning of the word 'junction'. While Slovenia interpreted 'junction to the High Sea' as a direct geographical contact to the High Sea, Croatia argued that the term 'junction' did not amount to territorial contact with the High Sea.[46]

The Tribunal determines that "the core meaning of 'junction' is the place where two or more things come together or join" and that in the present case the word 'junction' stands for physical location that connects Slovenia's territorial sea with the area beyond the territorial seas of Italy and Croatia.

---

44 The Hague (2017a), pp.10-11.
45 The Hague (2017a), p.12.
46 The Hague (2017a), p.13.

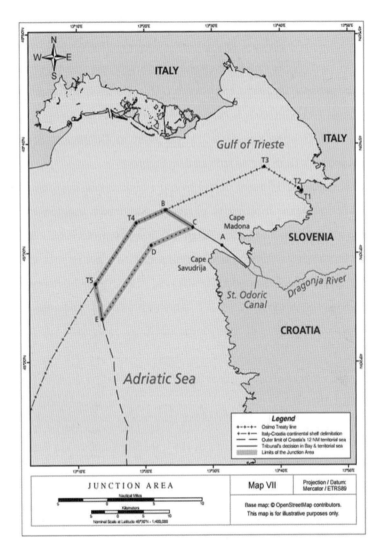

<Figure 4> Junction Area. Source: The Hague (2017a. p.15)

Turning to the geographical location of that connection between Slovenia's territorial sea and the 'High Sea', the Tribunal observes that there is presently no place where Slovenian's territorial sea is immediately adjacent to the area in which the applicable legal regime preserves the freedoms referred in UNCLOS Article 58 and Article 87.[47] The Tribunal thus determines that Slovenia's junction to the High Sea must be established by creating an area in Croatian territorial waters where "ships and aircraft enjoy essentially the same rights of access to and from Slovenia as they enjoy on the high seas". The established Junction Area is approximately 2.5 NM wide and connects Slovenia's territorial sea with High Sea as indicated on Figure 4.[48]

Furthermore, the Tribunal determines the regime that is going to apply to the Junction Area: In order to guarantee Slovenia's uninterrupted and complete access from and to the "High Sea", and to protect the integrity of Croatia's territorial sea, the Tribunal recommends a special regime unlike any other previously established under UNCLOS.[49] The Tribunal determines "the content and scope of the freedom of communication" and "guarantees of, and limitations to, the freedom of communication."[50]

VI. Conclusion

Since the collapse of Yugoslavia in 1991, the formation of six independent states has created new issues, such as the emergence of groups of ethnic minorities within their respective borders.[51] The ethnic conflict among the once-same citizens has seen further escalation with the matter of redrawing new frontiers among the recently- independent nations. In general, border

---

47 The Hague (2017a), pp.13-14; The Hague (2017b), p.3.
48 The Hague (2017a), p.15
49 The Hague (2017b), p.3.
50 The Hague (2017a), pp.16-17.
51 Gojkošek, Matjaž · Jeong, Moon-Soo · Chung, Chin-Sung (2017), op. cit., p.278.

disputes in the sea are much more complicated than border disputes on land, where the principle of *uti possidetis* applies, because they require consideration of a variety of precedents and circumstances, including the principle of *effectiviton*. Regarding the maritime territorial dispute between Croatia and Slovenia, both of whom became independent after the breakup of Yugoslavia, the article has presented the efforts to resolve disputes between the two countries and analyzed the principles and laws applied in the course of the PCI ruling.

The PCA's determination with respect to the land boundary was decided by the principle of *uti possidetis*, which does not face the irreconcilable confrontation of arguments from both sides. The determination on the boundary with respect to the Bay of Piran (or Savudrija/Piran) was determined on the basis of *uti possidetis*, and *effectivités* at the date of independence, especially with regard to the fisheries regulation and police patrols in the Bay of Piran. The determination of Slovenia's 'Junction to the High Sea' was determined by applying international law, equity and the principle of good neighborly relations. With accordance to freedom of communication referred in UNCLOS Article 58 and 87, the Tribunal determines Slovenia's 'junction to the High Sea' must be established by creating an area in Croatian territorial seas in which "ships and aircraft enjoy essentially the same rights of access to and from Slovenia as they enjoy on the high seas." Furthermore, the Tribunal determines "the content and scope of the freedom of communication" and "guarantees of, and limitations to, the freedom of communication."[52]

The PCA's determinations on the maritime boundary and Slovenia's "Junction to the High Sea" are welcomed by Slovenia but rejected by Croatia.

---

52 The Hague (2017a), pp.16-17.

On 29 December 29th, 2017, Slovenia started implementing the arbitration ruling but only at sea, while Croatia continued to oppose it.[53]

As with the case of China's absolute rejection of the PCI decisions in China and the Philippines,[54] the reality is, that the PCI's rulings on Croatia and Slovenia are not currently fully legally binding due to Croatia's opposition. But the parties to the dispute have an obligation under international law to negotiate faithfully to resolve the dispute. It is hopeful that a peaceful resolution to this dispute may be found. Therefore, it is very important to analyze the laws and the principles of the PCI's ruling on the disputed areas of the land border, the drawing of the border in the Gulf of Piran (or Savudrija/Piran), and the determination of Slovenia's 'Junction to the High Sea'. This is because it is essential that the maritime territorial dispute be resolved through consultation among the parties and arbitration at the ICJ and PCA, rather than through military engagement.

53 RTV Slovenia (2017), "Hrvaška policija ribičem svetovala lovljenje še naprej," Ljubljana: Radiotelevizija Slovenija (RTV Slovenia) retrieved Oct. 2019 at: https://www.rtvslo.si/slovenija/hrvaska-policija-ribicem-svetovala-lovljenje-se-naprej/441677

54 Lee, Jung Tae (2016), "China's the Construction of Artificial Islands in the South China Sea and PCA Ruling," *Korea Political Science Society*, vol. 24, no. 4. pp.163-186.

A Study on the Maritime Jurisdictions in the Constitutions of Asian Countries

Han, Byung-Ho

I. Introduction

The land has long been the fundamental base of human life, and it is still valid. Today, however, the resources of the land alone cannot meet the demands of human life as even the finite resources of land are gradually being exhausted. On the contrary, the utility of maritime resources is further increasing, and scientific techniques to preserve, manage, use, and develop them continue to improve. South Korea has long been interested in maritime resources, and the Article 2 of the Framework Act on Maritime Fishery Development says:

Recognizing that the sea is a rich repository of natural resources and a ground for living as well as a passage of logistics, and as such it exerts considerable influence on the national economy and national life, the basic ideology of this Act is to cultivate opulent and vibrant seas to be bequeathed to the future generations, by creating an environment where the marine fisheries can become more knowledge- and information-based and create higher added value, protecting the life and property of the people in the sea, and seeking the environment-friendly and sustainable development or use of the marine fishery resources.

However, increasing and spreading awareness of the utility of the sea rather causes or intensifies conflicts between countries over maritime jurisdiction. In fact, it became clear in the 20th century that many countries were endeavoring to expand the breadth of their territorial waters, traditional maritime jurisdiction, or claimed new maritime jurisdiction.[1] In such a difficult situation, international efforts continued to regulate maritime jurisdiction uniformly. As a result, the United Nations Convention on the Law of the Sea (UNCLOS) was finally adopted in 1982.[2] By March 2020, a total of 168 countries had ratified or acceded to UNCLOS.[3]

It is still common, on the other hand, for coastal countries to regulate their respective maritime jurisdictions by their own domestic laws in accordance with UNCLOS. Coastal countries usually prescribe the specific details of these maritime jurisdictions by their own domestic laws. This domestic legislation on maritime jurisdiction can be affected by various factors such as the principles and rules of international law, the country's interests in maritime jurisdiction, relations with neighboring countries, and the other conditions under which maritime jurisdiction issues are posed. As a result, different countries have

---

1 Treves, Tullio, "Historical Development of the Law of the Sea", Donald R. Rothwell et al (ed. 2015), *The Oxford Handbook of the Law of the Sea*, Oxford: Oxford University Press, pp.4-13.

2 Treves, Tullio, op cit, pp.7-22; Churchill, Robin R., "The 1982 United Nations Convention on the Law of the Sea", Donald R. Rothwell et al (ed.), op. cit., pp.25-27; Donald R. Rothwell and Tim Stephens (2010), *The International Law of the Sea*, Oxford: Hart Publishing, pp.4-14.

3 https://www.un.org/Depts/los/reference_files/chronological_lists_of_ratifications. htm#The United Nations Convention on the Law of the Sea

different legislations on maritime jurisdiction.[4] South Korea has two laws which rule its maritime jurisdiction - the Territorial Sea and Contiguous Zone Act, and the Act on the Exclusive Economic Zone and Continental Shelf. These laws accept the principles and rules of UNCLOS as they are.

Sometimes these maritime jurisdictions may be regulated somewhat broadly by the Constitution, the supreme law of the state, although its content may not be as specific and detailed as that of the ordinary laws. If a coastal country regulates its maritime jurisdiction by its own Constitution, it can be said that its people are particularly interested in maritime jurisdiction. Because the Constitution is the fundamental and supreme law of the state, they must have great public interests in its contents. In South Korea, some recently argue for a constitutional amendment to clarify maritime jurisdiction in the Constitution by mentioning the concepts of maritime jurisdiction. However, constitutional reform is not easy because of the rigidity of the Constitution itself. In order to successfully amend the Constitution, public support is required. However it is just the first step in the procedure of constitutional revise to initiate a constitutional amendment. In order to prepare the amendment, it is first necessary to find a legislative-technical method, that is, how to describe in the Constitution which specific details of maritime jurisdiction. For this preparation, it is also useful to analyze the cases of constitutions of other countries.

This article will analyze how to regulate maritime jurisdiction by the constitutions of Asian countries. It will specifically address the following: First, whether the concepts of maritime jurisdiction mentioned in UNCLOS, such as the territorial sea, the exclusive economic zone and the continental shelf, are referred to in the constitutions of Asian countries; Second, what kinds of

---

4 https://www.un.org/Depts/los/LEGISLATIONANDTREATIES/PDFFILES/table_
  summary_of_claims.pdf

matters are regulated by using such concepts in the constitutions; and third, how the extent or limits of maritime jurisdiction are regulated in the constitutions addressed.

As is well known, the Asian continent is surrounded by the Arctic, the Pacific, and Indian Oceans northwards, eastwards, and southwards respectively. To the west, it borders relatively smaller seas such as the Black Sea and the Mediterranean Sea. There are 47 members of the UN in Asia. Geographically, the Asian countries are classified into five countries in East Asia, eleven countries in Southeast Asia, nine countries in South Asia, five countries in Central Asia, and 17 countries in West Asia.[5] There are 12 landlocked countries,[6] and 35 coastal countries,[7] including 10 island countries,[8] in Asia. Of 47 members of the UN in Asia, 33 countries, including 28 coastal countries, are state parties to UNCLOS,[9] however seven coastal countries are not. [10]

The objects of analysis in this paper are the Constitutions of 34 coastal

---

5 Department of Economic and Social Affairs Statistics Division (2019), *World Statistics Pocketbook 2019 edition*, New York: Unites Nations, pp.17-22. Palestine in West Asia and Taiwan in East Asia are not the members of the United Nations.

6 Landlocked Countries in Asia: Mongolia in East Asia; Laos in Southeast Asia; Afghanistan, Bhutan, and Nepal in South Asia; Kazakhstan, Kyrgyzstan, Tajikistan, Turkmenistan, and Uzbekistan in Central Asia; Armenia and Azerbaijan in West Asia.

7 Coastal Countries in Asia: China, Japan, South Korea, and North Korea in East Asia; Brunei, Cambodia, Indonesia, Malaysia, Myanmar, Philippines, Singapore, Thailand, Timor-Leste, and Viet Nam in Southeast Asia; Bangladesh, Maldives, India, Iran, Pakistan, and Sri Lanka in South Asia; Bahrain, Cyprus, Georgia, Iraq, Israel, Jordan, Kuwait, Lebanon, Oman, Qatar, Saudi Arabia, Syria, Turkey, UAE, and Yemen in West Asia.

8 Island Countries in Asia: Japan, Philippines, Indonesia, Timor-Leste, Brunei, Singapore, Maldives, Sri Lanka, Bahrain, and Cyprus. Taiwan, which is not a member of the United Nations, is also an island country.

9 http://www.un.org/Depts/los/reference_files/status2019.pdf.

10 North Korea, Cambodia, Iran, Syria, UAE, Israel, and Turkey are coastal countries, which have not been the state parties to the UNCLOS yet.

countries in Asia.[11] Israel, which does not have a written constitution, is excluded from analysis.

II. The Concepts of Maritime Jurisdiction in the Constitutions

UNCLOS refers to the concepts of maritime jurisdiction of coastal countries as follows: the Territorial Sea (Art. 2), the Internal Waters (Art. 8), the Contiguous Zone (Art. 33), the Exclusive Economic Zone [EEZ] (Art. 55), the Continental Shelf (Art. 76), and the Archipelagic Waters of archipelagic states (Art. 49). It is

[Table 1] The Concepts of Maritime Jurisdiction in the Constitutions

Concepts	Countries	Number
Territorial Sea	SE: Brunei, Myanmar, Philippines, Timor-Leste, Viet Nam S: Bangladesh, India, Maldives, Pakistan, Sri Lanka W: Georgia, Saudi Arabia, UAE, Yemen	14
Continental Shelf	SE: Cambodia, Philippines, Timor-Leste S: Bangladesh, India, Pakistan, Sri Lanka W: Georgia, Yemen	9
EEZ	SE: Timor-Leste S: India, Maldives, Sri Lanka W: Georgia, Yemen	6
Contiguous Zone	SE: Timor-Leste	1
Internal Waters	SE: Philippines S: Sri Lanka	2
Archipelagic Waters	SE: Indonesia, Philippines S: Maldives	3
None	E: South Korea, North Korea, China, Japan SE: Malaysia, Singapore, Thailand S: Iran W: Bahrain, Cyprus, Iraq, Jordan, Kuwait, Lebanon, Oman, Qatar, Syria, Turkey	18

※ In this table, E, SE, S, and W mean East Asia, Southeast Asia, South Asia, and West Asia, respectively, and it also applies to the tables below.

---

11 The texts of the constitutions used here are English versions or translations provided by the Comparative Constitutions Project. https://www.constituteproject.org/search?lang=en.

First of all, there are 16 countries, including six island countries,[12] whose constitutions mention one or more of these concepts of maritime jurisdiction. This number is equivalent to 47 percent of 34 coastal countries in Asia. No concepts of maritime jurisdiction are mentioned at all in the constitutions of the other 18 coastal countries, though ([Table 1]). No concepts of maritime jurisdiction are mentioned at all in the constitutions of 12 landlocked countries, either. Of the 28 Asian coastal countries which are state parties to UNCLOS, the constitutions of half - 14 countries, mention concepts of maritime jurisdiction, while the other half make no mention of the concepts of maritime jurisdiction at all. With regard to the six Asian coastal countries (excluding Israel), which are not the state parties to UNCLOS, concepts of maritime jurisdiction are mentioned only in the constitutions of two countries, Cambodia and the UAE.

Secondly, in analyzing which concepts of maritime jurisdictions are mentioned in the constitutions of the Asian coastal countries, we can see that of those referred to in UNCLOS, the concept of Territorial Sea[13] is cited in the constitutions of 14 countries - much more than any other concept ([Table 1]). This is natural because the territorial sea is not only a component of the territory, over which the state exercises its own sovereignty, but also because this concept has been the most traditionally recognized of maritime jurisdiction. The question could be asked then, as to why the constitutions of the remaining 20 coastal countries make no mention of the Territorial Sea

---

12 Philippines, Indonesia, Timor-Leste, Brunei, Maldives, and Sri Lanka. This number is equivalent to 60 percent of the 10 Asian island countries. However, the Constitutions of Japan, Singapore, Bahrain, and Cyprus mention no concepts of maritime jurisdiction.

13 The word of Territorial Sea is used in the Constitution of Philippines; the words of Territorial Sea and Territorial Waters are used together in that of Sri Lanka; the word of Territorial Waters is used in the Constitutions of all the other countries.

concept at all.

With regard to concepts of other maritime jurisdiction, the Continental Shelf is mentioned in the constitutions of nine countries; the EEZ in those of six countries; Internal Waters in those of two countries; the Archipelagic Waters or the Archipelagic State in those of three countries. The concept of Contiguous Zone is only mentioned in the constitution of one country ([Table 1]).

In particular, various combinations of the three concepts of Territorial Sea, EEZ, and Continental Shelf are analyzed here. All three of these concepts are mentioned in the constitutions of five countries (Georgia, India, Sri Lanka, Timor-Leste, and Yemen). Combinations of two concepts are mentioned in the constitutions of four countries: Territorial Sea and Continental Shelf are found in the constitutions of three countries (Bangladesh, Pakistan, Philippines); while Territorial Sea and EEZ are only mentioned together in the constitution of one country (Maldives). EEZ and Continental Shelf concepts in combination are not mentioned in the constitutions of any countries. Only one of the three concepts is mentioned in the constitution of six countries: Territorial Sea is referred to in the constitutions of five countries (Brunei, Myanmar, Vietnam, Saudi Arabia and UAE), and Continental Shelf in the constitution of one country (Cambodia). In addition, only Indonesia mentions the concept of Archipelagic State. There are no constitutions of any Asian coastal country that mention only the concept of EEZ. It is perhaps peculiar that the constitutions of two countries - Cambodia and Indonesia, mention other concepts of maritime jurisdiction, but disregard Territorial Sea.

When we compare the results in Asia to those in the Americas, we find that of the 33 American coastal countries, the constitutions of 18 mention one or more concepts of maritime jurisdiction. In particular, constitutions of 11 countries mention all three concepts (Territorial Sea, EEZ and

Continental Shelf). Among the 34 Asian coastal countries, on the other hand, the constitutions of 16 countries mention one or more concepts of maritime jurisdiction. All three concepts of Territorial Sea, EEZ, and Continental Shelf are mentioned in just the constitutions of five countries.

III. Usage of the Concepts of Maritime Jurisdiction in the Constitutions

The second purpose of this article is to analyze usage of the concepts of maritime jurisdiction as mentioned in a constitution. In other words, it seeks to analyze what matters a constitution regulates by using the concepts of maritime jurisdiction. The uses of maritime jurisdiction concepts mentioned in a constitution are classified into three types. In the case of the first type of usage, by mentioning the concepts of maritime jurisdiction, a constitution establishes the extent and limits of maritime space over which the state exercises its sovereignty or jurisdiction. In the case of the second type, a constitution determines who has ownership of the maritime space and the resources therein, which the sovereignty or jurisdiction of the coastal state extends to. In the case of the third type, a constitution establishes the distribution of powers over maritime jurisdiction between state organs, in particular, between federal and state governments, between central and local governments, or between parliament and other state organs. Logically, the first type of usage is more rudimentary than the other two because the national authority over maritime jurisdiction in the second and third types presupposes the existence of maritime jurisdiction of a state among nations in the first type. Of course, these three types are not mutually exclusive.

Nor do these three types cover all of the usage of the concepts of maritime jurisdiction in a constitution. To classify uses of the concepts of maritime jurisdiction mentioned in the constitutions of 16 coastal countries in Asia, the results are as follows ([Table 2]):

[Table 2] Usage of the Concepts of Maritime Jurisdiction in the Constitutions

Type	Name of countries	Number
Limits of Maritime Jurisdiction	SE: Indonesia, Philippines, Timor-Leste, Viet Nam S: Maldives, Sri Lanka W: UAE	7
Properties of Maritime Resources	SE: Cambodia , Philippines, Timor-Leste S: Bangladesh, India, Maldives, Pakistan W: Saudi Arabia, Yemen	9
Distribution of Powers to Maritime Jurisdiction	SE: Myanmar, Timor-Leste S: India, Pakistan, Sri Lanka W: Georgia, UAE	7
Unusual Case	SE: Brunei S: Maldives	2

The first type (Limits of Maritime Jurisdiction), corresponds to the constitutions of seven countries ([Table 2]).[14] These constitutions refer to Territorial Sea as a component of the territory, over which the state exercises its sovereignty, or they refer to the concepts of maritime jurisdiction in order to establish maritime spaces, over which the state exercises its jurisdiction. The second type (Properties of Maritime Resources), corresponds to the constitutions of nine countries ([Table 2]).[15] According to this type of the constitutions, the property of maritime space and resources, which sovereignty and jurisdiction of the state extends to, usually belongs

14 Indonesia: Article 25A; Philippines: Article 1; Timor-Leste: Article 4; Viet Nam: Article 1; Maldives: Article 3; Sri Lanka: Article 5 and Article 170; UAE: Article 2.

15 Cambodia: Article 58; Philippines: Article 12; Timor-Leste: Article 139; Bangladesh: Article 143; India: Article 297; Maldives: Article 248; Pakistan: Article 172; Saudi Arabia; Article 14; Yemen: Article 8.

exclusively to the federal government in federal countries, and central government in unitary countries. The third type (Distribution of Powers to Maritime Jurisdiction), corresponds to the constitutions of the seven countries ([Table 2]).[16] According to this type of the constitutions, a federal or central government exclusively exercises its authority over maritime space and maritime resources within maritime jurisdiction of the state. Parliament has exclusive legislative jurisdiction over its own space and maritime resources. In addition to these three types, unusually, the concepts of maritime jurisdiction are referred to in the Constitution of Brunei with respect to mandate under the State of Emergency, and in the Constitution of Maldives with regard to the mission of Military Service.[17] The usage in the constitutions of these two countries also presupposes the existence of maritime jurisdiction of the state according to the above-described first type usage.

Concerning the combinations of the three types of usage, Timor-Leste is the only coastal country which utilizes all three types of usage of maritime jurisdiction concepts, in the Constitution. Of the three types of usage, combinations of two types are used in the constitutions of six countries: The first and second types are applied in constitutions of two countries (Maldives, Philippines); the first and third types are used in the constitutions of two countries (Sri Lanka, UAE); the second and third types are adopted in the constitutions of two countries (India, Pakistan). Of the three types of usage, only one is used in the constitutions of eight countries. The first is utilized in

---

16 Myanmar: Article 254; Timor-Leste: Article 95; India: Article 246, Schedule 7; Pakistan: Article 70, Schedule 4; Sri Lanka: Article 154G, Schedule 9; Georgia: Article 3; UAE: Article 121.

17 Brunei: Article 83; Maldives: Article 243.

the constitutions of two countries (Indonesia, Viet Nam), while constitutions of four countries (Bangladesh, Cambodia, Saudi Arabia, Yemen) apply the second type; and only the third is used in the constitutions of two countries (Georgia, Myanmar). However, it is worth mentioning again that the maritime jurisdiction in the second or third types of usage presupposes the existence of maritime jurisdiction in the first type. Therefore, it is not appropriate that the constitution, which does not apply the first type, utilizes the second or third type of usage (Bangladesh, Cambodia, Georgia, India, Myanmar, Pakistan, Saudi Arabia, and Yemen).

IV. Constitutional Provisions on the Extent and Limits of Maritime Jurisdiction

According to UNCLOS, in principle, the maximum extent or outer limits of maritime jurisdiction of coastal countries, measured from the baseline of the Territorial Sea,[18] is as follows: Territorial Sea up to 12 nautical miles (Article 3); Contiguous zone up to 24 nautical miles (Article 33); EEZ up to 200 nautical miles (Article 57); and Continental Shelf up to 200 nautical miles or outer edge of the continental margin (Article 76). Most countries, whether they have ratified or accede to UNCLOS or not, determine the extent or limits of their own maritime jurisdiction by ordinary laws in accordance with the principles and rules of UNCLOS. This applies to South Korea, as well.

---

[18] The baseline of the territorial sea means the baseline for measuring the breadth of the territorial sea.

[Table 3] Constitutional Provisions on the Extent of Maritime Jurisdiction

Type	Countries	Number
Mandate of Legislation	SE: Indonesia, Timor-Leste S: Bangladesh, India, Maldives, Sri Lanka W: Georgia, UAE	8
Not Mentioned	SE: Brunei, Cambodia, Myanmar, Philippines, Viet Nam S: Pakistan W: Saudi Arabia, Yemen	8

However, another case is the Constitution as the fundamental and supreme law of the state, of which the texts should be expressed as simply and clearly as possible. At this level, it is arguably very difficult, if not impossible, to set the extent or limits of maritime jurisdiction in detail exclusively by a constitution. Rather, there are some alternative ways of constitutional provision for determining the extent or limits of maritime jurisdiction. One such method, as just mentioned, is the direct determination of the extent of maritime jurisdiction by a constitution, though this would be by specifying it broadly and not in detail. There are no constitutions of Asian countries that set the extents of maritime jurisdiction in this way. There are constitutions of four Central, and one South American countries,[19] that explicitly define the breadth of the maritime jurisdiction for themselves. With respect to the extent of maritime jurisdiction being established in accordance with international laws or treaties, there are no constitutions of Asian countries, but several Central and Southern American countries[20] that state this explicitly.

There remains two other methods for the constitutional provision for determining the extent or limits of maritime jurisdiction. The first is a method

---

19 Costa Rica, El Salvador, Honduras, Mexico, and Peru.
20 Colombia, Cuba, Dominican Republic, Ecuador, Guatemala, Mexico, Nicaragua, Panama, and Venezuela.

whereby the Constitution mandates legislation to determine the extent of maritime jurisdiction by ordinary laws. The other is the way the Constitution makes no explicit statement determining the extent of maritime jurisdiction. The constitutions of the 16 Asian coastal countries, which refer to the concepts of maritime jurisdiction, use either of these two methods. The constitutions of eight countries utilize the first method, that is, the way of legislative mandate or authority ([Table 3]).[21] These constitutions merely state that the extent of maritime jurisdiction shall be determined by ordinary laws. The constitutions of the remaining eight countries use the latter way, that is, the constitutions have no explicit statements about determining the extent of maritime jurisdiction ([Table 3]).[22] Nevertheless, in these latter countries, as in the formerly mentioned eight, the extent and limits of maritime jurisdiction are established by ordinary laws. In theory, in spite of silence of the Constitution even in the countries of the latter type, the extent of maritime jurisdiction ultimately falls within comprehensive legislative jurisdiction, because in a democratic state, Parliament has comprehensive legislative power as long as it does not violate the Constitution. Moreover, it is not only the extent and limits of maritime jurisdiction, but also the other general matters of maritime jurisdiction that fall within comprehensive legislative jurisdiction. This is true of the 18 Asian coastal countries, whose constitutions refer to no concepts of maritime jurisdiction ([Table 1]).

---

21 Indonesia: Article 25A; Timor-Leste: Article 4, Article 95; Bangladesh: Article 143; India: Article 297; Maldives: Article 3; Sri Lanka: Article 154G, Schedule 9 (List II); Georgia: Article 3; UAE: Article 121.

22 Compared with this in Asia, of 18 American countries, whose constitutions mention the concepts of maritime jurisdiction, those of two countries of Brazil and Haiti have no explicit statements about it.

V. Conclusion

This paper has been analyzed how maritime jurisdiction is regulated in the constitutions of the 34 Asian coastal countries, excluding Israel, which has no written constitution. The results are summarized as follows:

1. Of the concepts of maritime jurisdiction, such as Territorial Sea, EEZ, Continental Shelf, Contiguous Zone, Internal Waters, and Archipelagic Waters - one or more are mentioned in the constitutions of 16 coastal countries. Alternatively, none of these concepts are mentioned at all in the constitutions of 12 landlocked countries, nor in those of 18 coastal countries.

2. With respect to each of concepts of maritime jurisdiction mentioned in constitutions, Territorial Sea is referred to in the Constitutions of 14 countries; Continental Shelf is mentioned in the constitutions of nine countries; EEZ is referred to in the constitutions of six countries; Internal Waters is mentioned in the constitutions of three countries; Archipelagic Waters or Archipelagic State is addressed in the constitutions of three countries and Contiguous zone is referred to in the constitution of one country.

In particular, concerning, the three concepts of Territorial Sea, Continental Shelf, and the EEZ, these three in combination can only be seen in the constitutions of five countries (Georgia, India, Sri Lanka, Timor-Leste, Yemen). Next, of the three concepts, a combination of two can be found in four countries: Territorial Sea and Continental Shelf are mentioned in the Constitutions of three countries (Bangladesh, Pakistan, and the Philippines); the concepts of Territorial Sea and the EEZ are stated only in the constitution of one country (Maldives); but together the concepts of the EEZ and Continental Shelf are not stated in any constitution. Finally, only one of the three concepts of maritime jurisdiction is mentioned as follows: Territorial Sea is mentioned in the constitutions of five countries (Brunei, Myanmar, Saudi Arabia, UAE, and Viet Nam); Continental Shelf is mentioned in the constitution of one country (Cambodia). In addition, the concept of an Archipelagic state is only mentioned in the Indonesian Constitution. Lastly, there is an absence of Territorial Sea, while including other concepts, in the constitutions of two countries (Cambodia, Indonesia).

3. Regarding the usage of the concepts of maritime jurisdiction in constitutions, there are three methods of utilization: In the constitutions of seven countries, the concepts of maritime jurisdiction are used to establish the extent and limits of maritime spaces over which coastal countries exercise their own sovereignty or jurisdiction - while in the Constitutions of nine countries, the concepts of maritime jurisdiction are used to regulate the ownership of the maritime spaces and resources falling within the sovereignty or jurisdiction. In the constitutions of seven countries, the concepts of maritime jurisdiction are used to distribute power over maritime space and resources within maritime jurisdiction, between state organs, especially between federal and state governments or between central and local governments. With respect to integrating the types of methods used in constitutions, there are various combinations. The combination of three types can be seen only in the Timor-Leste constitution. Combinations of two types can be seen in the constitutions of six countries (India, Maldives, Pakistan, Philippines, Sri Lanka, UAE), while the combinations of only one type can be seen in the constitutions of eight countries (Bangladesh, Cambodia, Georgia, Indonesia, Myanmar, Saudi Arabia, Viet Nam, and Yemen). However, it is not systematic that the constitution does not use the first type of usage, but rather the second or third type of usage, for example, in eight countries (Bangladesh, Cambodia, Georgia, India, Myanmar, Pakistan, Saudi Arabia, and Yemen).

4. Finally, with regard to the extent and limits of maritime jurisdiction, there are no constitutions of Asian coastal countries, which directly and explicitly establish the extent of maritime jurisdiction. There are no constitutions which explicitly state extent and limits can be established in accordance with treaties and international laws. The constitutions of the eight countries, which refer to the concepts of maritime jurisdiction, however, are not mentioning the precise extent of maritime jurisdiction. After all, the constitutions of the eight countries entrusts or authorizes legislation on the scope of maritime jurisdiction. In this regard, the constitutions of Asian coastal countries do not have active attitudes toward the regulation of the extent of maritime jurisdiction.

Chapter

4

Discourse on Sea and Seaport Cities

A Critical Review on the Japanese Waegu/Wako

Lee, Soo-Yeol

I. Introduction

"Waegu plundering off the coast of Korea and China in the 13th and 16th centuries" is how Waegu/Wako is defined in "*Encyclopedia of Korean Culture* (한국민족문화대백과사전)." The invasion of Toyotomi Hideyoshi, which began before the scars of Waegu/Wako in the late Goryeo and early Joseon Dynasty healed, and the history of the Korean Peninsula, which degenerated into a Japanese colony over the years, made the term "Waegu" a common noun in our society that refers to Japan's invasion of Korea. Contrary to this general perception of Korean society, however, Waegu/Wako have changed their image with the times in Japan. This article examines these changes in Japanese society, focusing on the history of research.

II. Image of Waegu/Wako in Modern Japan

1. From "villains in a backwater" to "pioneers of foreign countries"

When the Japanese invaded the Korean Peninsula and southern China,

A Critical Review on the Japanese Waegu/Wako **231**

Japan was in a state of rebellion due to the division of domestic politics. Thus, it was impossible to control the Waegu/Wako based in the western part of Japan. Muromachi Bakufu, centered on Kyoto, was not a national government that controlled the entire Japanese archipelago. As such, the existence of Waegu/Wako, which disrupted the international order in East Asia and put the government in danger, was also a big nuisance for the Muromachi administration. The use of terms such as "semipublic," "villain," "pirate," and "thief" in the historical data at the time are examples of the Japanese government's negative thoughts on Waegu/Wako.

These images begin to change in modern times. To put it simply, it was a transition from a conventional invader to an embodiment of Japan's overseas development. The Waegu/Wako became a symbol of Japan's pioneers of foreign countries, along with the ancient myth of the Samhan(三韓), Three Provinces of Korea, and the invasion of the Korean Peninsula by Toyotomi Hideyoshi, the hero of the century. It was fairly predictable that this change stretched in the form of Japanese imperialism and invasions throughout Asia. Especially in the 1930s, when the entry into Southeast Asia was on everyone's lips, the fact that Waegu/Wako came to the fore as a pioneer in the construction of "the Greater East Asia Co-prosperity Sphere," clearly accounts for the situation at that time.

2. The National Defeat and the Study of Waegu/Wako

The image of Waegu/Wako, which had changed with the times, was the same even after the national defeat. Since 1945, Japan's research on Waegu/Wako has undergone several processes through the present day. Although there is already detailed prior research,[1] to summarize it briefly, it began with the regression to the negative image after the national defeat, followed by the theory of multi-ethnic union, and the theory of "marginal man" of the present time.

The nation's defeat had a profound impact on Japanese history. The atmosphere after the lost war was enough to send Waegu/Wako out of the forefront of historical research, reflecting on the imperialistic perspective that was prevalent during the war and thinking about Japanese history in connection with world history. Waegu/Wako were only briefly mentioned by some people who had previously continued their research in the field of Sino-Japanese history.

It was Ishihara Michihiro who pushed ahead with a full-scale study on Waegu/Wako after the war. He originally worked as a researcher in Chinese history from the late Ming to the early Qing Dynasty. He once discussed Waegu/Wako in connection with the Japanese occupation of the Korean peninsula. In a magazine in 1940,[2] Ishihara stressed that the majority of Waegu/Wako were Chinese. It can be argued however that most members were actually Japanese, so his assertion can be disputed. After making this assertion, he evaluated Toyotomi Hideyoshi's invasion of Joseon as a "general settlement" of the Waegu/Wako' advance into the continent and the southern sea. He inspired a dramatic increase in national morale during wartime. It was obvious that he has not been able to adhere to his idea since the national defeat. In a book published

---

1 As typical studies, Yoon, Sung-Ik (2008), "Image Making of the Japanese Pirates at Prewar and Mid-war Period in Japan (戰前·戰中期 日本에서의 倭寇像 構築)", *The Korea-Japan Historical Review* (韓日關係史研究) 31.

2 Ishihara Michihiro (石原道博, 1940), "Daitoakyoeiken to Wako (大東亞共榮圈と倭寇)", *Shukan Asahi* (週刊朝日) August.

in 1964,[3] Ishihara invariably raised the issue of real and fake Waegu/Wako, but the conclusion was the exact opposite. The Japanese academic communities overturned the claim that the real Waegu/Wako were Japanese, and emphasized the passive nature of the Japanese, citing their numerical inferiority.

III. The Trajectory of the Waegu/Wako discussion

1. The Advent of New Study of Waegu/Wako

This situation surrounding the evaluation of Waegu/Wako began to change little by little in the 1960s. Tanaka Takeo's *"Wako to Kangoboeki,"*[4] published in 1961, was a biography of the study of Waegu/Wako. In the preface of the book, he refused to associate Waegu/Wako with the history of "Brilliant Overseas Development." He vowed to reveal the history of the Waegu/Wako and the tributary trade with "the fact that the Japanese claimed their existence in some parts of East Asia and actively participated in international relations," organizing the study of Waegu/Wako as follows:

To begin with, Tanaka marked the year 1350, when "Waegu/Wako" began to appear as an idiom in *"Goryeosa"* or *"Goryeosa Jeolyo,"* as the time of the outbreak of Waegu/Wako. Furthermore, he divided Waegu/Wako into two, "former and later Waegu/Wako," as this was the biggest difference in his point of view, compared to the usual practice of discussing them in a bundle from the 13th to 16th centuries. The reason for the distinction was that the Waegu/Wako in the 14th to 15th centuries, as mostly plunderers, and the Waegu/Wako

---

3 Ishihara Michihiro (石原道博, 1964), *Wako* (倭寇), Yoshikawakobunkan (吉川弘文館).
4 Tanaka Takeo (田中健夫, 1961), *Wako to Kangoboeki* (倭寇と勘合貿易), Shibundo (至文堂).

in the 16th century, which focused on smuggling or commercial trade, had tremendous differences.

Wako to Kangoboeki presented the directions and frameworks in the subsequent study of Waegu/Wako in the following respects.

First of all, Tanaka raised the possibility of Waegu/Wako "not just pointing purely at Japanese behavior," which then led to the theory "Waegu/Wako are the alliance of Japan-Goryeo-Joseon." The existence of Chinese Waegu/Wako has been pointed out before, but Tanaka extended them to the former Waegu/Wako.

Secondly, he noted that the main body of the former Waegu/Wako was limited to the residents of three islands, namely Tsushima, Iki, and Matsuura. He tried to find the cause of the Waegu/Wako in the geographical conditions of the three islands or in the incompetence of the Goryeo government. This allows him to block the connection between the Waegu/Wako and the Japanese domestic political situation. As for the relationship between the Waegu/Wako and the South Chinese forces, there is already a long history of research.[5] However, Tanaka's opinion, which limited the main body of Waegu/Wako to residents of three islands and found the cause of the growth only in external factors, has since become an established theory in academia.

Third, he evaluated the latter Waegu/Wako' activities as "modified forms of trade in East Asia" by identifying the limited role of the Japanese and actively adopting the theory of Chinese Waegu/Wako. It has long been pointed out that many Chinese were included among the latter Waegu/Wako. On that basis, Ishihara Michihiro's effort to stress the passiveness of Waegu/Wako and

---

5 In this regard, Yi Young (2013), "The Fiction and the Truth of the Study of Waegu (Japanese Pirates) in Japan (민중사관을 가장한 식민사관: 일본 왜구 연구의 허구와 실체)", *Japanese Cultural Studies* (일본문화연구) 45.

improve the image of Waegu/Wako has been based on what this article already introduced. Tanaka cited the Chinese pirates based in Kyushu as concrete evidence of the theory of Chinese Waegu/Wako. This way, he stressed that the latter Waegu/Wako helped facilitate trade, which was qualitatively different from the former Waegu/Wako, whom only focused on looting. He also limited Japan's role as "providing a base and members" to the latter Waegu/Wako.

In 1982, Tanaka Takeo published another study, "*Wako: Umi no Rekishi* (倭寇: 海の歴史)."[6] This book shows both the continuation and change of his perception of Waegu/Wako. The distinction between the early and late Waegu/Wako, which was first claimed in "*Wako to Kangoboeki*," was changed in name but the thesis remained the same. He differentiated the pirates of the 14th and 15th centuries and the 16th century. If there is a difference, he clearly emphasized the difference between the 14th, 15th centuries Waegu/Wako, which was part of Japanese sin history, and the 16th-century Waegu/Wako, which were led by the Chinese.

Cases of reinforcing the claims of previous studies can also be found in descriptions of the causes of Waegu/Wako. One of the causes of Waegu/Wako in the 14th and 15th centuries, "the incompetence of Goryeo" was embodied in the confusion of domestic politics and the land system, comparatively, the coastal residents and geographical conditions of the three islands were neglected. Another important difference was that the previous book described the 16th-century Waegu/Wako as Chinese, citing the existence of Chinese pirates such as Wangzhi. However, the new study carried the tributary trading system and the Hai-jin policy of the Ming Dynasty as a "hotbed for the occurrence of Waegu/Wako." Another difference that cannot be overlooked

---

6 Tanaka Takeo (田中健夫, 1982), *Wako: Umi no Rekishi* (倭寇: 海の歴史), Kyoikusha (教育社).

was the fact that the study is trying to connect the 16th-century Waegu/Wako with European forces entering Asia and the global silver trade.

Moreover, there are some changes in the interpretation of the history of foreign relations in the middle Ages, but the biggest change concerning the Waegu/Wako was the issue of ethnic composition. The previous Tanaka's careful prediction of the theory of multi-ethnic union has already been introduced. However, in *"Wako: Umi no Rekishi,"* citing the example of the participation of the Korean in Waegu/Wako in *"Goryeosa Jeolyo,"* he claimed the theory Waegu/Wako are the alliance of Japan-Goryeo-Joseon. The aforementioned political turmoil or land system disorder in Goryeo was also a device to emphasize that "the social conditions under which the lowest class of people, such as Hwachuk (禾尺) and Jaein (才人), acted as Waegu/Wako were mature enough." The multi-ethnic theory of Waegu/Wako has now begun to apply to Waegu/Wako in the 14th and 15th centuries, beyond Waegu/Wako in the 16th century.

If the Waegu/Wako included Chinese as well as Goryeo and Joseon people, then it becomes such a "great movement of East Asian coastal groups." It was natural that it would become a "problem of East Asian history or world history rather than a problem of Japanese history." 'History of the Sea,' claimed by Tanaka, was proposed as a new methodology for considering Waegu/Wako as a matter of East Asian or world history.

2. 'The History of the sea' and Waegu/Wako

In the 1980s, the Japanese history community stood at a great turning point. The upheaval in the modern world and the relativization of 'modern knowledge' urged Japanese to reflect on Eurocentrism and nationalism, simultaneously created history in new areas. It was also in the 1980s that the discussion of the Intra-Asian Trade Area, which emphasized the relative originality against the European-centered world system and the transverse network between Asian seaport cities emerged. It was one of the representative examples of dismantling existing Asian history and presenting a new image of Asian history. Tanaka proposed 'the History of the Sea' in the form of being conscious of, and leading such a movement.

The paper "Wako to Higashi Ajia Tsukoken (倭寇と東アジア通交圏)"[7] published in 1987, showed more details of the Waegu/Wako seen in 'the History of the Sea.' Tanaka approached "the image of veiled Waegu/Wako" by pointing out the problems of the national history and the land-centered historical view, and raising once again the need for "a sea-centered viewpoint."

First of all, Tanaka notices the fact that Waegu/Wako in the 14th and 15th centuries were a large group. Therefore, he says it is "unnatural and has no choice but to discard" thinking of Waegu/Wako as a group of sole Japanese. He classified the possibility of a group of Waegu/Wako into three categories: ① a group of solely comprised Japanese, ② a group of Japanese, Goryeo and Joseon people, and ③ a group of just Goryeo and Joseon people. Considering the movement of large numbers of people, ships, and horses in the sea, he said that it is highly likely that ② and ③ seem "the main subject of Waegu/Wako," since ① is "too risky." Tanaka gave examples of Goryeo and Joseon people, Hwachuk and Jaein, who appeared in the previous study. He went a step further, saying that the participation of ordinary farmers and lower-level

---

7 Tanaka Takeo (田中健夫, 1987), "Wako to Higashi Ajia Tsukoken (倭寇と東アジア通交圏)", Asao Naohiro (朝尾直弘) (eds), *Nihon no Shakaishi* I (日本の社会史 I), Iwanami Shoten (岩波書店).

officials in Goryeo and Joseon was not "difficult to predict." It is possible to think from this point of view that "the number of Waegu/Wako composed of Goryeo and Joseon, which were mentioned earlier as ③, was unexpectedly high." Tanaka thought it was "easy to explain" the cause of the large number, the situation of infiltration into the interior of the Korean Peninsula, and the cause of long-term continuation only when the main forces of the members of the Waegu/Wako were assumed to be ② and ③.

Arguably, Tanaka's discussion of Waegu/Wako, which began with the theory of the Residents in the Three Islands, was trying to move beyond the theory of the Japanese, Goryeo and Joseon people's union to the theory of Goryeo and Joseon people only. He claimed that the main subject of Waegu/Wako was Korean, not Japanese. His discussions on East Asian commissary rights were also aimed at shifting the responsibility onto others and highlighting its character as a merchant by resolving the looting of Waegu/Wako as part of a trading practices. In Tanaka's discussion of Waegu/Wako, a sea-centered viewpoint served as a way to dilute "the part of a Japanese-Sin history" as opposed to its original purpose. It was a paradox that the "History of the Sea, which began with the slogan of crossing borders, returned to a nationalistic agenda.

3. The Intensification of the Study of Waegu/Wako

By combining the study of Waegu/Wako with the "History of the Sea," Tanaka Takeo has come to present the image of Waegu/Wako as a multi-ethnic group that acts as one of the East Asian traders. The theory has since been inherited by next-generation researchers, making it a cornerstone of the

Japanese historical community as well as the general public's perception of Waegu/Wako today.

Along with Tanaka's paper "Wako to Higashi Ajia Tsukoken," Takahashi Kimiaki published "Chusei Higashi Ajia Kaiiki ni okeru Kaimin to Koryu (中世東アジア海域における海民と交流)."[8] Takahashi pointed to Jeju Island as the supplier, wondering how a large number of horses mobilized by the Waegu/Wako could be transported from Japan. This has the same view as Tanaka's suggestion of the possibility that the residents in Jeju Island were Waegu/Wako. If there is a difference, Takahashi went further and even said that Jeju Island at the end of the Goryeo Dynasty was not an area where the Goryeo government could reign. Moreover, he stated that "residents in Jeju Island and Tsushima were almost the same in terms of the national order of Joseon at the time."

In addition to Hwachuk and Jaein, the main body of Waegu/Wako, including people in Jeju Island, was expanded across East Asian waters by Fujita Akiyoshi.[9] Fujita claimed that the Waegu/Wako were not solely Japanese but "multi-ethnic groups," citing the fact that some of the Chinese maritime forces who participated in The Revolt of Ranshu Island fled to Jeju Island and Gobu(古阜), North Jeolla Province, in 1368. His imagination of the 14th and 15th centuries of East Asian waters was place as follows: ①Tsushima, the "Chinese stronghold," ② the coastal area of Korean Peninsula as a "multi-

---

8 Takahashi Kimiaki (高橋公明, 1987), "Chusei Higasi Ajia Kaiiki ni okeru Kaimin to Koryu (中世東アジア海域における海民と交流)", *Nagoyadaigaku Bungakubu Kenkyu Ronshu* (名古屋大學文學部研究論集) 33.

9 Fujita Akiyoshi (藤田明良, 1997), "Ranshuzan no Ran to Higasi Ajia no Kaiiki Sekai (蘭水山の亂と東アジアの海域世界)", *Rekishigaku Kenkyu* (歷史學研究) 698; Fujita Akiyoshi (藤田明良, 1998), "Higasi Aajia ni okeru Kaiiki to Kokka (東アジアにおける海域と國家)", *Rekishi Hyoron* (歷史評論) 575.

ethnic mixed residence area," where Chinese maritime forces and Waegu/Wako were "closely connected and cooperating" with each other, and ③ the vast trade sphere maintained by Chinese maritime forces in the Zhoushan Islands.[10] Fujita evaluates Waegu/Wako as a multinational group of merchants. It inherited the study of Tanaka, which suggests Waegu/Wako as one of the main sources of East Asian trade, in the most concrete way.

However, these discussions, which explain the existence of Waegu/Wako simply because of trade, are merely conjecture. It is because, as Yi, Young pointed out, "active trade activities in certain waters may be one of the 'necessary conditions' for piracy, but they are not the 'sufficient condition.'"[11] Something else to point out is that the more Waegu/Wako were emphasized as merchants, the less meaningful the distinction between the periods of Waegu/Wako has become. As a result, the violence of Waegu/Wako has become a point of interest among researchers.

Takahashi and Fujita's discussions had a strong inference tendency to theorize based on fragmentary historical data, rather than from a foundation of solid empirical study. They created new hypotheses based on their own theories.[12] Nevertheless, the reason why the Waegu/Wako as merchants were widely accepted was that the East Asian maritime history they presented

---

10 Criticisms of Fujita's discussions includes Yi Young (2013), *The Disturbance of Pax Mongolica and Waegu in Late Goryeo Dynasty: PIRATES and CORSAIRS in East Asia* (팍스 몽골리카의 동요와 고려 말 왜구: 동아시아의 파이렛츠 (PIRATES)와 코르세어 (CORSAIRS), Hyean (혜안).

11 Ibid, p.99.

12 Tanaka Takeo alike. According to Yoon, Sung-Ik, "Image Making of the Japanese Pirates at Prewar and Mid-war Period in Japan (戰前·戰中期 日本에서의 倭寇像 構築)", the Hwachok and Jaein, which Tanaka presented as an example of Goryeo and Joseon Waegu/Wako, were only resubmitted, attaching new meaning to the facts already known before the defeat. What changed was the standard of the historian's assessment of the Waegu/Wako.

echoes the critical mind of the academic community of the time, which was seeking a new methodology.

There is no doubt Murai Shosuke's "*Chuseiwajinden* (中世倭人傳)"[13] is the most persuasive theory of Waegu/Wako published under these circumstances. As a way to relativize the existing 'history of interaction between Japan-Joseon' on the premise of the border, Murai first established a "region" as a "bounding area in which national or ethnic attribution is ambiguous" and a "marginal man" as person in which resides in the border area. His aim was "to seek the timing of relativizing the nation, the people, or 'Japan'" through the Japanese as marginal man. Murai said the relationship between Japan and Waegu/Wako was as follows:

> "Wa (倭)" in the case of "Wako (倭寇)," "Wajin (倭人)," "Wago (倭語)," and "Wafuku (倭服)" is by no means equivalent to 'Japan.' Ethnically, Koreans who were taken to Tsushima by Waegu/Wako and lived for a certain period, were called Waegu/Wako as well. Wafuku refers to the clothing of Waegu/Wako which became the mark of piracy. Wago means the common features of the people living in a certain coastal area and the common language. Both were not exactly the same as the attire or language of 'Japan.'[14]

Murai defines the Waegu/Wako as "a group of people on a level that transcends nationality or ethnicity." It was "nothing but meaningless" to find out the ethnic genesis of the Waegu/Wako, who were separated from the nation

---

13 Murai Shosuke (村井章介, 1993), *Chuseiwajinden* (中世倭人傳), Iwanami Shoten (岩波書店).
14 Ibid, p.4.

or ethnicity and "lived as a free people." From this point of view, Tanaka's paper, which caused an international dispute by the inclusion of Goryeo and Joseon people in the Waegu/Wako, was a "shocking view" but could not be seen as false. It does not point out the nature of Waegu/Wako since ethnic genesis in the study of Waegu/Wako was nothing more than a secondary element.

Murai's study recognizes Waegu/Wako as free peoples. He evaluates the Waegu/Wako as beyond ethnicity and the nation. As a marginal man belonging to the East Asian sea world itself, the Waegu/Wako embodied both a contradiction of the country and the region. They sometimes acted as a ruthless pirate group and sometimes as a "main agent of regional exchanges."[15] Murai had found "a character predominating modern 'cross-border'"[16] within these features of the Waegu/Wako beyond a boundary.

IV. Conclusion

After their national defeat, Japan's research of Waegu/Wako began with the theory of the Residents in the Three Islands, followed by the theory of Chinese Waegu/Wako in the 16th/17th centuries and that of a multi-ethnic union in the 14th/15th centuries. Now, it reached the theory of marginal man. In the process, the appearance of Waegu/Wako changed from violent aggressors to multi-ethnic merchants. The descriptions of the 'History of the Sea' and the Waegu/Wako of East Asian maritime history by Japanese historians, which

---

15 Murai Shosuke (村井章介, 1997), *Kokkyo wo Koete* (國境を超えて), Azekura Shobo (校倉書房), p.27.

16 Ibid, p.3.

have recently been widely introduced in Korea, show that Korea is accepting the results of their research. There are claims of the theory of multi-ethnic union by giving examples of Jeju residents who participated in the Waegu/Wako as well as the residents on the southern coast of the Korean Peninsula. There is a specific example of the Goryeo records on the invasion of Waegu/Wako, limiting it only to the position of the Goryeo Dynasty and implying a strong possibility of trade.

Naturally, the Japanese academic community's study of Waegu/Wako drew strong criticism from Korean researchers. The main point being that the evidence presented by the Japanese researcher was only an exceptional case and that the historical data of the time could not prove the theory of multi-ethnic union and the theory of marginal man. However, Japanese researchers did not respond to this, except for a few notable cases. Murai Shosuke even criticized the Korean researchers' criticism as an outdated view tied to the nationality and gave severe criticism that it had something in common with the "new history textbook." Such remarks are not only sophistry but also an undesirable attitude toward academic criticism, given that it is the Japanese academic community who first raised the issue of the Waegu/Wako' ethnicity.

The "History of the Sea" was originally a methodology submitted to correct land-centered historical views. The reason for paying attention to the sea was to reflect on the nationalistic point of view seen in history so far and seek new history beyond the borders and national frameworks. Today, however, the East Asian maritime history is ironically being re-subscribed and abused by the country, where it tries to overcome the point of view. The fact that no more invaders can be found in the Waegu/Wako described in the textbooks is in line with the Japanese government's current direction of revising its history. It would not be a mere groundless rumor to worry about the Waegu/Wako, who have transformed themselves from outlaws in East Asian seas to merchants, being presented with a positive image again. The footsteps of Japanese research in modern and contemporary Japan have been in line with the nation's foreign policy. In this regard, Waegu/Wako are still the subject of the present progressive form, which provides many implications for history.

The Imperial Eyes towards Busan as Contact Zone

Gu, Mo-Ryong

I. Introduction

After the Japan-Korea Treaty of 1876, Busan was the best place to represent colonial Joseon until liberation. As Yeom Sangseop once said in "*Mansaejeon*" 'Busan grew into a colonial city with the opening of the port'.[1] After the Choryang Waegwan was established as a Japanese Concession in Busan, the Japanese brought in an influx of Japanese people and formed a new city. However, compared to the many records and descriptions of the 'Waegwan',[2] there is little data on the development of colonial cities after the Concession was built up. Busan, which appears in the written novels, was going through a phase of change before and after the annexation of Korea by Japan. Now, is there any way to know about Busan at the end of the 19th

---

1 Gu Mo-Ryong (구모룡, 2011), "The Modern Scape of Port City, Busan as Represented in Korean Modern Novels", *Cultural Interaction Studies of Sea Port Cities*, Vol. 4, Institute of International Maritime Affairs, Korea Maritime and Ocean Univ. Press, pp.71-100.

2 Tashiro Katsui (田代和生, 2005), translated by Jeong Seongil, *Waegwan*, Seoul: Nonhyung.

century? This article begins with this question.

At the end of the 19th century, several countries, such as the United States, France, Japan, Austria, Britain, and Russia, paid attention to the opening of the port of Busan, sending their citizens and describing it through various forms of travel writing.[3] For example, there are the travel writings of American Percival Lowell (1883)[4], Frenchman Charles Varat (1888), Japanese Sakurai Gunnosuke (柵瀨軍之佐) (1894), Austrian Hesse-Wartegg (1894), the Brit Isabella Bishop (1894-1897), and Russian V.P. Karnev (1895).[5] Generally, the travelogues were written after 1894 post-war, reflecting the geopolitical situation of Joseon at that time. Busan, a seaport city, is a contact zone where cross-cultural groups meet, collide, and fight each other in asymmetrical relations. Travel writings reveal various routes from the seaport city of Busan and highlight it as a nodal point. There were many forces who wanted to intervene in both the city and natural landscape of Busan. The esthetics of hierarchy describing the landscape are repeated in a way that demonstrates racial discrimination. The imperial eye is well illustrated in the contact zone.[6] There is also a subtle difference in

---

3 Casey Blanton (2002), *Travel Writing the self and the world*, Routledge. Travel writings are various forms of writing. Rather than defining the genre, it makes us look at the workings of social, political, and philosophical forces that intervene in relationships with the worlds visited by various egos.

4 The year in parentheses is the year of travel to Joseon.

5 Percival Lowell, translated by Jo Gyung-Chul (2001), *Choson, the land of the morning calm*, Yedam; Charles Varat, translated by Seong Gui-Soo (2001), *Voyage en Corée*, Noonbit; Sakurai Gunnosuke, translated by Han Sang-Il (1993), *"朝鮮時事," Dreams Left Behind in Seoul*, Konkuk Univ. Press; Hesse-Wartegg, translated by Jeong Hyun-Gyu (2012), *Korea: eine Sommerreise nach dem Lande der Morgenruhe*, CUM LIBRO; Isabella Bishop, translated by Lee In-Hwa (1994), *Korea and Her Neighb ours*, Sallim; Karnev V.P., translated by Kim Jeong-Hwa et al. (2003), *po koree puteshestbiia*, Gayanet.

6 The terms, "Contact Zone" and "Imperial Eye," are from Mary Louise Pratt, translated by Kim Nam-Hyuk (2015), *Imperial Eyes: Travel Writing and Transculturation*, Seoul: Hyunsilbook, p.32.

perspective depending on the subject who describes the travelogue. This is because the so-called "perspective-oriented view" or "world view" intervenes.[7] There is always a limit to perception of whether the subject is a principal-agent or not. Perceptual limits are formed by the environment and learning, and differences in world views create differences in understanding. It is obvious that the views of foreigners in Joseon and Busan at the end of the 19th century are different from each other. The formation of a discriminatory image by the imperial eye and the colonization of knowledge is widespread. Through the travelogues, the empire was able to build an image of the colonial landscape, through which the empire's inner subject was produced.[8]

It is meaningful to extract aspects of Busan, as an early colonial city, amid conflicting views from each subject. On one hand, it fills the gap of knowledge during the formation of the city and on the other hand, it gives us a chance to look back on our global perceptions. Besides this, it can be taken as a process of expanding the extension of local studies developed after the spatial evolution. If the research so far has been limited to one-nationalism, the analysis of contact zones reproduced in the travel writings is not only regional but also global. This is one innovative way to understand a locality. The travelogue of foreigners can be transferred by reinterpreting the present through its reversed image.

---

7 Elaine Baldwin, translated by Cho Ae-Ri et al. (2008), *Introducing Cultural Studies*, Seoul: Hangilsa, p.30.

8 Mary Louise Pratt, op. cit., p.24.

II. Travel Writing for Busan and the Route

There are frequent discussions about the process of railway construction and the installation of a ferry line connecting the islands and the peninsula. The history of the "Gwanbu ferry line (關釜連絡船)" linking Busan and Shimonoseki has been somewhat corroborated.[9] Before this, however, there was a lack of clearance for routes that guaranteed the mobility of East Asian waters. Foreign travel writings described the routes of the end of the 19th century. According to the writings, there were three routes that reached Busan. One was the route run by the British Jardine, Matheson & Company based in Shanghai and another was the route of the Japanese Mitsubishi Steamship Company based in Nagasaki. The former operated the routes of Shanghai - Nagasaki - Busan - Jemulpo and the latter operated the routes of Nagasaki - Busan - Wonsan - Vladivostock/Nagasaki - Busan - Jemulpo. In 1885, Mitsubishi Mail Steamship Company (郵便汽船三菱会社) and a joint transportation company (Kyodo Unyu Kaisha, 共同運輸会社) merged to become Japan Mail Shipping Line (Nippon Yusen Kaisha; NYK Line, 日本郵船). Most of the ships boarded by foreigners who traveled to and from Joseon after October 1885, belonged to the NYK Line.[10] The third route was Russia-run and used Vladivostok as its base port. It operated between Busan and Nagasaki, but it had fewer passengers than those of the Japanese.

Percival Lowell came to Joseon in December 1883. While serving as a diplomatic representative to Japan, he served as a guide to the special envoys of Joseon in 1883, following the United States-Korea Treaty of 1882. He

---

9 Choi, Young-Ho et al. (2007), *and Busan*, Seoul: Nonhyung.

10 Gu Mo-Ryong (2016), "Contact Zone and Chronotope of Ship", *Journal of North-East Asian Cultures*, No.49, The Association of North-east Asian Cultures.

went to the United States, came back to Yokohama, and headed for Joseon in December. He described Busan as "the first land on which people trying to reach Joseon arrive" and that it is "located below a high hill", referring to an area between Yongdusan (龍頭山) and Yongmisan (龍尾山). "The steamers first make Nagasaki their starting point, whether they come from Shanghai or Yokohama," he said, indicating that Shanghai - Nagasaki - Busan, Yokohama - Nagasaki - Busan were the basic routes and Nagasaki was the outport of a steamer's departure to Busan. The voyage from Nagasaki to Busan took about 13-15 hours. His travel route was from the US to Yokohama, then to Nagasaki and from Nagasaki to Busan. After a long voyage from Marseilles to Yokohama in 1888, the Frenchman Charles Varat stopped by Beijing via Tianjin from Shanghai before entering Jemulpo from Yantai. He arrived at Busan via a land route and departed to Nagasaki from Busan from where he headed to Siberia by ship with a layover in Wonsan and Vladivostok. At that time, ships passing through Busan went in three directions: China, Japan, and Russia. The route to China was bound for Tianjin or Shanghai from Nagasaki via Busan, Jemulpo, or Yantai. In order to go to Russia, Charles Varat departed Nagasaki to Vladivostok via Busan and Wonsan. This shows that Nagasaki was the hub port of East Asian waters. Ships set sail from Nagasaki to China, Joseon, and Russia. The Japanese Sakurai Gunnosuke came to Busan in mid-June in the middle of the Donghak Peasant War. He went to Osaka from Tokyo and stayed for a few days before heading to Nagasaki on June 12 taking the "*Asahikawamaru* (旭川丸)" leaving Kobe. At the dawn of the 14th, he waited for the "*Higomaru* (日向丸),*" which departed from Kobe, to arrive in Nagasaki. The Higomaru passed through Shimonoseki and Hakata, then crossed the Genkai Sea (玄海灘) to Busan via Izuhara of Tsushima. The Austrian Hesse-Wartegg described Busan on the eve of the Sino-Japanese War specifying the route through Busan. "Steamships, sailboats, junk ships, and warships travel from Japan to Busan". In the midst of the Sino-Japanese War, it is hard to find a narrative as detailed as Hesse-Wartegg among the travel writings from Japan to Hanyang via Busan and Jemulpo. He respectively described the journey from Nagasaki to Busan in chapter 1, Busan in Chapter 2, and the surrounding provincial cities in Chapter 3. The colorful descriptions of the route and ship's chronotope, race composition, and landscape reflect the fact that he was a professional travel writer. However, in his observation Joseon was the "Worst barbaric country." The Catholic persecution, which appeared in "*Histoire de l'Église de Corée (1874)*" written by Claude-Charles Dallet (1829-1878), which had earlier been introduced to Europe, was already imprinted in his mind. The imperial eye and the rhetoric of the Empire governed his travel writings. He received "an indescribable sad impression" from "a bleak and sad coast." The coast of Busan, which is reflected in his gaze comparing Japan's inland waters with the "classical ideal landscape inhabited by the Paeacians of East Asia," is desolate and gruesome. His view of the landscape overlaps with the perception that Korea was a semi-civilized country. Along with the discovery of the landscape, Hesse-Wartegg thoroughly converts knowledge acquired locally into European perspective and knowledge, showing an attitude of interpretation and explanation. The eyes of European centralism and the manifestation of Orientalism are intertwined through his narrative. Ernst von Hesse-Wartegg's travel writing illustrates the density of meaning and an aesthetic appreciation of the landscape. This implies a dominant relationship between the beholder and the sighted people. He places Joseon and Japan (Europe) at the end of both categories of beauty and ugliness, stating the meanings of desolate and brutal/

marvelous and lovely, anti-civilization/civilization.[11] His narrative attitude is similarly repeated, although there may be differences in degree to other's travel writings.

Isabella Bird Bishop first came to Busan around the winter of 1894. She was also on board the *Higomaru* from the NYK Line. Regarding the route, she pointed out the fact that Japan's dominance in East Asia had grown and the geopolitical status of Busan had also increased during the Sino-Japanese War. From 1885 to 1896, Russia sent a Joseon expedition team, led by five elite members. Karnev, one of the team members, described the southern part of Joseon. He was on board "*Isemaru* (伊勢丸)" and traveled from Vladivostok on November 8, 1895, via Nagasaki, to Busan on December 7, 1895. At 8 p.m. on December 7, "I passed three cliffs to the right and entered Busan Port, located between the bare mountains. The ship anchored about 85 meters away from the small breakwater of the Busan Customs." (page 19) He explored the southern part of Joseon by land route from Busan. Russia's official dispatch of large-scale expeditions reflects their interests in Joseon. Considering the Joseon government allowed and cooperated with these expeditions, helps to understand Joseon's position toward Russia at the time. Karnev also focused on objective narrative, which tells us that his writing was more like an exploration report.

---

11 Mary Louise Pratt, op.cit., pp.454-456. Hesse-Wartegg illustrates the rhetoric of discovery into three steps: 1) aesthetic appreciation of the landscape 2) density of meaning 3) dominant relationship between the beholder and the sighted people.

III. Hierarchical discourse on natural scenery and race

Busan's first impression in the eyes of Percival Lowell was "darkness." This was because of the rocky coast and bare mountains in Busan. He believed the reason why there were no trees in the mountain was that the soil was not fertile enough to grow trees or that they had been cut down for firewood. It was a reasonable analysis based on the characteristics of rocky coastal areas and the lifestyle of those days. Nevertheless, there was a bias of "rhetoric of discovery" towards the landscape. Lowell was making aesthetic judgments about the landscape of Busan in one category, "desolation" (page 38). The impression, which used to be seen as "Blue Island," translates into desolation, unmanned state, and barrenness, adding to the density of the gaze. The landscape, which began as a distant landscape, is reproduced as a richer entity with hills, gulfs, peaks, waves, and rocks, but does not arouse the sympathy of the beholder. The relationship of asymmetrical dominance between the beholder and the sought people works, which Louise Pratt associates with "pictorial writing."[12] If the landscape is a picture, Lowell is in a position to open it to appreciate and examine the picture. Lowell's view of the landscape extends to racial discourse. "The residence of the Joseon people is about two miles off the bay. The first thing that stands out there is the brown rice straw-thatched roofs. The road that passes through the seaside hill stretches from Hushan to Busan. When I saw ghost-like people in white clothes walking along the road here, I could tell that we had arrived at Joseon." In the expression 'ghosts-like people in white clothes,' the power of the gaze targeting strangers is clear.

In 1888, five years after Lowell's visit, Charles Varat arrived at Jemulpo and

---

12 Ibid, p.456.

reached Busan by land route from Hanyang. If Lowell was landscape-oriented, Charles Varat paid more attention to the lifestyles of the Joseon people. This is also the result of land travel, which required him to meet and maintain a conversational relationship, but above all, it stems from a good anthropological attitude to understand others. He summarized Busan's view of the sea as "the best" (page 200) when he crossed the mountain along the land route. It is a reflection of the position that empathizes with the differences in exotic scenery. Charles Varat, a geographer and folklorist, was a professional traveler. For him, cultural and anthropological exploration came before geopolitical interest. In this way, his travel writing has a value of requesting cultural and anthropological analysis. Sakurai Gunnosuke, who came to cover the Sino-Japanese War in 1884, had little interest in the landscape. "Busan is the largest port among the open ports of Joseon. Located in the southeastern part of Gyeongsang-Province, there is Yongmisan with dense old pine trees. Deer Island (絕影島) is in front of it, forming a large bay. Large ships and sailboats always converge to form a forest of masts. Ships sailing to Tianjin, Incheon, Wonsan, and Yeompo, in particular, anchor at this port whether they go or come. The prosperity of Busan's streets is incomparable to that of Shimonoseki or Misumi (三角). However, what is concerning is that it would be fair to say that the port's commerce and trade are just limited to commercial transactions within Japanese Concessions rather than shipbuilding trade," he said (page 269). He also expresses concerns about the "Joseon trade" that is still insufficient or criticizes the behavior of the Japanese in Joseon ("the Japanese people seem to be mostly trying to make a fuss"). Besides this, in the following descriptions, a disparaging expression of Joseon people appears on pages 273-274. Hygiene discourse is entwined in colonial policy studies. Cleanliness and smuttiness, the dichotomy of civilization and barbarism are planned as strategies of domination. As such, Japan's Orientalism is revealed as a racial prejudice against the Joseon people. Sakurai Gunnosuke's point of view already presupposes failure of understanding. If understanding is a passage into a never-expected complexity, he blocks this passage of understanding.[13] This is because the identity of Koreans is downscaled to only one characteristic.

The Busan, which Hesse-Wartegg had encountered, was no different from "a port of Japan." This is because the area was built as a Japanese-style city around the Japanese Concession and it was already similar to the cityscape he encountered in Japan. The perception of landscape, like any travelers, was 'desolation'. The contrast between the city and nature soon leads to racial discourse, forming a hierarchy. The perception is that the Joseon people are closer to barbarism than the civilized Japanese. This is based on the logic of European-centered civilization. Comparing "steamships" as "part of European civilization floating in the sea to get information about the outside world," for Europeans staying in Busan, Busan suddenly becomes a "painful dwelling." Wartegg's narrative attitude implies his intention as a European to create and propagate the order of the empire. He attempts to place Busan's landscape in the 'imperial imagination' and own it. The view of Busan, reflected in Isabella Bishop's gaze, is also depicted as "a bare, brown hill." She also compares Tsushima's landscape which "remains vividly in hand until I arrived in Busan. I still remember the magnificent stone steps, turquoise pine forests, and the feathery golden leaves of bamboo, with red maple trees and blooming plum trees sitting on top, the highlands where the temple located, and the shrines enshrined in the forest" with Busan, which is "terrifying and menacing." She adds asymmetrical comparisons with the privileged position of the beholder. In this case, comparisons are not distinguished from layered Orientalism. The

---

13 Michael Cronin, translated by Lee, Hyo-Seok (2013), *The Expanding World*, Seoul: Hyunamsa, p.69.

landscape easily joins the logic of civilization and race.

Busan, seen by Karnev, is also "located among the bare mountains." However, he does not amplify this view with the discourse of civilization and race. This is due to the relatively objective view of the observers, which had nothing to do with Russia's position toward Joseon. He visited the house of Hunt, the collector of customs, located in the Japanese Concession. He also visited the governor of Dongnae, Ju, Seok-Yoon (Ji, Seok-Young's error). This was to obtain cooperation for the exploration of Joseon. The meeting, accompanied by an interpreter, showed faithful communication and trust. This is different from other travelers, which is understood to be a sign of friendly relations between Joseon and Russia, along with the aspect of conducting public exploration.

IV. The Japanese Concession and the Aspects of Busan

The year 1883 when Percival Lowell came to Busan was more than seven years after Busan opened its ports due to the Japan-Korea Treaty of 1876. To him, the 'Japanese Concession' "seems like Japan, not Joseon." From the port where Yongmisan is located, the city is formed from left to right, and the view from the port is on the right side. The town below Yongdusan is not yet visible. Percival Lowell calls the Concession 'Hushan'. He thought there was a place called Husan inside Busan. This was due to the fact that Busan (釜山) was also marked as Busan (富山), which was read in Japanese style. It is clear that the name Busan originates from the shape of a cauldron, but Lowell associates it with Yongdusan, as Dongbonwonsabyulwon (東本願寺別院) was not located at the top of Yongdusan but at the bottom, the "Jeol" mentioned in Lowell's statement was a shrine. Furthermore, the reference to the Waegwan was very distorted. The historical facts of the process of transition from Waegwan to Japanese Concession were not fully recognized. It seems that his knowledge of Busan was given to him by the Japanese or caused though a misunderstanding by his imperial eye. The asymmetry of Lowell's gaze is repeated until it reaches his description of the "Korean residence" outside the colonial city. As such, Lowell makes the Japanese Concession a place of privilege along with the name "Hushan."

There is no such distortion in Charles Varat's narrative. Nevertheless, his position of looking at the landscape was of superiority. The act of moving from low to high places and looking down implies the power of the gaze. "A fairly fine view from the top of the mountain" was obtained by aesthetic distance, erasing specific details. This compares with the consciousness, thought process, in which the Percival Lowell experienced the loss of scenery in the darkening process as mentioned earlier. Charles Varat had a bird's-eye view from the mountain where a shrine was located. Through this, his point of view reveals his ideology of civilization. By highlighting the immediate Japanese shrine and matching it with the Catholic Church, the discovery of local landscapes was linked to European style. This is no different from confirming the commandments of the "Europe-Japan-Joseon" power relationship. Charles Varat summarizes the Japanese Concession in way of a panoramic view of the shrine and foreign settlement while avoiding describing specific aspects from the point of view of the traveler. This soon leads to a statement that "in fact, all commercial transactions at this port are monopolized by the Japanese (page 200)." The aesthetic perception through that of a bird's eye view makes us re-identify his privileged position in the process of describing Joseon people's dwellings contrasting with the scenery of the sea marveled with "oppression."

"On the other hand, the zone I call the Joseon side of Busan is almost ten miles away from the port. To get there, I have to walk along a low hillside by the coastline, where the ocean view is overwhelming. The place where the indigenous people of this area live is very poor and some are local fishermen," he said. He also added that Joseon fishermen store "a lot of sardine fertilizer" to be exported to Japan and fish around coastal waters ("a huge wooden frame is set up in the waters of a shallow beach so that seawater can be carried in through only one entrance, and then catch the fish all at once.") With the clear division of space between the Japanese Concession and the Joseon people's dwellings, the dual urban aspect of the colonial city is not seen in Charles Varat's travel writing.[14]

Sakurai Gunnosuke, who came to Busan on June 18, 1894, faced the Sino-Japanese War, and had the purpose of newsgathering. He was on duty to describe the exact situation of Joseon. This position gives him a view of the situation in the Concession from the Japanese perspective. Sakurai Gunnosuke externally presupposes a correspondent's objective point of view. It is described from the perspective of a reporter as the delivery of facts. His writings show the main facilities and population of the Concession. Facilities and institutions are in line with the impression that "it cannot be said to be complete, but it cannot be said to be incomplete." In other words, the requirements of colonial cities have been met. In addition, it is possible to see the development of a dual city by holding the "village of Joseon people located in the middle of the two Concessions of Japan and the Qing" (page 274). Since land reclamation from the sea (北濱埋築工事) had yet to begin, the

---

14 The complexity of colonial cities means duality or contradiction in a different way. Kim Baek-Young (2007), "A Theoretical Study on the Comparative Study of Colonial Cities", *Time in space*, compiled by Urban History Research Society, Seoul: Simsan, p.330.

contrast between the Concession and the residential area of the Joseon people was clearly described. As previously seen in racial discourse, his dual urban view reveals the dichotomous manifestation of civilization/barbarian, health/disease, cleanliness/dirtiness. Sakurai looks at Busan with a privileged view of the imperial eye, as seen in his statement, "The filthy house of the governor in Busan." In reality, the interrelationship between the two cities is also pointed out.[15] In the eyes of Gunnosuke Sakurai, the hybridity of these landscapes is not properly captured.

When he describes the Concession, the observer's gaze disappears, and his description is written in the first person. He not only distorts the Joseon people's view of Japan but also describes the reality of Joseon in a very negative way. The view of corruption and exploitation of officials is not limited to Japanese but reproduced in most Western travel writings. The widespread pre-understanding of Joseon may have served as the basis for this position. Gunnosuke Sakurai's statement in the quotation above makes us recognize the process of Joseon's colonization as a historical order. It proves that he is

---

15 Kim, Jong-Geun (2011), "Discussion and Practice of Separation of Residence in Incheon", *The Journal of Incheon Studies*, No. 14, Institute of Incheon Studies Press. A lot of evidence is needed to overcome the view of colonial cities as dual urbanism. For example, Kim, Jong-Geun is trying to dismantle the view of Incheon as a dual city. However, the interconnectedness of the dual cities appears in the process of expanding the city center of the former residence. Busan will have the meaning of "a city within a colonized society" at a time when Busan Port is being modernized. As the homogeneity of the Concession is somewhat dismantled, the process of heterogeneousization develops. The city is first defined by the perspective of a foreigner with the imperial eye and then repeated from a decolonist perspective. Nevertheless, one thing that should not be missed is the process of uneven development. It is also a problem to dichotomically simplify the space and culture of colonial residents and indigenous people, but there is a limit to highlighting only the mixing between them. It is necessary to describe the process of cultural hybridization without overlooking the uneven development seen in these boundaries.

responding to Joseon as with a view of Japanese Colonialism that was popular in Japan at that time.

For Hesse-Wartegg, the first impression of the Japanese Concession was presented as "white houses." This contrasts with the 'dark, brutal rocky coast' and meant "a comfortable trip" along with the 'steamboat.' For him, steamboats were a symbol of European civilization, as previously said. He describes various systems in Busan, which are close to those in colonial cities, with the view that the world is enlightened and liberated by Europe. He shows compassion to the Europeans who work at customs under China's jurisdiction ("The Customs Supervisor in Busan is British, and his subordinates are German and Danish.") He also highlights the presence of the "Missionary Hill" in the south of the city where they reside. "There was a beautiful house where American missionaries and Canadian missionaries gathered together," he said. Having reached the "Japanese Concession" through customs, he treated Japan, which has embraced European modernity, in an amicable manner. Along with the admiration of Japanese-style buildings, shops, and streets, the compliments to European-style consulates and consuls stand out. On the other hand, Joseon officials are disparaged as exploiting their subordinates. The hierarchy of Orientalism, Europe-Japan-Joseon is well disclosed. The view of scenery and landscape cannot be separated from the perception of the person living in it. Citing the case of a Joseon official, he made a critical statement (regarding the purchase of the national flag) discriminatingly saying, "The situation was better for Japanese people under the control of the Japanese consul." This was intended to add to the charm of the Japanese Concession. Repeatedly comparing the Japanese (European)/Korean, Japanese residence/ Joseon residence, and Japanese life/Joseon life, Hesse-Wartegg described the landscape and lifestyle of colonial cities as less civilized. There were also many distortions in a story of sharks and sea cucumbers. Such as the statement that sharks are "rumbling" in the bay of Busan. In addition to the distortion of facts, anti-civilization discourse also appears as a wild discovery. For example, he described the "Haenyeo (female diver)" as "a woman diverting a strong and different charm in a short skirt with her exposed, voluminous breasts." "Koreans would eat raw very hard shellfish," or "fishermen in Busan catch dolphins and whales and eat the meat." There is no careful distinction between Japanese haenyeo and fishermen who emigrated, and Korean haenyeo and fishermen. Nevertheless, he said that the Concession is composed of dual cities. This is supplemented by a detailed description of the daily lives of Joseon porters around customs. The boundaries of dual cities are dismantled through hybridization. Hesse-Wartegg clearly distinguishes the location of the Concession from the outside, and at the same time does not miss out on hybridization, for example, the circulation of money. The fact is that "the most circulated coin in the Japanese Concession is Joseon's coin," which was being used to hire Joseon laborers. Wartegg's description of "the miserable lives of Joseon people living in and around Busan" is very specific. However, his view on the situation in Joseon, which demands Joseon people to live, is biased. By adhering to the cognitive framework of the citizen's misery and the corruption of the ruling class, he makes the readers think of the colonization of Joseon as an inevitable process.

Hesse-Wartegg's travelogue differs from others in that it contains the most detailed contents In particular, his statements that the duality and hybridity of colonial cities formed with the Concession are considered to be beneficial, although there is a distortion by his subjective point of view. There were some Joseon people and Chinese working in the Concession, but "I have not seen a single Chinese-style house or Joseon-style house," which means that, by saying this, the Concession was a thoroughly Japanese-style city. In addition, the exterior of the dual city was described as five districts: the Japanese Concession, Bumin-dong, Choryang, Gogwan, and Yeongdo in sequence. By doing so, he compared very clearly both inside and outside. The exterior was described as a "high and steep bare mountain," "a shabby wall similar in color to the mountain, thatched houses that are almost indistinguishable from the mountain," "the chaos of irregularly dense mud houses," "a ruined fortress," and "shabby mud houses that were never seen in China or Japan." While missionary Hill and the Chinese residence have been embossed, most of the Joseon people's residences have been intagliated. With such pictorial writing, he exaggerated that Joseon exists in darkness. He summarized that "the total population of these five areas that form Busan is roughly 30,000 and they mostly depend on fishing and small trade. This is Busan, the second largest port in Joseon, which has been talked about so often recently!" (page 26).

As Hesse-Wartegg's travel writing states, the Concession has been thoroughly created as a Japanese city. Travelers familiar with the Japanese urban landscape via Nagasaki would have been shocked when they found a Japanese-style city in Busan.

Isabella Bishop's perception of Busan also shows little distance from Hesse's. "The foreign residence in Busan is a place overlooking a steep cape, with Buddhist temples hidden by a large number of cedar trees planted during the Japanese occupation of 1592," she mentions. Here, her pre-understanding of Joseon is also distorted. Her description of Busan is in 1897 after the Sino-Japanese War.

The Japanese Concession reflected in Bishop's view was a modern city. There was an urban infrastructure in the mix of British and Japanese houses. The water supply and sewage system were well equipped to prevent a cholera epidemic. The city was not only beautiful but clean. The presence of Japanese fishermen and the manufacture of sardine-based fertilizers were introduced as a part of the outer Concession. She described the exterior of the colonial city where Koreans live from the perspective of the ship. "From the boat, I saw a narrow road going up and down, maintaining a constant height over the sea, along the edge of a hill about 4.8 kilometers from Busan. The road ends with the indigenous village, which surrounds a very old castle built by the Japanese, according to the engineering concept of three centuries ago. There were white creatures resembling a pelican or penguin on the rocks along the beach next to the road. Since the white things were constantly moving around between the old and new cities of Busan, I thought the white creatures would be Koreans. My guess was not wrong," (pages 34-35) she said. The viewpoint when she visited the Japanese Concession was changed to the perspective view (遠近法) while observing Joseon people's residences, and historical facts (extension of Busanjin-castle) were distorted. She continued to provide favorable supplementary descriptions of impressions of Joseon people, but it is hard to expect a description of the trend toward hybridization, a specific aspect of a colonial city space. This is not irrelevant to her attitude of recognizing Busan as a dual city between the new and old cities but appears to be an act of investigating the new and old cities separately. The old town was a "scary place" for her. In a survey here, she highlighted the activities of three Australian female missionaries. The "Missionary Hill," that Hesse mentioned, was also revealed in detail. "There is a very small Roman Catholic mission center between the Japanese Concession and the Korean residence," she said. "However, Australian female missionaries live and work with Joseon people in villages of Joseon people".

Compared to Hesse and Isabella, Karnev's eyes were more attentive to the landscape of Busan. They reflected the position that he was focused on a concrete investigation into Joseon and its people. His narrative attitude was microscopic and balanced, as the subheadings read "Japanese Consul protecting its country" and "Busan mixed with Joseon and Japan". Karnev described it by moving from west to south through the interior of the Concession. He listed the various institutions, shops, streets, and buildings that make up the interior Japanese-style cities, reaching the boundary between the Joseon and Japanese shops. As buildings in the Concession were a mixture of Japanese and European styles, Japanese and European goods were displayed and sold together. If this hybridity represented the Japanese modern era, the western boundary of the Concession revealed the mix of Joseon and Japanese stores. Japanese and Joseon people on the streets also refer to daily life in the region, where they were mostly porters looking for work or women carrying goods in heavy pouches. Inside the border area, there is a "Consul" followed by a "Japanese shrine and a "Japanese school attended by some 100 students." Karnev records the demographic status of the 1895 period as follows: "As of the end of 1895, the number of Japanese residents in Busan was 4,953 and the number of temporary residents was 126. In addition, there were 7,600 Japanese fishermen sailing on their own boats and 32 more foreigners, including male and female missionaries." (page 26) So he figured that about 13,000 Japanese and Western Europeans lived there. Karnev also refers to the "water supply" essential to modern cities and then shifts his eyes to the southern seaside fish market. Sharks and shark-hunting have been mentioned by many travelers. Karnev also adds folklore descriptions of shark-hunting conducted on the "Southern Coast of Joseon." "First, lure the shark into a narrow bay by throwing food," and then "block the exit to the sea with a hard net with heavy objects, and pull the net toward the shore when the shark is caught" (page

28). In the southern narrative, Karnev adds a reference to Youngdo. Here, a noteworthy statement was made, "there were two coal warehouse buildings built by the Japanese in 1887, where there was a cholera hospital established by the Joseon Customs Service to the west". However, "according to Mr. Hunt, 10 years ago, in 1886, the island was covered with dense forests. Now, just as all the mountains near Busan are, not a single tree can be found here." The statement, "Joseon people cut down all the trees because they did not want to hand over the island to the Japanese," is controversial. (page 28) As many people have stated, many mountains in Busan have become bare mountains because they used trees for firewood. Karnev's statements usually relied on the British sea captain J. H. Hunt. Records of Busan history, current situation, and trade status were mostly based on Hunt's statements and documents from the maritime customs.

V. Colonial City and Neighborhood Dongnae

Percival Lowell's travel writing describes the route directed to Jemulpo via Busan. Hanyang, the capital, is the destination. His description of Busan is bound to be limited to Busan Port and its vicinity. Charles Varat journeyed through Busan to Vladivostok as well. The view that came into his sight was all about Busanpo (Busan port). He took the *Takachiho Lake* (高千穂町) and headed for the port of Wonsan, the intermediate port of call. Gunnosuke Sakurai headed to Jemulpo Port. "On my departure from Busan, I was able to sail happily while looking all around because the calm sea below Yongmi Mountain stretched far and there were no waves hitting the boat. Just in time, I raised my head and looked at the field of Dongnae. The once magnificent fortress is now devastated, and it only reminds me of Konishi Yukinaga (小西行長)," he said. (page 276) However, it is questionable whether he was able to see Dongnae properly. The "Dongnae" seen on ships sailing to the South Sea would be only part of the coastal areas of Nam-gu today.

It was Hesse-Wartegg who attempted to make a full-fledged trip from the Japanese colonial city of Busan to Dongnae. His decision to travel to Dongnae was not planned.. "The postal ship was not scheduled to sail to Jemulpo and Tianjin until late in the evening," so he decided to "look around the Joseon area around Busan." The contact zone is also a translation zone, so he found a "Japanese who spoke Korean to communicate with Joseon people." However, he also needed a "Chinese crew member as another interpreter to communicate with the Japanese interpreter." "When I spoke to the Chinese crew member, he delivered it to the Japanese, and the Japanese again gave instructions to the two Joseon people on the big ferry." "The Japanese do not know English and the Chinese do not know Korean." It is a companion in consideration of these circumstances. Hesse-Wartegg headed from a steamship to Dongnae via a river ferry, "Passing through Jaulin, a Chinese residence, and to the Gugwan (舊館), the old town of Joseon in Busan, he sought a horse to ride." In this process, he looked at Joseon people and customs from an ethnological perspective and revealed his prejudice against Joseon officials. His gaze targeting the Joseon people and the landscape was as superior as the "binary glasses" he used. He had an "good view (概觀)" of the landscape.

The rhetoric of Hesse-Wartegg's discovery was being "collaborated in a way that converts local knowledge into European and continental knowledge that is linked to European forms and power relationships."[16] Wartegg, the

---

16 Mary Louise Pratt, op. cit., p.453.

subject with the perspective view, looks at the landscape of Joseon people and Joseon from the perspective of a man. As such, the point where the male-centered view of Europe is maximized is when it is directed at women. The discourse on the beauty of young women forgetting 'racial defects' has a strategy of strengthening governance through aesthetic transformation. These aesthetic ideas extend to discourse that highlights the disorder and dirtiness of villages and streets and reveals the laziness of men. Hesse's discriminatory gaze is not collected, despite the saying, "Every country has its own customs." This is also reenacted in the process of dealing with officials in charge of the Busanjin Fortress, which stands out in the phrase "I spoke international Volapuk language, not Korean or Chinese," in the process of borrowing a horse. On his way to Dongnae, Hesse wrote many empirical descriptions. It is himself who blocks his intention to seek cooperation in travel through a Chinese interpreter. By substituting silver for communication, cultural negotiations are suspended, while confirming the corruption of Joseon officials and the status of Europe's civilized economy. There is no interactive and symmetrical communication that acknowledges conflict. On the level of binary logic, he gave back Joseon people to their unchanging identity.[17] His journey toward the periphery of the colonial city eventually enhances his reign by otherizing the Joseon people while owning the scenery. They rode horses for two hours and headed to Dongnae. Considering the situation at that time and the departure time of the steamboat, he looks back at Dongnae from far away. "The city and its great buildings are clearly in our sight thanks to the clear and clean atmosphere", he only describes the Dongnae government building, "the front porch, where buildings and columns that look like big temples

---

17 Michael Cronin, op. cit., p.71.

stand in rows, and the Dongnae government office, a fortress once played an important role in the country's history but is now in ruins." Dongnae, reflected in his gaze, is degenerating into a subject of domination, as the word "waste" implies. As it heralds an imminent Sino-Japanese war, it is used as an indicator of the fate of Joseon. The situation contrasts with the colonial city, the Japanese Concession.

Isabella Bishop, who heads from Busan to Jemulpo, also stops at describing the dual city of Busan and does not seek Dongnae. However, the Russian group of Karnev rented 14 horses and went on an investigation, and the first journey was to Dongnae.[18] The horses shall be leased under the terms of six articles of contract in consultation with the governor through the medium of the head of the maritime police, Mr. Hunt. In this process, the exchange rate and currency in circulation at that time are well described. "500 Nyang (a unit of old Korean coinage), for a dollar or yen" is the exchange rate, and "the exchange was made by Japanese officials, whose money was sold out in 500 nyang or 1,000 nyang. 100 nyang is divided in knots, unlike other bundles." When Karnev was heading for Dongnae in 1885, it was said that the road from Busan to Dongnae was "a road easy for wheels to roll." Descriptions of Dongnae are mainly aimed at "Joseon's houses and lifestyles." Unlike Busan, many houses in the town are tile-roofed, while most farmhouses have thatch-roofed houses. Karnev's description of lifestyle is meticulous, including the structure of farms, the structure of tile houses where officials live, and the kitchen and food. Just as in 1883 from Percival Lowell to Charles Varat in 1888, Gunnosuke Sakurai

---

18 Karnev's route; Busan-Dongnae-Yangsan-Ulsan-Gyeongju-Youngil-Heunghae-Yeongcheon-Punggi-Danyang-Jecheon-Chungju-Yeoju-Yangpyeong-Seoul-Jemulpo-Suwon-Dangjin-Cheonan-Gongju-Unjin-Jeonju-Sunchang-Damyang-Gwangju-Naju-Muan-Mokpo-Yeongam-Gangjin-Jangheung-Boseong-Sunchon-Gwangyang-Hadong-Sachon-Goseong-Masan-Changwon-Kimhae-Busan, Karnev et al., op. cit., p.12.

before and after the Sino-Japanese War in 1894, Hesse-Wartegg, Isabella Bishop, Karnev's travelogue also recognizes Busan and Dongnae as distinctly different regions. This provides an important cognitive map of the formation of the colonial city of Busan in the late 19th century. The colonial cities of Busan and Dongnae are placed in a different region on the map.

VI. Conclusion

At the end of the 19th century, foreign tourists from various countries described the multi-dimensional routes via Busan. If Nagasaki was a hub route for East Asian waters, Busan was a node. Through the Sino-Japanese War, Busan emerges as a regional and global space. The imperial eyes towards Busan were intense. The travel writings of Percival Lowell, Charles Varat, Gunnosuke Sakurai, Hesse-Wartegg, Isabella Bishop, and Karnev represent geopolitical interests in Joseon and Busan. Their eyes on the Japanese Concession were creating an image of the Japanese city. This was because they could be reminded of the experiences of Japanese cities like Nagasaki when they arrived at Busan. Their eyes reveal various dualities. The colonial cities of Busan/the natural landscape, Japanese Concession/Joseon people's residences, and Busan/Dongnae are asymmetrical. Civilization discourse and Orientalism work in a layered form. The attitude of approaching the city and the landscape also maintains a view from above or utilizes perspectival perception. This creates a dominant relationship between the beholder and the sighted people. At this point, racial hierarchical discourse is implicated. Depending on the timing of the trip and the traveler's position, the perspective of the colonial city's dual space appears to vary. Hesse Wartegg and Karnev clearly distinguish between Japanese and Joseon people as well as their residences, while paying attention to the mixed patterns of boundaries. Dual city and hybridization are two essential aspects of understanding the colonial city. However, the imperial eyes cover up and block differences and conflicts with binomial logic. By opening the landscape, scenery, and lifestyle through pictorial writing, the control and ownership of others are strengthened.

The five travel writings help us understand the shape of Busan as a contact zone. The development of the Concession into a colonial city is described in detail. There is no way to avoid the fact that they are biased in their descriptions or draw false cognitive maps with the imagination of the Empire. This was because the possibility of translation and cultural negotiation was blocked by asymmetrical power relations. If the Japanese modernity inherent in the colonial city of Busan can be understood as a mixture of Europe and Japan, the outside should also be recognized in a different way. It can be seen that Busan and Dongnae are depicted as completely different spaces. This is a big difference to Joseon's viewpoint. It asks for follow-up work to compare and analyze descriptions of Busan from the perspective of the Joseon people. At the current level, it is hard to find the description of the Concession written by Joseon people in the late 19th century. Therefore, the important goal was to understand the imperial eye, which intervened in the formation and development of the colonial city of Busan, on a multi-layered scale. Localness expands with regional and global intervention. The process of changes in the colonial city, Busan, is well described in various travel writings.

Life on the Sea: The Merchant Vessel as a Cultural Interaction Space

Choi, Jin-Chul

I. Introduction

No other professional world on Earth is more directly affected by the flow of globalization than merchant ships based on work and life at sea. Despite the development of transportation and communication technology, more than 80 percent of the world's cargo is transported by sea, and 99 percent of the goods exported from South Korea are shipped abroad by ship. Therefore, the merchant ship is a workspace at the forefront of globalization, which plays a pivotal role in local and international economies. As such, the global shipping industry, affected by global trade flows, is like a silent battleground for global shipping companies around the world.

Due to the local and international economic recession, Hanjin Shipping's bankruptcy, and changes in values for a job favoring a "work-and-life balance," the shipping environment has recently experienced drastic changes in the composition of the crew of the national flag carrier, and the working environment. The merchant ship, formerly recognized only as a "romantic

Life on the Sea: The Merchant Vessel as a Cultural Interaction Space **273** space of Matroos," now has a wide range of human beings, including crew members of various nationalities with wage competitiveness, young ship officers (deck/engineering officers) for Onboard Ship Reserve Service[1], a few female seafarers who ventured into the traditional male-dominated professional world, and the captain and the chief engineer who have more than 20 to 30 years of experience in the sea. It is a cultural contact zone where various human groups conduct highly intensive work and temporarily called home, including housing and relaxation, in a space that is physically and psychologically narrow. Therefore, today's merchant ships are not just romantic spaces where you can see and experience various cultures around the world, but highly stressful and culturally challenging spaces for subordinates to endure.

The working environment of merchant ships, where the distinction between work and life has traditionally been indistinct, becomes hardscrabble because of the pressure to transport cargo as quickly, accurately, and safely as possible within the fierce global competition system. The working environment in which more than 20 members have to live in limited spaces and relationships for three months up to a year, and Port State Control, which strictly checks the structure and facilities of foreign ships entering ports to prevent maritime accidents and protect the marine environment are other reasons and factors that contribute to the challenging environment. On top of that, various stakeholders, including ship owners, ship management companies, and crew

---

1 The term "onboard ship reserve service" means personnel who are mariners or engineers under Article 4 (2) 1 and 2 of the Ship Personnel Act, and who are called for taking charge of works to transport goods essential for the national economy and military supplies as well as works related thereto during a war, civil war, or an emergency similar thereto in accordance with the Emergency Resources Management Act or the International Ship Registration Act to perform their service aboard a ship.

manning companies, are attempting to manage ships and seafarers in their own way from their respective perspectives.

In this study, a merchant ship is regarded as a space of "cultural interaction" dominated by diversity and plurality, or a "small society on the sea." Moreover, it contemplates various behavioral aspects in merchant ships. For example, environmental changes caused by multinational crew members, ship management centered on non-human technology and duties, to be stricken with the illusion of the "Fourth Industrial Revolution," cultural conflicts between older and younger seafarers, ship owners, and ship management companies that emphasize safety but intend to maintain minimum capacity for economic reasons.

This unique workplace of the 'merchant ship' is faced with a variety of challenges as follows; rapid demographic changes of ship crew members with different nationalities, ship management captured by an illusion of the 4th industrial revolution, duties that are carried out only skill- and task-oriented, not human-oriented, a generation conflict between junior and senior crew members, a ship owner and a ship management company that emphasizes safety at sea but eventually seeks to keep the minimum crew requirement for economic reasons, among other issues. This study examines the behavior of various actors surrounding merchant vessels.

It will show that the merchant vessel is a workplace under the constant tension between the supporting team on land (ship owner or ship management company) and the ship at sea. Furthermore, this will shed light on the ship as a multicultural space where not only differences in nationality and language among its members, but also differences in generations, schools of origin, genders, ranks and work areas, and even in sexual orientation are revealed. In doing so, it will prove that ships are actually a space dominated by cultural diversity. The first goal of this study is to represent this diversity manifestations through the diverse voices found in the working environment on board of ships. A more in-depth analysis will be conducted in subsequent research on each issue.

The study describes the true nature of merchant ships as a cultural contact zone through the voices and episodes of various people related to this work place inside and outside the ship, which the author collected while conducting intercultural training for ship officers. The findings are based on conversations and in-depth interviews with the staff of ship management companies and ship officers. The paper is based on ethnographic field work about merchant vessels.

II. Characteristics of Work on a Merchant Ship

Shipping was part of various exchanges and interactions between regional, national, and coastal communities from early stages of ancient times to the present, past the age of sailing ships and steamboats. With globalization, shipping is expanding its scope into the realm of "global" beyond "regional" and "international." Not only from the macroscopic perspective of the global response strategy of shipping companies preparing for the long-term shipping recession, but also from the composition of multinational crew members, the encounter and hybridization situation of plural identities on shipboard, make ships a global space, a workspace that shares work and life on the sea. Thus, the location of the headquarters or the nationality of shipping companies and ship owners today does not have much significance compared to the past in the composition of the crew and in-ship work culture. The following example explains the complexity of global stakeholders surrounding a singular vessel:

'The Italian ship owner registers its ships as Italian ship, entrusts management to a ship management company in Malta, takes ship insurance to a British insurance company, and reinsure ship from a Norwegian reinsurance company. Among the crew members of the ship, the officer is from Denmark, and the ratings are Filipinos and Indonesians. The German shipping company charters the vessel and operates it all over the world.'

Korean shipping companies are also taking the lead in cutting costs and generating profits to compete with global shipping companies. Solving the shortage of crew members and reducing labor costs due to global competition has led to the multinational crews being utilized by Korean-flag vessels. In fact, stakeholders of Korean shipping companies say:

"We can employ 1.5 foreign seafarers on board with the budget of a newly appointed Korean third deck/engine officer, and it is highly cost-effective to ship three foreign seafarers on board with the same budget as two Korean seafarers. Many low-paying foreign seafarers want to be on board."

Therefore, a Korean flagged ship boarded by only Korean crew members is recognized as an exceptional situation, and even the term 'mixed ship,' which refers to ships that board with foreign seafarers, now has become obsolete.

The merchant ship is already forming a 'microcosmos' by itself. From the moment when a merchant ship sails out of the harbor, it is a completely physically blocked space from the outside world. The specificity of the merchant ship provides the crew members both advantages and numerous disadvantages simultaneously. In particular, the work on the merchant ship has different situations, when a minor situation can result in a fatal accident if the members of the ship do not properly recognize and communicate information in a timely manner. Unlike work on land where people can leave after work, the crew members spend almost 24 hours working and living together in the ship where the opportunity to go home is fundamentally blocked (In case of watch officers, they should be on standby after they are relieved of their watch, other onboard officers should be on standby after their daily duties as well.). In fact, many crewmen say that their total working hours are "from the moment they board the ship to the moment when a voyage ends and they get off." Thus, more than 20 members of the ship are exposed to a special situation in which they are forced to "actively" depend on each other, both in a professional and a personal capacity. The three-month or one-year voyage makes them share everything. They are forced to share not only the official daily lives of sailing with other members of the ship, but also the extremely private aspects of individual life, such as free time, meals, birthdays, and illness.

The work in the land is based on specific work plans and work processes specified in the manual, such as business and leisure hours, workdays, and holidays. However, seafarers are required to get out of the normal life rhythms that on land life provides. After suspending the vacation and personal leisure time which could have been used easily on land, the crew will be able to enjoy such relaxation and leisure on land after a voyage is completed. Thus, the relatively long vacation after the voyage is a sweet break given as a result of enduring the arduous, lonely, and dangerous work and life on merchant ships, which cannot be compared with the office work of general companies on land. Crewmen on the sea have no choice but to give up a certain amount of private time and space under the shift work system, which constantly changes their life rhythms, and the working conditions on weekends, holidays, and national holidays. Additionally, the exotic atmosphere of foreign ports and the time to experience the ports are not properly given due to the complicated inspection and control done by the local port authorities. If not for the supply of daily necessities and medical supplies or equipment repairs, the crew has little more than a short stay before a journey to another berth, all while standing at the gates of other countries. In the end, the image of a romantic seafarer, such as the chance to stay abroad and experience foreign countries, appears only in movies and dramas in the 1960s and 1970s because of the heavy workload and duties related to various international agreements and conventions, such as port state control, which checks the compliance of various international standards with respect to ship safety, as well as the economic logic of reducing costs through minimizing the time of each berth stay.

Regardless of the size and type of ships, ships have traditionally been hierarchical spaces. These features have not changed much in the past or today. The merchant vessel is a thoroughly compartmentalized and standardized organization that operates according to its responsibilities and authority as stipulated in the International Maritime Organization (IMO) regulations. There is the management level, officer level, from the captain and the chief engineer, to the deck cadet and the engineering cadet. There is also the operational level, hands-on sailing staff level from boatswain to minor foreign ratings. This clear difference in rank and status also is evident in the living space, dining space, and leisure space.

The characteristics of work on board compared to the work on land can be summarized as follows.

- ○ Limitations and closeness of space
- ○ Limited relationships and restrictions on social/cultural activities
- ○ Inability to leave the work space

(Hard to make a clear distinction between duty and off-duty time, 24/7 on watch)

○ No distinction between public and private matters

○ Shiftwork (watch-keeping), No weekends/holidays

○ Possibility of sporadic stay in foreign ports and contact with outside-ship people

○ Hierarchical work structure

○ Highly dangerous work environment

III. Aspects of Cultural Interaction Onboard

1. Multinational Crew Members: 'Koreans vs. Non-Koreans'

Just as foreign workers are being put into dangerous on-shore work and low-wage labor, foreign seafarers working on Korean-flagged ships already have become indispensable members. According to the Korean Seafarers Statistical Year Book in 2019, a total of 61,072 Korean seafarers were employed at the end of 2018, with 34,751 (57%) native Korean and 26,321 foreign seafarers working on Korean ships, accounting for 43% of the total crew members (see Table 1). The number of foreign seafarers doubled from 12,777, 13 years ago, in 2005 to more than 137 times higher in 1992. While the number of Korean seafarers has steadily declined at an annual average rate of about 0.5 percent over the past decade, the number of foreign seafarers has increased by about 12 percent every year, a sharp contrast. The number of foreign seafarers onboard the Korean-flagged vessel has steadily increased since 1991, when 58 ethnic Chinese-Koreans were on board for the first time, due to the gradual employment of foreign seafarers and the avoidance of working onboard by young indigenous Koreans. In particular, the number of foreign seafarers has increased significantly since the mid-to-late 2000s when the open-door policy for foreign seafarers was rapidly developed.

<Table 1> Employment Status of Foreign seafarers in Korean-flag Vessels

Year	Management State					Seafarer's Nationality						
	Total	Ocean -going vessel	Ocean -going fishing vessel	Coastal vessel	Coastal & Near- ocean Fishing vessel	Total	China	Indonesia	Vietnam	Myanmar	Philippines	others
2010	17,558	7,899 (74)	4,006	497	5,156	17,558	4,457	4,248	1,907	3,221	3,653	72
2011	19,550	9,037 (125)	4,540	564	5,409	19,550	4,002	5,339	2,385	3,856	3,880	88
2012	21,327	9,672 (57)	4,647	597	6,411	21,327	3,654	6,275	2,628	4,031	4,587	152
2013	20,789	9,691 (159)	4,298	607	6,193	20,789	2,341	6,073	3,282	3,687	5,175	231
2014	22,695	10,576 (157)	3,551	655	7,913	22,695	2,179	6,731	4,208	4,001	5,504	72
2015	24,624	12,136 (70)	3,374	673	8,441	24,624	2,000	6,895	4,697	4,619	6,321	92
2016	23,307	11,211 (70)	2,991	791	8,314	23,307	1,737	6,991	4,642	4,235	5,503	199
2017	25,301	12,184 (75)	3,810	823	8,484	25,301	1,669	8,275	4,720	4,512	5,903	222
2018	26,321	11,860 (47)	3,850	878	9,733	26,321	1,501	9,084	5,355	4,346	5,779	256

※ Remark: Number in ( ) is the ocean-going passenger vessels and included in the total number
Source: Korean Seafarers Statistical Year Book in 2019

With the increased number of foreign (non-Korean) seafarers, the problems of communication and (cultural) conflict among seafarers sharing the limited spaces of ships have worsened seriously in recent years. The mental and physical instability caused by conflicts or disputes between the crew members with different national and cultural identities has led to large and small maritime accidents such as onboard violence, unauthorized departures of foreign seafarers, and onboard safety accidents. Therefore, communication between on-board members and mutual respect for multicultural situations on-board became an important issue due to the increase of multinational seafarers. However, neither the main body managing the ship nor the members of the ship have access to systematic research and analysis and constructive approaches in terms of this multinational and multicultural makeup onboard. Moreover, the management system in the shipping industry, which is based on hardware-oriented (technical) thinking, such as ship operation technology, has many difficulties and limitations in devising a software-based (non-technical) management system or problem-solving method that approaches these problems between humans. Therefore, shipping personnel-management experts are trying to strengthen the soft capabilities of the officers by preparing manuals to deal with recent problems, such as foreign seafarers' issues and suicide accidents, or by preparing short-term training programs for leadership and organizational revitalization in the existing technology-oriented job training, rather than preparing solutions based on in-depth analysis of conflicts and communication patterns among ship crew members. Such in-house training programs are only applicable to large shipping companies and ship management companies. These officers' on-the-job training usually emphasizes the need to strengthen standardized seafarer education to minimize conflicts caused by cultural differences, such as limitations in English-mediated communication, differences in eating habits, and religious consciousness of Muslim seafarers. However, the onboard conflict prevention education, which is based on such cultural differences, has side effects that could encourage excessively generalized stereotypes and prejudice against foreign seafarers.

Through the voices of the Korean seafarers talking about their boarding experiences with the foreign (non-Korean) seafarers, the pattern of communication between the Korean and foreign (non-Korean) seafarers on the mixed ship shows the need to find and analyze the cause from various aspects and perspectives, including the use of an official language, labor contracts, onboard work culture, food culture, and religious rituals etc.

Language Problem

"I have little difficulty communicating in English, the official language of the ship. But some old captains or chief engineers often don't speak English well."

Differences in Onboard Work Culture

"There are many problems in terms of culture. Although Korean seafarers work overtime without any remarks, but Filipino insist on working overtime only if it does not violate the Marine Labor Convention (MLC). They keep grumbling while working overtime. Korea has a deep-rooted military and Confucian culture, but Filipino's do not. They don't see the necessity to be loyal to their bosses."

"In situations such as working beyond the working hours specified in the contract or yelling at the crew when they are scolded, Filipino seafarers often report these issues to the management offices on land and incur disadvantages."

"It is kind of our routine to help other colleagues or bosses even after our work is done, which foreign seafarers don't understand. They don't help unless it's their job. Once, a Korean seafarer entrusted his work to an Indonesian seafarer, and the mood had turned so bad that the chief engineer mediated."

Differences in Food Culture

"The cook was Indonesian, so it was very difficult for Koreans to adapt to the food."

"After the voyage, I took a cooking class during my vacation, learned how to cook Korean food. I cook for myself onboard."

Religious Rituals

"The Islamic coast pilot boarded to enter the port of Kuwait, and suddenly he began to bow during the port entry. It was strange to see them not neglect their religious rituals even during their work. I found that religion was the most important thing in their mind."

"On one occasion, a Myanmar seafarer burned incense on board during a Buddhist prayer ceremony, but the other seafarers mistook the smell of incense for smoke from a fire, and it caused a difficult situation on the ship."

2. Majority and Minority: 'Men vs. Women'

Today, more and more women are jumping into the realm of 'forbidden to women' as men enter the realm of jobs previously considered to be meant for women as well. In the job world of seafarers, which is traditionally classified as a male occupation, like the military, police, and firefighting sectors, the glass ceiling is also on the verge of being shattered. Since the Middle Ages, seafarers have believed in the superstition that 'It is unlucky when women are on board ship,' which has led to women rarely participating in navigation. Ships on the sea, especially in the shipping sector, were not open to women until recently when compared to other occupations. Of course, in the early 19th century, stewardesses boarded cruise ships in Europe and elsewhere, but it was only around the 1970s that women took over the rank of officer in merchant ships and began to work as deck and engineering officers in earnest. Although it is still regarded as an exceptional situation in Korean-flagged vessels, the number of female mates and engineers has been increasing since the 1990s.

While many men who have entered fields where women once specialized are building relatively successful careers by taking advantage of their own favorable conditions, women in the field of shipping are still struggling. This is because female ship officers are prone to suffer from prejudice created by the male-dominated job world, which is fostered and developed from the beginning of their careers. Even if they succeeded to disprove the prejudices, they encounter limitations breaking through the glass ceiling. Moreover, it is extremely rare for several female officers to be on board a merchant ship at the same time. Thus, female officers are forced to board with the invisible stigma of being the only woman or minority among the more than 20 members of the ship. The situation is not only in Korea, but also for the shipping industry in Europe and North America, which is a relatively well-established institutionally encouraging system for the entry of women into public affairs.[2]

---

2 Cristina Dragomir et al. (2018), Final Report IAMU 2017 Research Project No. 20170305, *Gender Equality and Cultural Awareness in Maritime Education and Training*

In general, compared to the employment of women on land that somewhat follows the trend of gender equality, shipping and ship management companies are still forced to remain reserved in hiring female ship officers in the special working environment of merchant ships, where work and living spaces coexist. First of all, the employment of female seafarers makes the shipping companies think about additional problems compared to male seafarers such as whether there is a job competency to handle the workload of male seafarers of the same rank, changing the on-board structure for female seafarers, and even securing substitutes in areas at risk of piracy, as well as sexual harassment that can occur when a large number of male seafarers are on board for a relatively long period. Additionally, male-centered prejudice and stereotypes are prevalent in the shipping industry that "female officers board the ship as a means to get a more stable job on land, and the long-term voyage is impossible due to marriage and childbirth even if they want it." Therefore, the ratio of female seafarers and officers on the deck, and in the engineering department of the Korean flag carrier remains low. Although there have been signs of change in recent years, with Korean-born female captains being produced from Korean and foreign shipping companies, the female captain still remains exceptional in Korean merchant vessels. Nevertheless, the percentage of female students applying to MET (Maritime Education and Training) institutions for ship officers such as Korea Maritime & Ocean University has remained steady.

The following are statements by employment recruiters at the ship management companies and male officers with onboard experience with female officers. Here, it reveals that the short history of female ship officers' voyage and employment, which has only existed in the Korean shipping

---

(GECAMET), IAMU, Tokyo.

industry since the 1990s, unilaterally generalized the positions of females from a male-centered perspective, creating a fixed image of them.

"Most young female officers board to qualify for the Ministry of Maritime Affairs and Fisheries in Korea. Therefore, they often get off the ship after a certain period. So you can't trust the female officers."

"(Women officers) say they will board for a long time at first, but if the job on board is a little tough for them, they tend to easily give up."

"They'll quit anyway if they get married."

"On one occasion, a female and a male officer onboard had sex, and when the woman's parents protested against the shipping company after they learned about the pregnancy of their daughter, the captain was held responsible."

"The shipping companies have so far been fooled enough by female ship officers."

"To say it simply, female mates don't want to do chipping work (to remove debris from the ship's corroded surface). But men do. Because as a breadwinner, men have to endure it so that they can be promoted. The sense of responsibility is bound to be different between men and women."

3. Generational Conflicts: 'Ubervisor vs. Non-ubervisor'

According to a recent survey, nine out of every ten office workers in Korea have experienced a generation gap at work, and the most likely part of the generation gap is the "communication method." In accordance with a survey of 475 office workers conducted by Job Korea, a job portal, 92.2 percent of the respondents said they had experienced a generation gap in the workplace. "Communication method" (53.2 percent) topped the list according to a survey of how they feel about the generation gap (multiple responses). This was followed by "work lifestyle such as commuting time, attire, etc." (36.3 percent), "work style such as dining out" (32.6 percent), "meeting, reporting, etc." (28.5 percent), and "daily conversation topics such as TV programs" (21 percent).[3]

Various job preference surveys also show the growing tendency among young people to prefer jobs like teacher, serviceman, and government employee, which have a better balance between work and life. In addition, in July 2018, the Korean government introduced a 52-hour workweek to try to change the working culture of the society, which has the longest working hours among OECD countries, and in line with this trend, more and more large companies and venture companies are introducing a flexible work system. This indicates that Koreans' perception of work and values are increasingly changing in a way that makes a clear distinction between what is public and private. Unlike in the past when they were forced to sacrifice and support the state and organization, now they focus on individual fulfillment and family life.

---

3 Job Korea (2017), "Nine out of every ten office workers have experienced a generation gap at work," September 21.

As mentioned earlier, the job of seamen, who works onboard where it is almost impossible to find a work-life balance, are becoming jobs that the younger generation does not prefer. Seafarers are largely divided into "officers" of the manager-level, who are trained professionally by mates and engineers, and "ratings" who are in charge of the operation of ships under the direction of the officer. Ship officer is a specialized maritime workforce supported and nurtured by the state, including the National Maritime High School (Busan, Incheon), the National Maritime University (Korea Maritime and Ocean University, Mokpo National Maritime University), and the Ocean Polytech Course of Korea Institute of Maritime and Fisheries Technology. Although new ship officers are graduating from these institutions every year, the number of officers who actually board ships and the long-term voyage is gradually decreasing. This trend closely correlates with the most important aspects of recent job-seeking: 'Work-life balance,' which is virtually impossible to realize, due to limited human relationships, isolation from society, restrictions on civilized living and internet use, and long-term voyages. At least until the 1990s, there was an incentive for maritime jobs to have higher wages than land jobs, but recently, as the wage gap between them has narrowed, the entire shipping industry is currently suffering from manpower shortages.

Nevertheless, one of the important systems that has so far been able to maintain the supply the demand of professionally well-trained seafarers, such as ship officers is the "Onboard Ship Reserve Service."[4] The system has been

---

4 Onboard Ship Reserve Service is a system in which service is substituted for military service by convening and boarding services to support the transport of essential materials and military supplies to the national economy in wartime, accident, or an emergency equivalent thereto. 1,000 people are serving on board a year, not a replacement or conversion service, and if they graduate from a school designated by the Minister of Maritime Affairs and Fisheries and qualify, the person will serve on the designated ship

an important incentive for young people to choose a special profession, ship officer. However, the Ministry of National Defense plans to scale down and abolish the special or alternative military service system, which began under the previous administration. This is based on a decrease in military resources due to the low birth rate, subsequently, the maritime and fishing industries are expressing serious concern over the possibility of abolishing the Onboard Ship Reserve Service. Young people avoid working in the fisheries industry, as well as on board merchant vessel. Particularly, the fisheries industry is expected to face further setbacks in securing human resources. In fact, the Ministry of Maritime Affairs and Fisheries declared on November 21, 2019, that the "Plan for Improvement of the Alternative Military Service System" has been finalized, including reducing the number of people assigned to work onboard from the current 1,000, to 800 by 2026.

Additionally, seafarer statistics show that a large number of ship officers who graduated from maritime colleges or universities are leaving the industry after completing a three-year commitment. As of the end of 2018, the number of Korean seafarers aged 50 or older accounted for about 67 percent of the total. In particular, the aging of the crew is continuing and very rapidly progressing, with 12,833 people, or 36.9% of the total, nearly doubling from 6,505 at the end of 2010 (see Table 2). This highlights the fact that most male applicants from maritime college choose the unique and challenging job of ship officer because of the incentive to disengage their military service. They fulfill their military duty upon completing three years on board after their

---

for three years and will be forced to be transferred to the national essential ship in case of emergency such as war or national disaster. He is an active-duty soldier who is subject to special duties in case of emergency, unlike other alternative services, when he is released from service after three years.

graduation. After they are freed from this compulsory duty on board, they move to a land job where they can find a more favorable work-life balance. However, the more serious problem here is that these young officers' motives for boarding are directly affecting their work and human relationships on board. What's more, the difference of working values and career goals between the generations is enormous. Due to this, the older generation accounts for nearly 70% of all experienced crew members in the industry. The ship management companies cited that the very problem of "generation conflict" is currently the biggest issue in the management of maritime personnel.

<Table 2> Current Status of Seafarer Employment by Age

		2010	2011	2012	2013	2014	2015	2016	2017	2018
Age of Seafarer	Total	38,758	38,998	38,906	38,783	37,125	36,976	35,685	35,096	34,751
	Under 25	1,183	1,137	1,275	959	1,150	1,161	1,065	1,299	1,201
	Over 25 and Under 30	2,163	2,587	2,630	2,613	2,961	2,969	2,398	2,654	2,566
	Over 30 and Unde 40	4,032	4,054	3,940	4,388	3,771	3,909	3,299	3,154	3,131
	Over 40 and Under 50	9,329	8,610	8,125	8,864	7,156	6,902	5,116	4,747	4,640
	Over 50 and Under 60	15,546	14,506	14,466	14,233	12,742	12,252	11,429	10,454	10,380
	Over 60	6,505	8,104	8,470	7,726	9,345	9,783	12,378	12,797	12,833

Source: Korean Seafarers Statistical Year Book in 2019

The statements below illustrate how junior and senior officers in the merchant ship view one another. Senior officers point out the psychological weakness and lack of job competency of junior officers from the perspective of their generation. While junior officers criticize the anachronistic thinking and working style of seniors based on the current work attitude and life values oriented toward "work-life balance." Both groups are evaluating each other with their generation's work attitude and life values as their ideal goals.

Junior Officers Viewed by Senior Officers (Captain, Chief Engineer, First Mate, and First Engineer)

"Something that I never imagined before happens on a ship now. These days, young officers send their parents a message or contact the shipping company if they feel a little uncomfortable. There is too little patience or sense of hierarchy, as well as a working competency. In the past, juniors followed what their boss instructed without complaining, but nowadays I (as a boss) have to show how and what to do and give them specific instructions."

"We have to get rid of Maritime Universities in Korea. Isn't it up to the school to train the proper ship officer to build an upright character? Young officers these days have no attitude, willing or strength to work."

"I feel a generation gap. I don't know the terms they use in conversation, and we have significantly different interests to share."

"I'm so disappointed when they act irresponsibly. I have to decide instead of them and give instructions. It's so childish. They can't make any decisions by themselves and they are so irresponsible."

"There are many juniors who feel repulsed by the work instructions of superiors. They just hate to listen when their superiors explain safety-related precautions."

"In the old days, I went to the army, then graduated from school, and became a ship officer. Now I don't think young officers have enough spirit to unite with the collective action because the junior and even the first officers didn't go to the army."

"Even if the work instructions are well explained and clear, they just answer 'I can't do it!' when they find it difficult."

"After working hours, they act individually (because they have a laptop)."

"They have a poor work ethic. So many junior officers want to discontinue their career on the ship as soon as they finish their Onboard Ship Reserve Service."

"In accordance with the International Safety Manual (ISM) code, the responsibility and authority of each crew member are exactly assigned, but the juniors rather shift the responsibility on their superiors and interpret and utilize the ISM only to their own benefit."

"It is not just the captain and the chief engineer who should understand the new values or cultures of the younger generation."

"If there is a conflict on board, they try to avoid confrontation (leaving the ship or quitting the job) without trying to resolve it internally."

"They are not interested in forming a personal bond with colleagues on board, and focus just on life after the mandatory period of the voyage."

"No job is as good as a ship officer. On land, you have to be aware of various people and suffer from a lot of stress. But there is no such stress on the ship. You just do your job well. That's why former seafarers who worked on land, try to return to working on the ship. Young officers these days have to realize this quickly."

The senior officer viewed by junior officers (second and third mate and engineer)

"These days, we can use Kakao Talk (a free mobile instant messaging application for smartphones) or the internet on board. However, if the data allocated to each individual is exhausted, we should ask the captain. This part is so frustrating."

"We prefer to use the whistle-blowing system because the conflict situation could get bigger or worse if we talk directly to the senior officer or the captain (chief engineer) on the spot, with whom we have a conflict or misunderstanding. We also prefer sending messages directly to the head of the HR management department in our ship management company via Kakao Talk. And in some cases, there is no use to say something directly to the other person since the other is their senior. They just ignore it, not reporting it to superiors."

"You can't go against the flow of the times. The culture on board should also change with the times. What's wrong with being individualistic? It is positive because it can protect the privacy of individuals. Even though you work as a member of a group, your personal time should be guaranteed when you take a rest."

"Senior members confuse individualism with our desire to maintain some form of basic independence that our generation has become accustomed to. We simply feel that the culture on board should be respectful of individual differences. And the culture on shipboard should continuously be changed in the direction of respecting individual differences."

"The captains (the chief engineers) seem to put the company's interest ahead of the grievances of the members of the ship (e.g., a drastic cut in-store claims)."

"Some seniors are too insensitive to all kinds of changes (technology, the lineament of the time, etc.) and think of on-board cultural support expenses as personal pocket money."

"They (the seniors) force us to work even during break time. It is natural that you have personal time when you are off duty."

"If you're doing your job well, there's no problem. We take it (individualism) for granted because it is a social change as well as an on-board culture, but there are still many seniors who do not understand individualism, so we, junior officers also need to understand them and make efforts to be understood."

IV. 'Merchant Vessel', a Small Society on the Sea

Merchant vessels act as blood vessels for global trade that enable trade between countries, regions, companies, and individuals by transporting various kinds of goods, such as industrial goods/consumer goods, finished products/half-finished products, raw materials, or materials needed for industries such as crude oil, oil refining, grain, natural gas, and iron ore. However, the public awareness of the importance of the shipping industry is still lacking. Rose George, a British journalist who published a book about her six-month experience aboard a merchant vessel, notes that the general public is well aware of the U.S. computer software company called Microsoft, but not of the world's No. 1 shipping company Maersk in Denmark, which has a similar scale of business performance. She mentioned that the general public suffers from sea blindness.[5] In other words, more than 90 percent of everything that surrounds us is being delivered to us through ships, which highlights the paradox that we have no understanding and interest in what is going on in the sea, and what is going on in ships carrying most of the goods and food we encounter. This article also highlights the fundamental question of whether the space of merchant ships should be understood simply as an important global economic artery contributing to the movement of goods and commodities. A world view centered on land rather than sea forces merchant ships to be understood only as part of a corporate organization that contributes to the global supply chain. However, what is overlooked here are the stories of the human experiences from people working and living on the sea and ships. We should consider whether people's problems in the ship are being overlooked, overshadowed by the trend of discussions on rapid technological development

---

5 Rose George (2013), *Ninety Percent of Everything*, New York, Picador, p.4.

and high-tech development, such as autonomous ships and eco-friendly ships in the "Era of the Fourth Industrial Revolution."

As mentioned earlier, the view of ship owners, ship management companies, and maritime personnel management companies on merchant ships view situations only through the perspective of the management. It leans toward the interests of the shipping company rather than the interests of people on board, such as profit-driven prevention of safety accidents, job training, the highest turnover on minimum investment (such as hiring low-paying foreign seafarers, hiring contract seafarers, maintaining minimum capacity on board, etc.). This situation directly affects the work and living conditions, relationships, and safety issues of the members of the ship. Perhaps this situation is not much different from on-land corporations, either. Nevertheless, the various circumstances of the merchant ship revealed by this study call for an urgent change in understanding of managers' views that merchant ships are simply regarded as a part of the company. In other words, merchant ships are part of a corporation that seeks profit by achieving a specific goal of moving goods from A to B, but it should be recognized as a 'small society on the sea' where people of various levels, including foreigners/natives, minorities/ majorities, and new/old generations, meet, work, and live together. Based on this perception change, not only the crew members on board of the merchant ship, but also the ship management companies that manage and support the ship from the land should take a more systematic and analytical approach to the issues of relationships and interactions between humans representing the diversity and pluralistic identities on the merchant ship.

It is impossible to find a solution to the communication and coexistence patterns of crew members with different cultural identities based on nationality, gender, age, educational background, work area, etc. in the ships without thorough and clear analysis and understanding of the working environment of merchant ships. This is because the particular behavioral context of merchant ships themselves has a profound effect on interactions between members. Due to the specificity of the above-mentioned work and living space, the aspects of cultural interactions on the ship are distinct from those in general companies on land, and in that respect, the approach to "differences" among members revealed by multicultural manifestations should be different from the approach on land. Here, the "merchant vessel" is ostensibly part of a general corporation that exists to generate profits, but it implies the characteristics of a "multicultural society" in that it functions as a completely independent social space during the voyage. Therefore, the staff management, communication management, as well as the overall interaction in the merchant vessel should be done in full consideration of these distinct characteristics of merchant ships.

The vessel is a "transnational social space"[6] that moves beyond the physical and psychological boundaries of nation-states based on interactions between humans and humans, humans and the sea, humans and technology, and technology and technology. According to Ludger Pries, transnational social spaces are dense, stable, pluri-local and institutionalized frameworks composed of material artifacts, the social practices of everyday life, as well as systems of symbolic representation that are structured by and structure human life within a certain space for a certain period. These spaces are characterized as de-local and de-territorial. The aspects of these transnational social spaces are all found on merchant ships. Thus, various actors inside and outside of the ships including ship owners, ship management companies, ship operators, and seafarers, should strive to change their perception from the conventional

---

6 Ludger Pries (2001), *Internationale Migration*, Bielefeld, p.53.

technology-oriented perspective to the human-centered one. Only from that point of view, the work and life of members of various identities encountered on board can be viewed from a multi-layered basis. Furthermore, this view will help overcome the limitations of fragmented approaches to the problems such as "issues of foreign seafarer," "issues of female officers," and "issues of generational conflict." As shown in the figure below, it is the multi-layered multicultural identity of each individual member on the ship that must be understood within the space where each crew member must meet, work, and live together for a certain period. The important competence that the crew members must have is the ability to create a common cultural layer based on their understanding and recognition of the multicultural identity of the members on board the ship (see Figure 1).

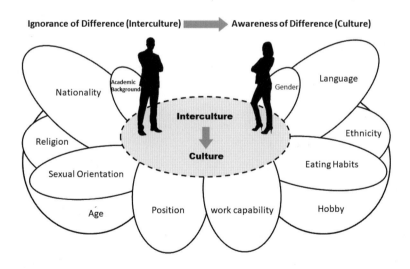

<Figure 1> Multi-layered Intercultural Communication Model

Thus, various actors in the shipping industry have to cultivate not only engineering expertise related to ships, but also interpersonal skills, as well as knowledge and competencies to embrace humanistic values. In an ever increasingly diverse and complicated world, careers are calling for new talents to understand and embrace others beyond their job competency and, by extension, create a synergetic work environment with them. Therefore, the humanities approach and qualitative analysis methods are necessary for discussing and analyzing the ship as a small society on the sea. For example, through the cultural anthropological approach of "thick description"[7] on the conditions and situations in the behavioral context, we will be able to improve the fragmentary and one-sided interpretation of a certain culture. Such cultures include but are not limited to national culture, generation culture, gender-based culture, and corporate culture and so on. Through various qualitative approaches such as in-depth interviews, participation observation, and life-history research methods, we will be able to address and solve complex issues that were overlooked by conventional quantitative research results. Beyond the simple comparison between the invented 'differences' among individuals, an approach that focuses on the generating causes and circumstances of conflict could be acquired through anthropological studies.

V. Conclusion

People in the shipping industry are already aware of the diversity on merchant vessels, and the consequences that may result from it, and the International Maritime Organization (IMO) is trying to cope with and develop strategies for such diversity. Unlike land-based (multinational) corporations,

---

7 Geertz, Clifford (1973), "Thick Description: Toward an Interpretive Theory of Culture", *The Interpretation of Cultures: Selected Essays*, New York: Basic Books, pp.3-30.

however, it seems that the diversity management strategy in the maritime sector focuses just on being busy to suppress the "problem" of diversity itself. The diversity, plurality, differences, and commonalities that exist among crew members on board tend to be put on the back burner, or are supposedly regarded as a totally separate issue from the workplace. Therefore, it seems that trying to cope with this challenge simply by further strengthening the collective identity of seafarers, could be helpful in overcoming the obstacles originating from the increasing diversity on shipboard.

This article demonstrated that the problem of diversity is manifested in the workplace of merchant ships includes not only the diversity of language and nationality of seafarers, but also various sub-components such as generation, gender, religion, academic background, rank on board, task area on board, and even sexual orientation. Therefore, serious discussions on "on-board diversity management" are needed in human resource management departments in the shipping industry. Efforts should be made to raise the self-esteem of seafarers, who play a pivotal role in the global economy, in various capacities. In other words, it should be noted that the lack of awareness of the important role of seafarers for the global economy and the absence of self-esteem as a seafarer is automatically creating the lack of "seamanship" among seafarers, and that the physical, psychological, and mental stresses and anxiety resulting from the lack of "seamanship" are causing problems of human relationships between crew members on board. Ship owners and ship management companies also need a fundamental change in their myopic perception: If problems arise due to foreign seafarers on board, they tend to ascribe that issue just to "national cultural differences" or in the case of misunderstanding between junior and senior officers, they impute those conflict issues on board simply to "generational differences." Therefore, a sincere movement of change in the shipping industry more urgently needed than "soulless" guidelines or policies, such as 'the foreign seafarer guidebook' and 'bullying solution manual' etc. This is precisely the field where the scholars in the humanities researching sea-related issues should make an important contribution. The keen insights provided by the humanities that highlight solutions to problems in society, can and should be applied to the shipping industry as well.

【Acknowledgements】
【Index】

Acknowledgements

This book is the result of HK⁺(Human Korea Plus) Project with the Agenda "Bada Humanities" from 2018 to now.

The First chapter is condensed from Jeong, Moon-Soo et al. (정문수 외, 2018), "Studies on the Relationship between Maritime/Marine Studies and Humanities," *Cultural Interaction Studies of Sea Port Cities*, No. 19, Institute of International Maritime Affairs, pp.1-37.

Kim's paper in the second chapter is condensed from Kim, Kang-Sik. (김강식, 2020), "The Drift and Sea Area of Gyeongsang-Province and Ryukyu Drifters during the Joseon Dynasty," *Korea-Japan Marine Exchange in the Daegaya Era and the Current Reproduction*, Sunin Publishing, pp.373-412.

Lee and Jeong's paper in the second chapter is condensed from Lee, Hak-Su et al. (이학수 외, 2018), "A Study on a British Sailing Ship Harbouring at Yongdanpo in 1797," *Cultural Interaction Studies of Sea Port Cities*, No. 20, Institute of International Maritime Affairs, pp.269-307.

Choi and An's paper in the second chapter is condensed from Choi, Eun-Soon et al. (최은순 외, 2018), "The National and Transnational Characteristics of Korean Merchant Seafarers - Focusing on the period of the shipping industry from 1960-1990," *Cultural Interaction Studies of Sea Port Cities*, No. 19, Institute of International Maritime Affairs, pp.113-143.

Kim's paper in the third chapter is condensed from Kim Seung (김승, 2019), "A Study on Russia's Deer Island (絶影島) Leased Territory in the Late 19th Century," *Cultural Interaction Studies of Sea Port Cities*, No. 21, Institute of International Maritime Affairs, pp.189-242.

Woo's paper in the third chapter is condensed from Woo Yang-Ho (우양호, 2019), "A Sea Agreed upon as a 'Sea' : Territorial Dispute and Settlement of the Caspian Sea," *Cultural Interaction Studies of Sea Port Cities*, No. 21, Institute of International Maritime Affairs, pp.149-188.

Gojkošek, Jeong, and Chung's paper is condensed from Gojkošek, Matjaž et al. (마티아즈 코이코섹 외, 2019) "The Maritime boundary dispute between Slovenia and Croatia," *Journal of Marine and Island Cultures*, Vol.8, No. 2, Institution for Marine and Island Cultures, pp.11-24.

Han's paper in the third chapter is condensed from Han Byung-Ho (한병호, 2019), "A Study on the Maritime Jurisdictions in the Constitutions of Asian Countries," *Maritime Law Review*, Vol. 31, No. 1, The Korea Institute of Maritime Law, pp.105-138.

Lee's paper in the forth chapter is condensed from Lee Soo-Yeol (이수열, 2019), "A Critical Review on the Japanese Waegu/Wako," *Cultural Interaction Studies of Sea Port Cities*, No. 21, Institute of International Maritime Affairs, pp.117-148.

Gu's paper in the forth chapter is condensed from Gu Mo-Ryong (구모룡, 2011), "The Imperial Eyes towards Busan as Contact Zone," *Cultural Interaction Studies of Sea Port Cities*, No. 4, Institute of International Maritime Affairs, pp.71-100.

Choi's paper in the forth chapter is condensed from Choi Jin-Chul (최진철, 2019), "Life on the Sea: The Merchant Vessel as a Cultural Interaction Space," *Cultural Interaction Studies of Sea Port Cities*, No. 20, Institute of International Maritime Affairs, pp.237-368.

Index

About Contributors

Jeong, Moon-Soo (jms@kmou.ac.kr)

    Director of Institute of International Maritime Affairs (IMA), Korea Maritime and Ocean University

An, Mi-Jeong (gasirian@hanmail.net)

    HK professor of Institute of International Maritime Affairs, Korea Maritime and Ocean University

Chung, Chinsung Dury (dury@kmou.ac.kr)

    Professor of Division of Global Maritime Studies, Korea Maritime and Ocean University

Choi, Eun-Soon (eschoi@kmou.ac.kr)

    Professor of Division of Global Maritime Studies, Korea Maritime and Ocean University

Choi, Jin-Chul (choi1@kmou.ac.kr)

    Professor of Division of Global Maritime Studies, Korea Maritime and Ocean University

Gu, Mo-Ryong (kmr@kmou.ac.kr)

    Professor of Division of East Asian Studies, Korea Maritime and Ocean University

Gojkošek, Matjaž

    Graduate School Student of Department of International Area & Cultural Studies, Graduate School of Korea Maritime and Ocean University

Kim, Kang-Sik (ks1592@hanmail.net)

HK Professor of Institute of International Maritime Affairs, Korea Maritime and Ocean University

Kim, Seung (namsan386@hanmail.net)

HK Professor of Institute of International Maritime Affairs, Korea Maritime and Ocean University

Lee, Soo-Yeol (sosoyo78@hanmail.net)

HK Professor of Institute of International Maritime Affairs, Korea Maritime and Ocean University

Lee, Hak-Su (leefrance@hanmail.net)

Visiting Professor of Institute of International Maritime Affairs, Korea Maritime and Ocean University

Han, Byung-Ho (ilgong@kmou.ac.kr)

Professor of Division of Maritime Law, Korea Maritime and Ocean University

Woo, Yang-Ho (woo8425@hanmail.net)

HK Professor of Institute of International Maritime Affairs, Korea Maritime and Ocean University